LEADING PUBLIC DESIGN

Discovering human-centred governance

Christian Bason

First published in Great Britain in 2017 by

Policy Press
University of Bristol
1-9 Old Park Hill
Bristol BS2 8BB
UK
t: +44 (0)117 954 5940
e: pp-info@bristol.ac.uk
www.policypress.co.uk

North American office:
Policy Press
c/o The University of Chicago Press
1427 East 60th Street
Chicago, IL 60637, USA
t: +1 773 702 7700
f: +1 773-702-9756
e:sales@press.uchicago.edu
www.press.uchicago.edu

British Library Cataloguing in Publication Data
A catalogue record for this book is available from the British Library.

Library of Congress Cataloging-in-Publication Data
A catalog record for this book has been requested.

ISBN 978-1-4473-2558-1 paperback
ISBN 978-1-4473-2560-4 ePub
ISBN 978-1-4473-2561-1 Kindle
ISBN 978-1-4473-2559-8 ePdf

Cover design by My Buemann, Danish Design Center
Front cover: image kindly supplied by Christian Bason

Printed and bound by CPI Group (UK) Ltd, Croydon, CR0 4YY

For Malene, with love.

Contents

List of figures and tables

Figures

Tables

Foreword

This book is the culmination of a journey over the past decade, starting in 2005, where I have become increasingly intrigued by the contribution of design to public sector innovation. This journey has been professional, personal and academic.

Professionally, I have authored a number of books on innovation and leadership in government, where design methods have featured an increasingly central role; I have led the Danish government's innovation team MindLab, which employs professionally trained designers; I have served on the European Commission's (EC) Design Leadership Board and been Chairman of a subsequent EC expert group on public sector innovation (European Commission, 2012; 2013b). My present job, since 2014, is to run the Danish Design Centre (DDC), a government-funded institution that aims to strengthen the use of design by business and society, nationally and globally. Across these professional activities, I have developed a deep personal interest in and curiosity about what design might offer to public organisations and public managers such as myself. As a public manager, what does it really take to engage with design approaches to enact change, not only in discrete projects but also on a wider scale? What are the implications and responsibilities for public managers, and the meaning and sense with which they conduct their jobs? This curiosity has finally led me to an academic journey, where since 2010 I have conducted a PhD project to explore in detail the significance of design work for public managers and for the future of public governance.

This book builds on all of these three journeys. In it, I propose that design approaches can contribute in powerful ways to innovation in the public sector and, potentially, transform how public organisations are governed.

With this foreword I wish to thank the many people who have accompanied me on the journeys and in numerous ways have inspired me to pursue what ultimately has become this book. First of all I wish to thank my thesis advisor at Copenhagen Business School, Robert Austin, who has guided the development of the project from the start. Also, I am indebted to co-advisors Rafael Ramirez of Oxford University's Saïd Bsuiness School, Banny Banerjee at Stanford University and Dick Boland at Case Western Reserve University's Weatherhead School of Management. Also a warm thank you to Eduardo Stazsowski at the New School's Parsons School for Design, with whom I conducted a visiting scholarship. Along my academic journey I have also been extremely grateful for inputs and ideas from Richard Buchanan, also at Case Western, from Sabine Junginger at the Hertie School of Governance and from Daniel Hjorth, Dorthe Pedersen and Lotte Jensen at Copenhagen Business School.

A range of people in my professional network have been instrumental in supporting and catalysing this work – with ideas, suggestions and opportunities to interact. Geoff Mulgan at Nesta has been an inspiration, as have David Halpern of the UK's Behavioural Insights team, and Ann Mettler and Peter Droell, both at the European Commission. Stephane Vincent and François Jegou of La 27ᵉ Region have been great collaborators. Martin Stewart-Weeks, Tom Bentley and Nina Terrey have, from their vantage points in Australia, provided many opportunities to present and discuss the work leading up to this book. Charlie Leadbeater, author and speaker, has always provided fresh perspectives and ideas. I must also mention Giulio Quagliotto who has recently challenged my thinking on the intersection of experimentation and design.

This book and the research behind it have depended on the professionalism and world-class work of my former colleagues at MindLab, where many of the networks and relations leading to this book were established. Not least Kit Lykketoft, then Deputy Director, was amazing in the day-to-day running of the organisation during research-intensive periods. Today I am supported by an incredible team at the DDC, where Chief of Staff Anne Christine Lyder Andersen makes sure everything runs smoothly, and COO Sune Knudsen takes care of day-to-day business. Also at DDC, project assistant Paw Wöhlk did an excellent job as background researcher for this work. MindLab and the DDC are institutions under the auspices of the Danish Ministry of Business and Growth, under the leadership of Permanent Secretary Michael Dithmer. I am grateful that he and his ministry have allowed me to prioritise a research project alongside my management duties.

It goes almost without saying that this book would not have been possible without the 15 public managers who have provided me with their personal leadership stories and experiences of using design. I wish to thank each of them for their time, commitment and openness in sharing their challenges and successes with me.

Once again it has been a pleasure working with the professional team at Policy Press. Last but not least, I must thank my wonderful family – my wife Malene and Christopher (12), Julia (9) and Lillian (3) for putting up with another project that turned out to be slightly more consuming than I originally promised!

Christian Bason
Copenhagen, January 2017

ONE

Introduction: design as a vehicle for exploration

To see that a situation requires inquiry is the first step in inquiry. (John Dewey, *Logic: The Theory of Inquiry*, 1938, p 111)

Carolyn Curtis is a public manager in Adelaide, South Australia. She has been seconded for nearly eight months to a project on how to redesign services for 'chaotic families'. These are families that are typically characterised by high levels of alcohol abuse, violence, unemployment and dysfunction. For the past eight months Carolyn has no longer acted formally as a manager, but has participated with a small team consisting of a designer and a sociologist in exploring how such families live their lives, with the aim of finding new opportunities for helping them to become 'thriving families'. Carolyn says:

> "I was trained as a social worker to assess and categorise various social events. Throughout this project I have needed to undo all that. And that is difficult. I have been given the space, time and resources to really reflect on what we have been doing in our agency. We have handled these problematic families as a pre-designed 'programme', with fixed criteria and no end-user involvement."

Carolyn describes the new families project as a 'resourcing model', which is radically different from how she has worked during her 10-year career as a manager. She says that by taking an end-user (family) perspective she has been able to critically reflect on the results of her agency's work:

> "It is bottom-up, it has end-user focus, and there is no fixed structure, criteria or categories. The work has been extremely intensive. We have focused on motivation and on strengths within the families – identifying the 'positive deviances' where some families are actually thriving, even though they shouldn't be, according to the government's expectations. We have focused on finding entry points and opportunities, rather than just trying to mediate risk. It is a co-design, or co-creation approach, and it has been entirely new to me. We are ourselves experiencing the actual interactions within and amongst the families, and breaking them down to examine in detail how they might look different. It is very concrete, capturing what words they use (...) It all looks, feels and sounds different than what I did before. Taking an ethnographic approach is entirely new to me. It has helped me experience how these citizens themselves experience their lives, and has allowed me to see the barriers. I have had to suspend my professional judgement. The whole iterative nature of the project, that it is OK to change, has made me understand how much of what we do is a matter of attitude. In this project, we are capturing their concrete stories, and allowing immersion into their reality. Doing my own ethnography in this way has been a phenomenal journey."

The quote above contains a wide range of interesting observations. Carolyn's experience, as a public manager and as a human being, of the Family by Family project raises a wide range of questions. What does it mean to 'undo' one's practice as a public manager? In what ways has the project been bottom-up and what does end-user focus imply in practice? Specifically, what does a co-design approach entail? How does ethnography come into play? What characterises the 'journey' that this manager has taken? Why does the process 'look, feel and sound' different than the types of development activities Carolyn Curtis has experienced before?

Carolyn goes on to elaborate the significance of the project for the organisation she is currently a part of, and the potential for more systemic change:

> "Today we as administrators meet the families reactively. We are trapped in a culture of risk. I can see we need a mind-set change in my profession. We are forgetting to see the potential. We are lacking openness and passion. (…) During this new project I have had to let go of myself as a manager and leader. Looking back now, I am seeing how the system could be very different. I have made decisions about removing new-born babies from their mothers that I now see weren't at all necessary. That recognition is really painful."

Carolyn Curtis's story leaves the impression that the methods she describes – user-centred, bottom-up, iterative, etc. – have had a major impact on not just herself as a person and as a manager, but potentially on her organisation's approach to its mission and role. In fact, her experience in some ways even questions some of our taken-for-granted expectations of government: the notion that public organisations are relatively stable, with predictable routines and practices, and that public managers in many ways are constrained by a range of powerful conditions: the rule of law, the operating principles of regulations, financial and budgetary demands, the identities, norms and roles of the professions public administration, of social work, of education, of nursing and so forth (Wilson, 1989; Simon, 1997). How is it at all possible, given these long-standing and embedded conditions, characteristic of bureaucracies, to disrupt the status quo?

If this brief narrative from a public sector design project were a single, isolated, random outlier, these questions would be of rather limited academic or practical interest. It could be that Carolyn Curtis had a particular personal characteristic that made her especially susceptible to the methods and processes that were employed; or it might well be that the particular institutional context of family services in Adelaide, Australia was somehow especially ripe for new insight, disruption and change along the lines Carolyn describes. It could even be that her project partners – a designer and a sociologist – were very extraordinary people who simply have a profound impact on those that they work with. Or could it be that Carolyn is at the forefront of a movement that leverages design approaches to truly make public sector innovation happen?

Design: an approach to innovation in government

As it turns out, Carolyn Curtis's story is not a single 'outlier'. Carolyn's work and Family by Family is one among a growing number of examples of managers using design approaches to innovation in public sector contexts (Parker and Heapy, 2006; Bate and Robert, 2007; Bason 2010, 2014b; Boyer et al, 2011; Cooper and Junginger, 2011; Manzini and Staszowski, 2013; Ansell and Torfing, 2014). By design approaches I mean systematic, creative processes that engage people in exploring problems and opportunities, develop new ideas and visualise, test and develop new solutions. In the public sector the use of such methods is often framed in the context of new forms of citizen involvement and collaborative innovation (Bourgon 2008, 2012; Ansell and Torfing, 2014).

Carolyn's story mentions a range of positive, but also challenging experiences from the collaboration with the design team. More broadly speaking, among the benefits of using design in public sector organisations, the following are often mentioned (see also Bason, 2010):

- better service experience for end-users, such as citizens or businesses
- higher productivity in public service production
- better outcomes for citizens and business
- enhanced democratic participation, openness and transparency.

These benefits are typically reached because design approaches help public managers and their organisations on a number of fronts, including:

- deeper and more nuanced understanding of problems and opportunities from a human perspective
- creation of tested and tried solutions, services, systems and strategies
- improving or rethinking organisation and governance models
- increased ownership of new ideas and of organisational change inside and outside the organisation.

Finally, a benefit of using design methods can be that the organisation is empowered to run faster, more effective and precise innovation processes.

Given this spectrum of potential benefits, which I explore further in this book, it is perhaps not surprising that more public managers are beginning to take notice and to try out design for themselves. International institutions, national government organisations, local government, foundations, philanthropies, voluntary and community organisations as well as educational institutions at all levels are taking up design approaches in various forms (Bason, 2010; 2013; 2014a; *The Economist*, 2014; Liedtka et al, 2013; Mulgan, 2014). The organisational anchoring (public or third sector) varies, as does the terminology: service design, strategic design, macro design, public design, design thinking, human-centred design, co-design and co-creation are among labels commonly used (Cooper and Junginger, 2011; Meroni and Sangiorgi, 2011; Liedtka et al, 2013).

In some instances, design capabilities are being organisationally embedded in the form of in-house studios or innovation labs. Just within the past few years, governments in the United States, Australia, Denmark, Singapore, the United Arab Emirates, the United Kingdom and Chile have set up their own Innovation Labs and 'i-Teams' (Bason, 2014c; Nesta, 2014; *The Economist*, 2014). Also, international bodies such as the European Commission, the World Bank and the United Nations (UNDP, UNICEF, others) are using labs and design methods. In terms of policy domains, nearly every thinkable corner of public service provision has in recent years been connected to design: from environmental, education, employment, business, finance and taxation issues to healthcare, mental health and social care at regional and local government level (Parker and Heapy, 2006; Meroni and Sangiorgi, 2011; Polaine et al, 2013; Manzini, 2015).

However, bringing design approaches into government is not without its challenges.

Design on the one hand, and the institutional and governance context of public organisations on the other, can be viewed as two waves crashing against each other, resulting in unpredictable ripple effects. Imagine the (admittedly somewhat clichéd) creative, fast-paced culture of designers as it meets the (equally clichéd) old-fashioned bureaucratic culture of civil servants. Although both descriptions are stereotypes, there is no doubt that the professionals who typically occupy the two domains – designers, artists, ethnographers and technologists on the one side and economists, lawyers and political scientists on the other – have very different views of and appetites for innovation and change (Michlewski, 2015). The relationship between designers and government officials, viewed empirically, is thus not always an easy one and is potentially ripe with contradictions, frustrations and conflict, as much as with positive change and value creation (Mulgan, 2014).

The relationship does not become less complicated when one considers the context in which it unfolds. As Hernes (2008) suggests, contemporary organisations can be viewed as 'tangled' and 'fuzzy'. Managers act in a fluid world where the changes they take part in (or create) change them in turn (Hernes, 2008, p 145). Public managers, being in the midst of the dynamics of change processes, are the witnesses who, with their stories, might help us to understand what unfolds and to interpret what matters.

So, in spite of the rise of design as a new approach to innovation in the public sector, much is still not known about how design approaches work in practice, and even less in known about how public managers most fruitfully commission, lead and benefit from design processes. As an important emerging agenda for government innovation – alongside other agendas such as new technology, social media, open government and evidence-based policy – the design field needs a further grounding to become a mature management practice in the public sector. Such grounding, which can strengthen the use of design in leading public sector innovation, is the aim of this book.

Before turning to the book's content, however, I'd like to share with you the background to the making of this book.

Advancing public sector innovation practice: the next agenda

I met Carolyn Curtis, and had the chance to interview her, on a trip to Australia where I launched my previous book, *Leading Public Sector Innovation: Co-creating for a Better Society* (Policy Press, 2010). Carolyn's story convinced me that I was already on to something important in that book, but also that the job wasn't quite finished. I had introduced a number of ideas about how to achieve more innovation in the public sector: the ability to create new ideas, implement them and create value for citizens and society. These ideas took the shape of a broad conceptual framework. The story of that framework and how I have worked with it over the past years is key to the book you are now holding. The framework I introduced in *Leading Public Sector Innovation* focused on four dimensions, which I characterised as 'the four Cs':

- *Consciousness*, which introduced key concepts and a new language about public sector innovation and value creation
- *Capacity*, which addressed the need to build explicit strategies for innovation in public institutions and to leverage organisational design, more diverse recruitment practices and new technology so as to power innovation
- *Co-creation*, which provided a first set of suggestions for how to bring design approaches into a systematic process for driving innovation in government
- *Courage*, which was how I addressed the issue of leading public sector innovation; I proposed that managers fundamentally need to balance between inspiration (or creativity) and execution (or implementation) in order to become successful in making public sector innovation happen.

I argued that all these four dimensions, properly developed and applied, could help to overcome the numerous and well-documented challenges to innovation in government, such as the lack of a common language, tools and methods, under-investment in competencies, aversion to risk, lack of skills and insufficient management engagement from the top down. When I published *Leading Public Sector Innovation*, and had the opportunity to introduce its core concepts to public managers world-wide, it was my impression that the framework was useful overall. It gave some structure and rigour to an emerging field that had otherwise perhaps been interesting to scholars of public management, but also rather elusive to many managers and employees in government.

Since *Leading Public Sector Innovation* was published its messages have thus been tested thoroughly. I have conducted hundreds of presentations and training sessions based on the book, combining its framework with the methods and approaches that emerged from my team's work at MindLab, the Danish government's innovation team. From top-level managers in the European Union institutions to managers in the municipality of Copenhagen to Singapore's Civil Service College, to the United States and Canada's federal governments, I have introduced the approaches and tools espoused in *Leading Public Sector Innovation*. In some instances the book was taken up as a way to embed innovation more systemically in public sector institutions. For example, it provided direct inspiration for Australia's first nation-wide innovation policy for the public sector (Australian Government, 2011). When the policy was published, an Australian colleague reached out to me and remarked how the document used the 'four Cs' as its foundation. "They even put in the courage part," he exclaimed, rather astounded. Consider this for a moment: a major government that explicitly encourages public managers and staff, nation-wide, to be more courageous in pursuing more innovation in government. That's pretty courageous in itself. However, if one reads the document it is also clear that that section of the policy was not particularly clear on how exactly to implement the recommendation!

And here's the rub. Although *Leading Public Sector Innovation* provided a starting point, more needed to be done to transform the attractive idea of a more innovative public sector into practice. Already within the first few years after its publication, I realised that although the book provided a relevant foundation some important elements were missing, or at least under-developed. This feedback was confirmed through my hands-on experience leading first MindLab, and now the Danish Design Centre, which is a public institution devoted to strengthening the use of design in business and society. First and foremost, I have learned that the leadership role is absolutely critical for positive change to happen. When I ran MindLab our team could usually identify a successful project up front by the type of dialogue and engagement shown by the responsible leader on the receiving side of our design and innovation work. And since shifting my role from being an advisor on innovation methods at MindLab to running a public institution applying these methods at the Danish Design Centre, it has been painfully clear to me how hard it is in practice to drive meaningful, citizen-centred innovation. It is more than a little bit ironic that I am learning how tough it is to take my own advice. But it has made me realise how much public managers need concrete leadership methods and tools if they are to have any chance of really placing citizens at the centre of public services.

Design-led innovation in government: three building blocks

Concretely, I've become aware of three elements that need more substance and elaboration. They form the building blocks of this book.

Design practice

As design approaches are now increasingly used in government settings across the globe, there is a need to map the current practice. What key methods are emerging, and how are they concretely being used by public managers to engage citizens, their staff, and wider stakeholders in driving innovation? This book defines and takes stock of the current state of design in the public sector. I propose three dimensions of design that reflect the cutting edge of public design approaches and that have been applied with success by managers to drive their innovation efforts.

Leadership engagement

When, in 2010, I suggested that courage is a necessary trait for public managers to truly make innovation happen, that was my best bet. However, encouraging managers to be courageous is not only easier said than done; many public managers flinch at the word, as it obviously involves some unspecified degree of risk taking and what one might call civil disobedience. Could there not be some more precise and operational behaviours that public managers might use to drive innovation? As public managers commission designers (whether as external consultants or internal teams) to work with them and their organisations, what kinds of leadership behaviour and engagement are critical to the projects' becoming successful? What happens *between* managers and designers as innovative projects unfold? To what extent does it make sense to speak of *managing as designing* – the use of attitudes and methods of designers as part of one's own management practice? Based on rich empirical data – stories from 15 public managers who have led and experienced design processes in public organisations – I suggest six behaviours, or engagements, that public managers can deploy to drive innovation and change forward. This focus on leadership engagement with design practice is at the heart of the book.

Public governance

Third, as more and more solutions are developed using design methods, what are the wider implications for public governance? Could design approaches, over time, make an impact on how we conduct the overall strategic business of government? Could design help managers and their staff to discover a more impactful mode of running their organisations? In this book I argue that design projects can form a powerful pathway, enabling the transition to a different way of governing. Drawing on the empirical research as well as a range of academic literature, I suggest four defining characteristics of what I call *human-centred governance.* I discuss how this paradigm relates to the governance legacy we have inherited and I examine the potential dilemmas and pitfalls of bringing such principles into the context of existing governance arrangements.

Finally, in terms of context, this book explores the implications of the current policy environment for innovation approaches. I have found that there is an urgent need for many public managers to be more reflective, and nuanced, about the types of problems public institutions face. Scholars as well as policy practitioners and public managers have increasingly come to realise that not all problems are alike, and that issues of emergence, complexity and 'wickedness' of problems need to be taken very seriously. This does not mean that all public problems are complex and 'wicked', or that design approaches are suited for only certain problem types; but it might mean that design methods become even more relevant when many actors need to collaborate to find solutions under conditions of high interdependence, turbulence and complexity. In fact, you could argue that public managers today are facing a double complexity: as the external policy and societal environment has become more complex, so have the internal structures, processes, technologies, professions and governance arrangements established within and by public organisations. Managers who wish to innovate therefore have to deal actively with complexity on two fronts: externally as well as internally. My proposal is that design methods can help cut through them both, creating new meaning both for end-users and for internal staff.

Leading Public Design: Discovering Human-Centred Governance is thus essentially a companion, or extension, to *Leading Public Sector Innovation* that develops these three key elements – *design, leadership* and *governance* – in the context of complexity. This book is in that sense deeper, but also wider in scope, in its ambition to advance the practice of public sector innovation.

Research foundation and audience

The three strands in this book, the underlying case studies and its key insights derive from a comprehensive academic research project anchored at Copenhagen Business School (CBS). This research has been conducted as a PhD project in parallel with my daily work running MindLab and the Danish Design Centre. The research ran from 2010 to 2016 and explored how public managers in practice have engaged with design-led approaches to public sector innovation. A range of additional university partners have been involved, including Case Western Reserve University's Weatherhead School of Management, Oxford Saïd Business School, Stanford University and Parsons School of Design.

The main data material informing the book derives from this academic research and includes 15 case studies on public managers who have commissioned and experienced design processes at first hand. The cases, which are based on personal, qualitative interviews with the managers, cover five countries: Denmark, the UK, Australia, Finland and the United States. About a third of the cases are projects that were carried out by my team at MindLab, and where I therefore had some direct or indirect involvement. My relation to these cases is thus a reflection of *engaged scholarship* (van de Ven, 2007): 'a participatory form of research for obtaining different perspectives of key stakeholders (researchers, users, clients, sponsors, and practitioners) in studying complex problems' (2007, p 9).

The case interviews have been supplemented by secondary documentation relating to the specific design projects, such as process documentation, evaluations, business cases and impact assessments. The research approach has drawn on grounded theory, implying that the emphasis has been on identifying emerging patterns, archetypes, categories and relationships bottom–up, building on the empirical data (Suddaby, 2006; Corbin and Strauss, 2008). The ambition has been to develop new insights into how design can contribute to catalysing change in the public sector, with a particular view to the role of managers (Edmondson and McManus, 2007, p 1158). The research has provided a unique window not only into the relative importance of design methods for public managers, but also in particular into their personal leadership practices as they leveraged design approaches to address their organisations' challenges and capture new opportunities.

Although the research and PhD thesis form its backbone, it is important to say that this book deviates from the academic research project in certain important ways. First, for the purpose of clarity, much of the text has been updated, and in some instances I draw sharper and more pointed conclusions. Second, the more normative parts of this book – recommendations, suggestions and advice – do not derive directly from the research but have been added to give more direction and guidance to the reader. Not all recommendations can be traced to the research; rather, they are based on my practical experience and the experience of others I have worked with.

Who is this book for? The normative character of the recommendations implies that this is intended first as a book for practitioners. The main audience for this book are policy makers, managers and innovation specialists in public and social organisations who wish to make change happen in a reflective, meaningful and sustainable way. Designers and design firms, management consultants and other advisers who work closely with government agencies and organisations are also obvious audiences. Leaders in private firms who contract with public organisations or who are interested in bidding for new innovative partnerships with government should also find the book useful. Finally, it is my hope that the book will be a contribution to the academic community – scholars and students both within public management, within design research and more widely in innovation management.

Content and structure of the book

Beyond this introduction, the book is structured into three parts. Part One provides the background, definitions and context; Part Two develops the practice of leadership engagement with design; and Part Three suggests the building blocks of a new form of public governance. Each of the book's chapters concludes with a practical 'How to do it' set of suggestions and recommendations.

Part One: Complexity, design and governance

This part of the book introduces the context in which design approaches unfold in government settings.

In Chapter Two I explore the nature of public problems. I argue that the use of design is linked to a wider and evolving set of policy problems that may not be sufficiently addressed today. The current attempts of many nations, in the wake of the global financial crisis, to control public finances happen at the same time as the very same societies are facing seemingly intractable social challenges such as chronic health problems, ageing, unemployment – in particular among young people – and growing income disparity and poverty. Even though 'wicked problems' (Churchman, 1967; Rittel and Webber, 1973) are not unique to the public sector, they characterise many of these particular challenges. To understand the potential value of design, as well as the need for a different way of governing, we must first understand the nature of the problems and challenges that designers are invited to help to address.

In Chapter Three I map the rise of new, collaborative and more socially oriented methods and forms of design. I discuss alternative design definitions and briefly examine design history from its roots in craft towards today's use of design as an increasingly recognised approach to collaborative innovation also in the public sector. Along this analysis I reflect on how design in some ways is coming 'full circle' to a re-integration of production (craft) and user experience, enabled by new technology. The chapter further discusses the concepts of design management and design *as* management; and I consider *design attitude* as a perspective through which to understand how managers relate to design processes as they unfold in their organisations.

In Chapter Four I briefly chart the emergence of public management from its bureaucratic foundations to the new public management and up to the present. In particular, I characterise contemporary discussions of new networked and co-productive paradigms of public governance and I examine how the development is linked to questions of the nature of public problems and complexity. Finally, the chapter shows and explores some surprising similarities between innovations in governance and in the design profession.

Part Two: Leading design for public innovation

The second part of this book has to do with the real challenge of leveraging design for public sector innovation: *the role of leadership*. In much of the current literature and research in the area, the issue of leadership behaviour in relation to public sector innovation is under-developed. However, if public managers, their staff and, ultimately, the citizens they serve are to gain the most from design methods, they need guidance and practical advice on what it takes to lead the processes involved.

Building on my empirical case research among public managers, this book unfolds the leadership dimension and breaks it down into six concrete engagements, or practices. With design approaches as the opportunity, I map and analyse how these six practices are deployed by public managers in very different contexts, often with similar aims and intentions. My hope is that by sharing the stories of these managers, others can be inspired, draw on their practices and avoid some of the pitfalls they encountered. Who knows, perhaps basing oneself on these practices might even stimulate some additional courage to make innovation happen.

Chapter Five provides an overview of the design methodologies and processes that have been applied across the case studies. What, in practice, characterises the design work? How was it commissioned? The chapter also presents the overall analytical framework for the book as a whole. In Chapters Five through Eight I unfold the key concepts that may contribute to our understanding of the significance of design approaches, and how public managers relate to them. A key theme across these chapters is the notion of 'engagement' between managers and the design methodologies, tools and processes. I have structured this part so that three dimensions of design are the organising principle, while the six key management behaviours are presented as pairs, two in each chapter. In this vein, Chapter Six considers design as the exploration of public problems, Chapter Seven expands the role of design in establishing alternative scenarios and Chapter Eight analyses how design can catalyse the enactment of new futures.

Finally, Chapter Nine provides an overview of the types of outputs that result from the design processes and how they lead to the creation of public value. In it, I ask what the solutions flowing from design processes look like, and what the evidence is that design approaches really make a difference.

Part Three: Towards human-centred governance

This third part of the book discusses the emerging governance agenda and analyses the potential rise of a more human-centred governance, building on the characteristics of design approaches and outputs. In the course of my work and research I have found that the use of design can be considered a reflection of the quest of public managers not just to identify new service 'solutions' but to explore new and possibly more effective ways of *governing*. In other words, whereas the aim of much innovation work in government is to 'solve' discrete problems – or sometimes to address a particular new opportunity – the wider game that is at stake is how we run our public institutions. This game, the game of governance, is important for two main reasons, the first being because well-designed solutions to discrete problems usually cannot be effectively implemented without also changing the governance context in which they are to function. Take for instance a more flexible, citizen-centred service that empowers users to achieve better outcomes and that in order to do so cuts across the domains of two different government agencies. For that service to work, new arrangements might need to be found not only for the day-to-day running of the service but also for funding it and allocating resources across the two different organisations, for documenting and evaluating the service, for holding the staff and managers accountable and so on. It might *seem* that design approaches lead to singular new solutions, but often these solutions challenge the governance context as well. Or, one could say, these solutions open up new questions – and may even provide some tentative answers – about how we run our organisations.

Second, for more public managers to begin to work effectively with design methods, so their governance context might need to change. How are they held accountable, how are they evaluated, how much space, time and resources do they have for innovation work? As I will discuss in the book, some governance frameworks function to stimulate and enable innovation and change; others may very well stifle it. If we wish to embed design approaches more firmly into the fabric of public organisations as an approach to dealing with change, then do we not need to examine our current governance mechanisms as well?

Chapter Ten discusses the role of design in catalysing not only particular new 'solutions' but also the emergence of a new and more relational, collaborative and co-productive public governance model: *human-centred governance*. The chapter explores what characterises the types of changes in governance that are implied (at least in part) through design approaches. What are the particular patterns? What are the defining characteristics of a new form of human-centred governance that is catalysed by design?

Chapter Eleven brings human-centred governance into context. I discuss to what extent this model really might be different: at an overall level, what distinguishes it from other contemporary models? I also consider to what extent this model can be as effective at achieving desired public objectives and outcomes as the models we have inherited. I conclude the chapter by proposing how a positive, reinforcing cycle combining design approaches (innovation processes), management engagement (leadership action) and human-centred governance (organisational context) might work.

Chapter Twelve shifts the attention back to the particular roles of public managers in engaging with, and leading, the design process. I summarise how these roles have been presented in this book and how they can be understood. What is the nature of the particular management behaviours the book has shown? How can the role of the public manager be seen more as that of a future-maker rather than (only) that of decision-maker?

PART ONE

COMPLEXITY, DESIGN AND GOVERNANCE

TWO

The public sector and its problems

> Where the facts are most obscure, where precedents are lacking, where novelty and confusion pervade everything, the public in all its unfitness is compelled to make its most important decisions. The hardest problems are those, which institutions cannot handle. These are public problems. (Walter Lippmann, *The Phantom Public*, 1925, p 121)

Governments are paradoxically, and often in equal parts, seen as part of the problem and part of the solution.[1] Famously, then president-elect Ronald Reagan stated in 1981: 'In this present crisis, government is not the solution to our problem; government is the problem.'[2] The inability of public organisations to effectively address societal challenges has again and again been a fundamental point of contestation. In what was possibly the defining work on public governance in the 1990s, Osborne and Gaebler (1992, p 1) called for a 'reinvention of government', stating rather cataclysmically that in the United States,

> Our public schools are the worst in the developed world. Our health care system is out of control. Our courts and prisons are so overcrowded that convicted felons walk free. And many of our proudest cities are virtually bankrupt.

Viewing US society today, and considering contemporary debates on public schools, on healthcare reform, on terrorism, crime and city budgets, this all sounds eerily familiar. Europe is not much different. In a 2013 policy paper the European Commission, the executive body of the European Union, likewise highlights enduring challenges, but also new forms of problems, stating that: 'The evolution of society requires public administrations to tackle many new challenges, including those around demographic change, employment, mobility, security, environment and many others' (European Commission, 2013a, p 1).

The difficulty for institutions, expressed in this chapter's introductory quote by American journalist and writer Walter Lippmann in his 1925 work *The Phantom Public*, to 'handle' public problems, has thus not become less pressing with time. Why haven't we made more progress in our ability to address them? One prevalent argument is that the very nature of the problems the public sector faces is changing faster and more profoundly than our institutions are able to reform. This also entails that current modes of public management are out of touch with the challenges they are intended to address. There is no shortage of research and literature that raises this point (Carlsson, 2004; Seddon, 2008; Eggers and Singh, 2009; Mulgan, 2009; Parsons, 2010; Bourgon, 2012; Ansell and Torfing, 2014; Colander and Kupers, 2014; Doz and Koskonen, 2014; Hassan, 2014). To understand the need for public organisations to reinvent, to innovate – to redesign – we must first try to understand their current context better.

This chapter thus examines the context of present-day governance. I discuss the character of contemporary government challenges, and the nature of the problem space in which public managers increasingly find themselves.

The inability of government to address 'the public's problems'

Nobel prize laureate in economics and professor at Carnegie Mellon University, Herbert Simon, wrote in his seminal work, *Administrative Behaviour*, that 'To the best of our current knowledge, the underlying processes used to solve ill-defined problems are not different from those used to solve well-defined problems' (1997, p 128). This could imply that the management tools and approaches that public managers have inherited are still good enough, and effective enough, in addressing our contemporary challenges.

However, a growing number of voices argue the opposite. Take, for instance, Jocelyne Bourgon, a former top-ranking civil servant in the Canadian public service, now turned author and teacher. She suggests in *A New Synthesis of Public Administration: Serving in the 21st Century* that in some cases public managers will be able to rely on tried and tested past approaches and tools; however, in most cases 'they will need to chart a new course as they face new circumstances and unique challenges' (2012, p 19). According to Bourgon and many of her contemporaries, these 'new circumstances' have to do partly with the volume and scope of the issues and challenges that governments are expected to deal with, and partly with the characteristic of 21st-century problems.

At the same time, the range of government activity has become all-encompassing. Bruno Latour (2007, p 133) points out that no domain of human life is today beyond the boundaries of government responsibility and attention: 'Every day we discover to our great dismay *more* elements to take into account and to throw into the melting pot of public life, not *less*.' In fact, whether it is the very climate we live in or the air we breathe, governments have in recent years been called to action. The vision paper I mentioned from the European Commission states how citizens today are more than ever aware of their rights and have better access to information via information technology – and hence, the more they know, the more they expect governments to do (European Commission, 2013a). Perhaps the shift over the last few decades has been a recognition that, for better or for worse, there is no single domain in our societies where governments are not expected to play some role. Even when it comes to stimulating innovation in industry and business, the role of government can be seen as essential (Mazzucato, 2014). The wider issue, however, is whether the nature of the problems faced by public decision makers has remained stable.

Wicked problems and complexity

Some scholars point out that the problem space, or context, within which public organisations operate, severely constrains and challenges effective government action. In 2004 a professor of innovation, Bo Carlsson, wrote a contribution to the excellent book *Managing as Designing* concerning 'Public policy as a form of design'. In this chapter Carlsson asked:

> How can you make sensible policy or strategy in a nondeterministic, evolutionary, highly complex world, that is, a world where the most desirable outcomes are unknown but there may be many possible acceptable outcomes, where change is characterized by both path dependence and unpredictability, and where there are many diverse components, interaction, and feedback among components and multiple dimensions to each problem? This is the design problem with respect to public policy. (2004, p 36)

Carlsson argues that 'sensible' policy (or public management, or strategy, or governance) might not be the same as 'rational' policy. But then what might it be? Framing the challenge of how to govern effectively as a *design problem* suggests that design may contribute to addressing it. Contextually, as Carlsson highlights above, there is a growing recognition that the social systems that governments seek to influence are 'complex and adaptive, and continuously evolving over time' (Colander and Kupers, 2014, p 5). This could imply that at least a significant set of the problems faced by public managers call for new or different kinds of policy and public service responses.

As discussed above, Herbert Simon (and many of his contemporaries) did not substantially believe that problems could differ in their nature. However, if some types of problems are fundamentally different than others, might it then also be that the way of addressing (if not solving) them would also have to differ fundamentally? Let me first consider the notion of 'complex problems' before returning to 'wicked problems', since the two concepts are related, but not the same.

Dealing with double-sided complexity

The last decade has seen a significant rise in interest in understanding complexity – the theory and dynamics of highly interconnected systems. Part of the reason is quite possibly, as discussed above, that our 21st-century world is in fact getting 'complexer and complexer' (Colander and Kupers, 2014, p 47). Goldsmith and Eggers, in their work on networked governance, underline that 'increasingly complex societies force public officials to develop new models of governance' (2004, p 7). Marco Steinberg (2014) likewise points out that the complexity at hand is caught between human behaviour, cultural traits, ideals, values, physical principles and perceived facts. The task, says Steinberg, is to find the right simplifiers for issues spanning many domains. From a policy practitioner's standpoint, this raises several questions, where one of the most pressing ones may concern the issue of diagnosis: how does one come to know what kind of problem space is in play – ranging from 'tame' to 'wicked' or perhaps 'super wicked'? Given the problem dynamics, the policy environment and the tools available, what kinds of process and potential solutions should we look for?

The claim made by most observers seems partly to be that policy makers and public managers have under-estimated (or simply not understood) the extent to which the problem space they find themselves in is fundamentally characterised by wicked and complex problems. Issues such as education, health and social policy are all characterised by a very large set of actors acting simultaneously, by extremely high numbers of users and thus interactions, and by unpredictable dynamics. Partly, the argument is that megatrends such as rapid changes to life-styles, health, globalisation, demography, immigration, mobility, deregulation, technology and so on all introduce new sources of dynamics and unexpected relationships. The social entrepreneur and activist Zaid Hassan, for instance, argues that 'our current challenges are profoundly different than those of the past. Our familiar modern responses no longer work because they're based on a fundamental misunderstanding of what we are facing' (Hassan, 2014, p 17). Similarly, Wayne Parsons (2010, p 27) suggests that:

We face problems for which causal relationships are so complex that we cannot know when one problem ends and another begins, or whether the problems themselves have been caused by previous or existing policies. We confront a world in which 'what works?' is a simplistic and nonsensical question. 'What works?' like probability, is a poor guide to action in a world in which 'problems' are not continuous over time and space.

Unfortunately, for all the recognition of the novelty brought forward by technology, globalisation and other megatrends, the sense that public problems are being ill-addressed is far from new. Donald Schön, in his 1983 treatise on reflective practice, asserts that 'Professionally designed solutions to public problems have had unanticipated consequences, sometimes worse than the problems they were designed to solve' (1983, p 4). An important point here is the phrase *professionally designed*, which points to the classical role of policy experts deriving 'solutions' and proposing decisions on the basis of rigorous data and analysis.

Characterising 'wicked'

Another characteristic of public problems is the notion of 'wicked problems'. One fundamental way of distinguishing between problem types is the following.

- *Tame problems, or well-defined, technical and engineering problems.* These problems can be understood and addressed through an appreciation and careful, systematic assessment of their constituent parts. Although they may be extremely 'difficult' or 'complicated' (Bourgon, 2012, pp 20–1) or 'hard' (Martin, 2009, p 95), they can be effectively addressed through rigorous analysis and it is relevant for decision makers to draw extensively on knowledge of existing evidence and 'best practice' (Snowden and Boone, 2007).
- *Wicked problems.* These are ill defined and can be addressed only by way of systematic experimentation. These types of problems, or contexts, were first articulated in some detail

by Horst Rittel and Melvin Webber (1973). They famously argued that a certain kind of problems, or planning dilemmas, are better understood through examining the interrelations and dependencies between the constituent parts and by 'probing' in order to generate dynamics that then reveal underlying and hidden relationships. Many public policy problems fall into this category, since, as paraphrased by Wayne Parsons (2010, p 17), the design of public policies is 'a very different matter from that of designing for a moon landing'.

Originally, Rittel and Webber (1973) put forward 10 criteria to characterise wicked problems, the first among these being that they have no clear or final definition, and so can be continuously redefined. The original list contains some overlap and repetition; for the sake of clarity Martin (2009) suggests that, ultimately, wicked problems can be identified by four dimensions, which are presented here, with some additional substance provided from other sources:

- *Causal relationships are unclear and dynamic.* Root causes of the problem are difficult, if not impossible, to identify; they are ambiguous and elusive. Part of the reason for the confusion around causality is also that many public problems are ultimately *behavioural*. In particular during the last decade, research ranging from Nobel laureate Daniel Kahneman's work on how people make decisions, *Thinking Fast and Slow* (2011), to Dan Ariely's *Predictably Irrational* (2009) and Thaler and Sunstein's runaway success *Nudge* (2008) and Sunstein's more recent *Simpler* (2013), has pointed out that human behaviour is not as easily understood as we might like to think and cannot be predicted with much accuracy. Following the ostensible failings of traditional economics in the wake of the 2008 global financial crisis, fields such as behavioural economics and psychology have gained prominence. Another part of the confusion around causality is more political. In a public sector context the root causes, and thus the very definition of the nature of the problem, can be highly prone to ideological contention: Is immigration a problem or a resource for a society? Is climate change a problem or just a manageable consequence of the quest for growth?

- *The problem does not fit into a known category*; in fact there are no 'classes' of wicked problems. Snowden and Boone (2007) have argued that this implies that available 'good' or 'best' practices cannot be applied effectively as a course of problem solving. This poses particular and important limitations to the public management notion of 'evidence-based policy', which implies that policy decisions should be based on solid knowledge of 'what works'.

- *Attempts at problem solving change the problem.* Devising potential approaches to the problem tend to change how it is understood; and implemented solutions are consequential in the sense that they create a new situation for the next trial; so all solutions are 'one shots'. This is not least the case in the highly exposed domain of public policy, where as soon as stakeholders learn of potential ideas, plans, laws or initiatives they start acting strategically and thus influence the policy landscape even before any action has been undertaken. This prompts the need for more iterative, non-linear and possibly more inclusive approaches – what Halse et al (2010) call *generative* – ways of exploring and addressing the problem.

- *No stopping rule.* Further, wicked problems do not have any firm basis for judging whether they are 'solved' or not; as Rowe (1987, p 41) formulates it, they have no 'stopping rule'. Solutions cannot be judged as true or false, but merely as 'better or worse' (Ritchey, 2011, p 92). Whenever a solution is proposed, it can always be improved upon. Due to the indeterminacy of the problem definition, alternative problem definitions will always be possible, and thus entirely new solution spaces can be envisaged. In fact, one can question whether wicked problems can ever truly be 'solved'. In a public sector context this issue is hardened by the many stakeholders often engaged in a particular policy field, who can have wildly divergent notions of what is 'good' or 'bad' – based not on empirical or 'objective' data, but on ideology, power calculations or institutional interests.

At times of rapid change and increased turbulence, Rittel and Webber's notion of 'wicked problems' may even be too limited a notion; Stanford University's Banny Banerjee (2014, p 71) characterises some contemporary public challenges as 'super-wicked' in that they:

> Have most notably the additional attributes of massive scale, urgency and complex interactions between many subsystems that are themselves wicked problems. A 'Grand Challenge' such as ensuring global water security certainly transcends our current disciplinary limitations but the real difficulty lies in the possibility that the nature of these challenges is emblematic of deeply entrenched flaws in our institutional structures, our underlying theories, definitions of success and our inability to act.

Andrea Siodmok, who holds a PhD in design and currently runs the Policy Lab in the UK Cabinet Office, similarly proposes that the public sector is facing more ill-defined problems than it used to. She argues that such 'mega-challenges' require a more holistic, qualitative, contextual and experience-based approach to policy making (Siodmok, 2014).

The problems with wicked problems

The implications of these insights for the issue of innovation, change and governance in the public sector are potentially significant.

Let me briefly discuss two perspectives. The first perspective entails a shift from attempting to apply 'best practices' through evidence-based policy and benchmarking, to exploring possible new practices. The second perspective entails a questioning of the problem-oriented frame of many public decision makers: a shift from reacting to problems to enacting new futures.

From applying best practice to probing for next practice

First, as Parsons (2010) underlines, recognising that many of the challenges facing public organisations are akin to complex, wicked problems, runs counter to the notion that accumulating and applying rigorous evidence of 'what works' is the key to public service reform. The movement around evaluation research and evidence-based policy making, which has been strongly associated with the rise of the new public management governance paradigm (Hood, 1991; Osborne and Gaebler, 1992; Rist, 2004), is challenged. The same is true, one might argue, with the big data and analytics movement. David Snowden, in his now-famous *Harvard Business Review* article 'A leader's framework for decision-making', makes a similar point when it comes to decision making under conditions of complexity and emergence (Snowden and Boone, 2007). He asserts that the character of the problem space defines what are the most appropriate approaches to decision making. Again, here he is in opposition to Simon (1997), who does not believe that the appropriate decision making process differs between problem types. In his so-called Cynefin framework Snowden suggests that under conditions of relatively simple or even 'complicated' problems the application of 'best' or 'good' practices is relevant. As Bourgon contends, in such situations 'governments know what actions are possible, and have relatively good knowledge about their most likely impacts' (2012, p 20). Public managers can relatively comfortably stick with their usual ways of doing things.

But, under conditions of a high level of complexity managers cannot pull existing solutions off the shelf. Here, the problem is characterised by multiple actors and a high degree of interdependence. As Bourgon (2012) underlines, power is highly dispersed, and the problem space manifests a high degree of unpredictability and emergent characteristics. Instead, say Snowden and Boone (2007), decision makers must 'probe' their way to relevant insights about what would constitute effective action. In other words, managers need to act to the best of their ability, even if tentatively, then 'sense' or register the changes and results coming from their actions, and then rapidly adapt their efforts accordingly. One could call this approach an ability to embrace uncertainty and ambiguity (Michlewski, 2015). This understanding of management under conditions of complexity is in many ways at odds with the analytical, data-driven and rational approaches to management that are prevalent in public organisations, and indeed in many business organisations. As Michlewski (2015) dryly observes, it is hardly surprising that the notion of 'embracing uncertainty and ambiguity' goes against their very foundations.

From reacting to problems to enacting new futures

Second, what if the tendency to frame public policy in terms of 'problems' is in itself problematic? By suggesting that the business of government is to deal with 'problems' – whether they are wicked or not – casts the public manager into a particular role. As Junginger (2014) argues, the *problem frame* renders governments in a reactive position, one of analysing problems and trying to deduce 'solutions', rather than one of truly appreciating situations that can give rise to creative new visions. Henry Mintzberg (2009) has made a similar argument when it comes to business strategy: by emphasising how organisations must address problems through their strategy, there has been so much emphasis on analysis that people have forgotten that analysis is not synthesis. So, whereas there is a powerful argument for a new type of governing because of the changing nature of the problems faced by government, there is also a narrative suggesting that governments might need to become more future oriented than problem oriented. Or, as I will discuss later, less focused on minimising risk, less concerned with optimisation and decision-making procedure, more focused on the ability to produce the outcomes society longs for. One might even call it *a shift from a decision-making stance to a future-making stance*, as a way of being effective, relevant and legitimate in a 21st-century context. Essentially, it is a quest for a new paradigm.

How to do it: embracing complexity

This chapter has argued that the types of problems facing many public managers are probably characterised by a high degree of complexity and 'wickedness'. One could think that this difficult and seemingly intractable nature of many of the problems that public managers face is disturbing. However, in my experience, to many public managers it is also a bit of a relief to recognise that the job really is not supposed to be easy. Recognising the problem space can be the beginning of an exploration and concrete use of new tools of management, which may offer better chances of success. As a public manager, it can be worthwhile to reflect on the following.

- **Reflect on the mission, role and tasks of your organisation in the context in which it operates.** How would you characterise the landscape in which your organisation operates? Who are the key user groups and constituencies, who are the main stakeholders internally within the public sector and in wider society? You might even map the set of stakeholders visually. And you might ask what changes these actors are experiencing, and how these changes and complexities influence your own organisation's role and ability to act. On the dimensions spanning from simple to complex, and tame to wicked, roughly where is your organisation placed?
- **To what extent is your organisation successfully addressing the challenges it currently faces?** Are there domains or activities or user groups where your organisation is somehow performing inadequately, or even failing to accomplish its objectives? What do your data and current feedback mechanisms tell you? How would you know if your organisation was failing? Might you need different or better data to know?

The next chapter presents design as a profession and as a set of emerging methodologies that may be uniquely positioned to contribute to addressing a range of public problems.

Notes

[1] This section builds in part in Bason (2014b).
[2] Inaugural address, 20 January 1981 (Reagan, 1981).

THREE

The changing nature
of design

Design is one of the basic characteristics of what it
means to be human, and an essential determinant of
the quality of human life. (John Heskett, *Toothpicks
and logos*, 2002, p 5)

On 26 May 2011 the international news magazine *The Economist*
featured the cover headline 'Welcome to the Anthropocene',
depicting an artificially created Earth. The issue noted that,
according to geologists, humankind is entering a new era
where the majority of our planet's geological, ecological and
atmospheric processes are affected by humans. Our civilization's
entry into the Anthropocene, literally meaning 'The Age of
Man', underlines how our species is increasingly shaping our
environments not only locally but also at a global scale to meet
our needs. This shift is characterised by some as 'the human turn',
a world in which 'man has increasingly moved to the centre as a
creature that has set itself above and beyond, and even reshaped,
its natural surroundings' (Raffnsøe, 2013, p 5). This fact has
wide-reaching implications for many of our natural scientific
disciplines and for our understanding of our role on the planet.

The human turn can be construed from a range of angles –
geological, philosophical, social and industrial. The coming of
the Anthropocene might also be seen as the culmination of the
last several hundred years' *design* of the increasingly human-
made environments in which we live: 'The capacity to shape
our world has now reached such a pitch that few aspects of the
planet are left in pristine condition, and, on a detailed level, life

is entirely conditioned by designed outcomes of one kind or another' (Heskett, 2002, p 8). The notion that our planet can be transformed by design is by no means new. In fact, the universality of design is a key strand in much thinking and writing on design. Buckminster Fuller, the futurist, architect and designer suggested already in the early 1970s, in Victor Papaneks' *Design for the real world*, that 'Design is everything'. C. West Churchman, in 1971, asserted that 'We believe we can change our environment in ways that will better serve our purposes' (1971, p 3). Norman Potter opens his influential book, *What is a Designer?*, with the statement that 'Every human being is a designer' (Potter, 2002).

Behind much of the contemporary understanding of design is a notion of design as a problem-solving activity. Famously, when asked about the boundaries of design, the renowned furniture designer Charles Eames answered 'What are the boundaries of problems?' (Moggridge, 2007, p 648). Design thus cuts across all other human activities as a particular concept that addresses how physical, commercial, social and public outcomes are created. Much of this design activity is not explicit, or intentional. As the digital, social and physical tools for designing are becoming democratised, 'everybody designs'. Professor Ezio Manzini at Milan Polytechnic, a leading design school, distinguishes between 'diffuse design', by non-experts or ordinary people, and 'expert design', by professionally trained designers (Manzini, 2015, p 37).

While it can be debated whether design is 'everything', it seems without doubt that 'life in contemporary society is saturated by design' (Simonsen et al, 2014, p 1). However, as design has reached this saturation point, not least through the proliferation of physical objects and expressions, it has begun to undergo significant change. Forms and objects of design move towards services and systems, design practice is changing with notions of strengthened end-user and stakeholder involvement, and with new ideas about the contributions of design to the theory and practice of management. At a deeper level, the context for design is changing. Design as a discipline is being redefined by technological and social megatrends that have significance for how organisations are run, how products and services are shaped and how value is created. As part of this shift in context, design is finding its way into the public sector.

This chapter provides an overview of the context, history, development and definition of design towards 'new' forms and meanings of design, and the emergent application of design in the public sector. It aims to unwrap the various definitions and directions and to distil some characteristics or sensibilities of design approaches. It develops the idea of design management and the notion of public managers as designers – a key theme in this book. Finally I discuss the notion and role of design as a particular 'attitude'.

The splintering of design

The rise of design as a distinct profession in contemporary society was historically linked to industrialisation and the rise of mass production, which in turn was driven by developments in technology and in the organisation of work (Sparke, 2004; Manzini, 2015). In this perspective, design is a key factor linking consumption and new technological opportunities. As designers found ways to create marketable products that fulfilled people's tastes and demands, these in turn influenced modern society's culture of consumption.

Just plainly observing everyday life in our current society, it seems clear that objects of consumption, ranging from the clothes we wear to the mobile phones we carry and to our preferred forms of transportation, are powerful signifiers of our identity. In other words, there has historically been a 'close-coupled, recursive relation between the design profession and the structure of capitalist society' (Shove et al, 2007, p 120). Not only that, but designed products influence how we behave in our daily lives. As is recognised in fields as diverse as sociology, anthropology, behavioural science and technology, material objects make particular social and practical arrangements possible in our lives and in society. According to Shove et al (2007), this means that design is located as a medium through which social and commercial ambitions are materialised and realised. Friedman and Stolterman (2014, p viii) say that design 'is always more than a general, abstract way of working. Design takes concrete form in the work of the service professions that meet human needs, a broad range of making and planning disciplines.'

Even as we note that much of our current world is essentially designed and shaped by humans, and as the context for design has shifted markedly over time, there is no clear picture of what exactly characterises design activity.[1] Richard Buchanan proposes that design can be thought of as *a liberal art of technological culture*. In this definition, design is viewed as an integrative, supple discipline, 'amenable to radically different interpretations in philosophy as well as in practice' (1990, p 18). As Buchanan suggests, the history of design, as well as contemporary developments in design, shows that design has not one, but many shapes. Part of this challenge, but perhaps also the richness of the term, is that design can be treated 'ambiguously both as a process and as a result of that process' (Sparke, 2004, p 3). According to others, design holds substantially more than these two dimensions, so that '"design" has so many levels of meaning that it is itself a source of confusion' (Heskett, 2002, p 5).

Heskett points out that since design has never grown to be a unified profession like law, engineering or medicine, the field has 'splintered into ever-greater subdivisions of practice' (Heskett, 2002, p 7). In spite of this splintering, some overall patterns in the meaning of design may none the less be identified. These patterns are very closely related to the history of design and its relations to industrial society laid out in the preceding section.

For the purpose of understanding what it is to design, in the context of this book I suggest that design can be viewed as (1) a *plan* for achieving a particular change; (2) a *practice* with a particular set of approaches, methods, tools and processes for creating such plans; (3) a certain way of *reasoning* underlying or guiding these processes. Each of these understandings of design has been, and still is, undergoing significant development, and I address each of those emergent patterns, or 'layerings' to use another term suggested by Heskett, relating to planning, practices and reasoning, respectively. The definitions pave the way for considering design more explicitly as a particular approach to management and to leading organisational change, which I consider in more detail in the final section in this chapter.

Design as plan: towards the social

The late Bill Moggridge, a co-founder of the design firm IDEO and director of the Cooper-Hewitt design museum in New York, suggests that we look to the famous design couple Charles and Ray Eames for a useful definition of design. According to Charles Eames, design can be defined as 'A plan for arranging elements in such a way as to best accomplish a particular purpose' (quoted in Moggridge, 2007, p 648). Eames hereby highlights the emphasis in design of arrangement, construction of various parts as well as purposefulness: design is concerned with achieving a particular intent. Roughly in line with this definition, Herbert Simon proposed in the late 1960s in his work *The sciences of the artificial* that 'everyone designs who devises courses of action aimed at changing existing situations into preferred ones' (Simon, 1996, p 111). In Simon's definition the plan has to do with establishing possible actions, again with the intent to change the current order. Whether that intent is for a commercial or a social purpose is left open.

The question of what the design plan is *for*, or what the nature of the intended change is supposed to be, has developed significantly over time in terms of variation and refinement. The objective of design has moved far beyond the creation of physical products or graphics, towards services and systems. 'Historically, design changed "things". More recently it's changed services and interactions. Looking ahead it will change companies, industries and countries. Perhaps it will eventually change the climate and our genetic code,' claims a book on the new features of design (Giudice and Ireland, 2014). However, the notion that design addresses a broader set of objectives is by no means new. Donald Schön, in his 1983 seminal work, *The reflective practitioner: How professionals think in action*, quips that 'Increasingly there has been a tendency to think of policies, institutions, and behaviour itself, as objects of design' (1983, p 77). While he was sceptical of the risk of blurring the differences and specific properties across professions spanning from architecture and media to policy making, Schön acknowledged that 'we may discover, at a deeper level, a generic design process which underlies these differences' (1983, p 77).

According to Richard Buchanan, design affects contemporary life in at least four areas: symbolic and visual design (*communication*), the design of material objects (*construction*), design of activities and organised services (*strategic planning*) and the design of complex systems or environments for living, working, playing and learning (*systemic integration*) (Buchanan, 1990). Elizabeth Sanders and Pieter Jan Stappers (2008) similarly argue that design as a discipline is undergoing a significant transformation, which incidentally places it more squarely at the heart of an organisation's ability to create new valuable solutions.

Design is also increasingly embracing 'the social'. Ezio Manzini (2011, p 1) emphasises that design in the 21st century has followed the evolution of economic thinking in reflecting '*the loss of the illusion of control, or the discovery of complexity*' [original emphasis]. This has contributed to a wider change in design culture that has arguably been under way since the late 1960s and that could be characterised as 'design for social good'. Although he has been criticised for an overly rational and perhaps reductionist interpretation of design as a 'science of the artificial', Herbert Simon himself addressed design for social planning. He proposed that there are wider implications of design activity, which requires careful consideration of issues such as problem representation, data, client relationships, the designer's time and attention, and ambiguity of goals and objectives (Simon, 1996, p 141).

The intersection of the recognition of social complexity, which might be understood as the characteristic of highly interconnected systems (Colander and Kupers, 2014) on the one hand, and the ambition to design for positive social change on the other, has led to multiple new strands of design. This is in part captured by the movement of social entrepreneurship and social innovation (Mulgan et al, 2006; Murray et al, 2009; Ellis, 2010; Manzini, 2015), and in part by the growing interest in public sector innovation (Mulgan and Albury, 2003; Eggers and O'Leary, 2009; Bason, 2010; Boyer et al, 2011; Manzini and Staszowski, 2013; Bason, 2014a). One of the foremost observers and documenters of the transformation of the design discipline, Liz Sanders, suggests that today, 'Design can bring the foundational skills of visualization, problem solving and creativity to a collective level and seed the emergence of transdisciplinary approaches to addressing the complex issues critical to society today' (2014, p 133).

Design as practice: more 'co'

Shifting to understanding design as practice, or capacity, numerous definitions come to the surface. John Heskett proposes that design is best defined as 'the human capacity to shape and make our environments in ways unprecedented in nature, to serve our needs and give meaning to our lives' (2002, p 7). Others contend that design practice can be considered as the discipline of melding the sensibility and methods of a designer with what is technologically feasible to meet people's real-world needs (Norman, 1988; Sanders and Stappers, 2008; Brown, 2009; Halse et al, 2010; Michlewski, 2015). This definition highlights tools and concrete practices connected to running specific design projects and shaping new products or services. One might characterise this as much as a capability (Heskett, 2002; Jenkins, 2008; Cooper et al, 2011).

As with recent developments in design as plan, design practice has developed tremendously in the past few decades. Meyer (2014) pragmatically notes that design must be understood as a set of activities: 'methods, approaches and techniques that provide its practitioners with a way of working together in a highly productive way' (2014, p 188). The perhaps most fundamental shift has been that of questioning the role of the gifted, single 'heroic' designer as the key agent in design practice, and viewing design practice much more as a social, collaborative process. This certainly does not mean that the iconic, gifted designer is no longer a key figure in our Western commercial culture; one might even argue that superstar designers have never been more celebrated. Further, it does not mean that there is no difference between highly professional expert designers, on the one hand, and 'everday designers', on the other (Boland and Collopy, 2004; Verganti, 2009; Manzini, 2015)

However, across business and government significant strands of design practice are simultaneously shifting to 'co': To *col*-laboration, *co*-creation and *co*-design as central features, emphasising the explicit and systematic involvement of users, clients, partners, suppliers and other stakeholders in the design process and, in essence, challenging the role of the single designer (von Hippel, 2005; Shove et al, 2007; Michlewski, 2008, 2015; Sanders and Stappers, 2008; Bason, 2010; Halse et al, 2010; Meroni and Sangiorgi, 2011; Ansell and Torfing, 2014). Variations such as participatory design and service design, which focus on (re)designing service processes, are rapidly growing (Bate and Robert, 2007; Shove et al, 2007; Brown, 2009; Cooper and Junginger, 2011; Polaine et al, 2013; Manzini, 2015). In particular, the new shapes of design 'for' a variety of purposes are usually associated with such a social or collaborative approach where outcomes are co-created or co-designed together with a variety of actors, often taking the perspectives of end-users such as consumers or citizens as their point of departure. In fact, design is increasingly explicitly characterised as 'human centred' (Brown, 2009; European Commission, 2012). This in turn has brought more research-oriented activities to design practice, including methods drawing on anthropology and ethnography. Halse et al (2010, p 27) suggest three major strategies that embody the notion of a design-anthropological approach.

- *Exploratory inquiry:* researching without a prior hypothesis to be tested but, rather, aiming at understanding purpose and intent: why, for whom, and for what is a certain understanding directed?
- *Sustained participation:* 'No design team will possess all the relevant knowledge by itself', claim Halse et al (2010), and they suggest that clients and stakeholders must be engaged in a continuous dialogue.
- *Generative prototyping:* taking problems and solutions as the basic elements of continuous loops of iterations. By experimenting and trying out different thoughts and actions, generative prototypes evaluate not only whether a solution will work, but also whether the understanding is right and allows new meanings to evolve within the network of stakeholders.

So the tools applied for collaborative design include, for instance, methods for creative problem solving, user research and involvement, visualisation, concept development, rapid prototyping, test and experimentation, all of which help designers to 'rehearse the future' (Halse et al, 2010). In the context of the emerging field of design it also seems clear that the role of the (specialist) designer is shifting towards one as process facilitator or coach (Shove et al, 2007; Sanders and Stappers, 2008; Meyer, 2011). The change here cannot be over-estimated: the traditional role of the designer was to work with a client, either as an external consultant or in a design function within a firm, to provide design 'input' based on a brief or problem specification. In the collaborative mode of design, the role of the designer – while still drawing on his or her professional practices, attitudes and ways of reasoning – is essentially to involve actors from end-users to managers to staff in a process of discovery and co-creation. Table 3.1, first suggested by Sherry Arnstein (1969) and later developed by Sabine Junginger, seeks to illustrate the span of roles of citizens' engagement with public authorities on a 'ladder' from highly subordinate to highly empowered.[2]

Table 3.1: Ladder of citizen involvement in decision making

Level	Role of citizen
Citizen control Delegated power	Decision making *by* citizen
Placation Consultation Informing	Decision making *with* citizen
Therapy Manipulation	Decision making *for* citizen

The table illustrates that citizens can be cast into widely different roles, depending on the way in which government bodies choose to engage with them. Creating the right conditions for enabling these citizen roles can be viewed as a design task.

Design as a way of reasoning: design thinking and beyond

This set of definitions include design as a *mind-set* (Sanders, 2014), a way of *thinking* (Buchanan, 1990; Brown, 2009; Martin 2009) or an *attitude* (Boland and Collopy, 2004; Michlewski 2008, 2015). Arguably, design thinking is the strand, or interpretation, of design which since the early 2000s has become almost a household term in business circles (Brown, 2009; Martin 2009). Roger Martin (2009) characterises design thinking as the ability to manage and move between the opposing processes of *analysis*, involving rigour and 'algorithmic' exploitation, on the one hand, and *synthesis*, involving interpretation and exploration of 'mysteries', on the other hand. At the heart of design thinking is thus, according to Martin, the balancing or bridging of two different cognitive styles: the analytical-logical mind-set that characterises many large organisations and professional bureaucracies, and the more interpretative, intuitive mind-set that characterises the arts and creative professions. Martin highlights the capacity for *abductive reasoning* – which he describes as the ability to detect and follow a 'hunch' about a possible solution, bridging the gap between analysis and synthesis (Martin, 2007; 2009).

As Piore and Lester (2006), as well as Verganti (2009), have argued, intuition and the ability to interpret information to form new solutions is the 'missing dimension' of innovation. Tim Brown also acknowledges explicitly, referring to Martin's *The Opposable Mind* (Martin, 2007), that 'design thinking is neither art nor science nor religion. It is the capacity, ultimately, for *integrative* thinking' (Brown, 2009). Perhaps the integrative nature of design has best been characterised by Dick Buchanan, who states that design thinking is about moving toward 'new integrations of signs, things, actions and environments that address the concrete needs and values of human beings in diverse circumstances' (1990, p 20). This directs our attention to understanding design as an approach to management, placing it 'at the core of effective strategy development, organizational change, and constraint-sensitive problem solving' (Boland and Collopy, 2004, p 17).

However, the term design thinking has also attracted wide criticism. One of its earliest and most vocal proponents, Bruce Nussbaum, distanced himself from the term in a widely read op-ed titled 'Design Thinking is a Failed Experiment. So What's Next?' (Nussbaum, 2011). Interestingly, his piece coincided with his launch of a new book titled *Creativity Quotient*, which argues that organisations need to foster creativity rather than embrace design.

More serious critique has been launched from design circles that argue that exactly the term 'thinking' misses the point, since design is as much a practice, even a craft, as it is a particular way of thinking. From this point of view design thinking is considered somewhat shallow. However, there is probably no doubt that the label 'thinking' has been instrumental in propelling design, as a discipline, into the awareness of managers, public as well as private. Design thinking, as a term and as it has been portrayed in a wide range of articles and books, has helped to popularise design far beyond the profession and related practices. Michlewski (2015, p 144) has sought to create some order in the various design 'frames' by suggesting that design thinking mainly places itself squarely between the *practical* concerns of design professionals, on the one hand, and the *epistemic* concerns of design researchers and philosophers, on the other. He characterises design thinking as 'a movement that promotes the philosophies, methods and tools that originate in the practice and culture of the design professions' (2015, p xviii).

In summary, this section has discussed three perspectives, which help define design. As shown in the table below, I have characterised each perspective and how it is undergoing change.

Table 3.2: Changing definitions of design

Design defined as	Characteristics	From	To
Plan	Plan for creating graphics, products, services, systems.	Commercial	Social
Practice	Methods for creative problem-solving, user research, involvement, visualisation, concept development, rapid prototyping, test and experimentation.	Expert	Collaborative
Reasoning	The cognitive ability to move between the opposing processes of *analysis*, involving rigour and 'algorithmic' exploitation, and *synthesis*, involving interpretation and exploration.	Thinking	Thinking-in-action

Increasingly, design is thus viewed as more than approaches and tools. It is also a discipline that has inspired non-designers to borrow some of its approaches and tools into the sphere of management. In the following I will consider two dimensions of this discussion. First, the management of design, and second, designing as managing, or as a particular attitude to managing that challenges our understanding of managers as decision makers.

From design management to managing as designing[3]

One of the insights I have found to resonate most powerfully with public managers (and, indeed, many leaders in business as well) is the following characterisation by Case Western professors Richard Boland and Fred Collopy:

> Managers, as designers, are thrown into situations that are not of their own making yet for which they are responsible to produce a desired outcome. They operate in a problem space with no firm basis for judging one solution as superior to another, and still they must proceed. (Boland and Collopy, 2004, p 17)

With the term 'thrownness', Boland and Collopy refer to the scholar of sense making in organisations, Karl Weick, who argues that any design activity must necessarily take place in an environment already ripe with 'designed' activities (Weick, 2004). Hereby the role of design becomes one of re-design, not of designing on a blank slate. The job of management, as designing, becomes one of balancing on-going decision making with efforts to design (new) practices. Boland and Collopy's edited volume further explores what a design vocabulary, a design 'attitude' and design practice might bring to the management profession.

Cooper and Junginger (2011, p 1) state that the intersection of design and management has generated decades of 'lively debate' in the design and business communities. What are the relationships between design and management, and between management of design and design management? As new and more collaborative approaches to innovation in the public sector are coming to the fore, this question is increasingly relevant to public managers. As service design, interaction design, human-centred design and strategic design approaches – in their various shapes and forms – are being applied to public problems, it becomes increasingly important to reflect on how managers relate to these strategies (Table 3.2).

Cooper and Junginger argue that the third paradigm – design capability – is particularly salient in public sector setting, as a reflection of the social and human nature of most, if not all, public policy concerns. A global environment characterised by intractable social, economic, environmental and political challenges calls for an increased use of design-led approaches to problem solving: 'Because the skills and methods that constitute design are useful in responding to the challenges facing us today, designing is now being recognized as a general human capability. As such, it can be harnessed by organizations and apply to a wide range of organizational problems' (Cooper and Junginger, 2011, p 27).

Table 3.3: Paradigms of design management

Function	Design practice	Design management	Design capability
Adds value through ...	Aesthetics, product innovation, differentiation	Interpreting the need, writing the brief, selecting the designer, managing the design and delivery process	Humanistic, comprehensive, integrative, visual approaches
Solves problems of design relating to ...	Products, brands, services	All aspects of design in the organization, but principally products, brands and services	Change in environment, society, economy, politics and organisations
Develops and fosters design competency among ...	Top management, board members, design leaders, design consultants, design team, cross-disciplinary design teams	Top management, board members, senior management, design management consultants	Every area of the organisation
Achieves objectives of ...	Managing design to deliver strategic goals	Managing design to deliver strategic goals	Delivering sustainable organisations in the context of societal and global well-being

Source: Cooper and Junginger (2011)

Of concern to this book is how public managers themselves engage with 'design' in their quest to proactively use their organisations to effect human and societal progress. The question then becomes not only how design approaches are in practice applied in public sector organisations to tackle public problems, but also the evolution of design capability: how public managers themselves 'design' in their quest to proactively affect human and societal progress (Boland and Collopy, 2004).

In search of design attitude

We have seen that design can be viewed as a particular way of reasoning; however, in considering 'design attitude' there is more to this perspective on design.

Richard Boland has argued that 'The way we narrate the story of our experience to ourselves and others as we engage in a series of events gives meaning to the problem space we construct and the calculations we make within it' (Boland and Collopy, 2004, p 107). In this book I will therefore examine how particular public managers tell their stories of innovation and change, which happens to be in contexts where design approaches have been utilised. How do they, as managers and leaders, think and act as part of that process? How do they 'design'?

The notion of 'managers designing' implies that they go about innovation activities in line with what Boland and Collopy (2004) have called a 'design attitude', In a somewhat similar vein, Tom Peters (1997) writes of 'design mindfulness' as a way to approach problems, questioning what the manager can do to make solutions work better for the organisation and/or those around it. Meyer (2011, p 197) points out that in change projects building on internal expertise, 'every organization has a few of these individuals who may not instinctively self-identify as designers or design thinkers but who display an immediately recognizable set of behaviours that tag them as design minded'. Similarly, the public managers I have interview for the present research do not generally think of themselves as designers, but they do seem to display attitudes or behaviours that are 'design minded'.

Boland and Collopy define design attitude as the 'expectations and orientations one brings to a design project' (Boland and Collopy, 2004, p 9). They make the point that 'a design attitude views each project as an opportunity for invention that includes a questioning of basic assumptions and a resolve to leave the world a better place than we found it' (Boland and Collopy, 2004, p 9). They hereby frame *design attitude* in opposition to a *decision attitude*, which portrays the manager as facing a fixed set of alternative courses of action from which a choice must be made. A decision attitude is suited for clearly defined and stable situations and when the feasible alternatives are well known. The highly influential Herbert Simon's scholarship across nearly half a century was to establish the role of management as that of representing problems and making decisions between a set of alternatives.

However, many of the problem sets facing managers – including public managers – in the current environment have vastly different, less stable and more complex characteristics, which may call for an increased focus on design attitude. By complex characteristics I refer to systems with large numbers of interacting elements; where interactions are non-linear so that minor changes can have disproportionately large consequences; which are dynamic and emergent; and where hindsight cannot lead to foresight because external conditions constantly change (Snowden and Boone, 2007; Bourgon, 2012). Not all public problems are like this, but many are. We could therefore ask whether the concept of design attitude can help us to understand the role of the public manager as someone who catalyses innovation, often in complex settings, by taking responsibility, in different ways, for designing organisational responses to the challenges and opportunities they face.

Such a break from the mainstream understanding of 'managing as making decisions' towards 'managing as designing' is significant, and essentially underlies the entire emerging paradigm of design as a discipline of management. In a nutshell, design methods offer the potential to reframe the role of management from 'decision making' (choosing from alternatives) to 'future making' (creating the alternatives from which to choose). The key question becomes whether managers possess, or can come to possess, the skills, tools and processes that allow them to address problems in designerly ways.

In a systematic exploration of what Boland and Collopy's notion of design attitude might entail, Kamil Michlewski (2008) undertook doctoral research in which he interviewed a number of design consultants and managers from firms like IDEO and Philips Design and mapped how these people viewed their roles and practices. On the basis of this study he subsequently proposed five characteristic dimensions of design attitude. More recently, he has developed his thesis into a book (Michlewski, 2015) and has tested a number of the design attitude dimensions statistically through a questionnaire-based survey among 235 designers and non-designers (174 classified themselves as designers). According to Michlewski (2015), the survey showed a statistically significant difference in the attitudinal dimensions between designers and non-designers.

These attitudinal dimensions are a useful conceptual frame for understanding public managers' approaches to problem solving and the generation of new ideas, innovations and governance models by engaging with design. The design attitudes as presented in Michlewski's most recent and developed (2015) work are as follows:[4]

- *Embracing uncertainty and ambiguity.* Michlewski perceives this dimension in terms of the willingness to engage in a process that is not pre-determined or planned ahead, and where outcomes are unknown or uncertain. It is an approach to change that is open to risk and the loss of control. According to Michlewski, really creative processes are 'wonky' and often stop-start. The challenge for managers is to not resist, but to allow for the creative process to unfold.[5] One might say that this reflects an acceptance of Boland and Collopy's (2004) point that managers operate in a problem space where the basis for judging one solution as superior to another is at best questionable. Managers who embrace uncertainty and ambiguity are likely to say 'why don't we just do it and see where it leads us?'
- *Engaging deep empathy.* Michlewski finds that designers intuitively 'tune in' to people's needs and how they as users

relate to signs, things, services and systems. What do people want, what kind of quality of life are they seeking? Using true empathy requires courage and honesty in abandoning one's mental models. Engaging personal and commercial empathy is, in Michlewski's interpretation, also about listening to better understand the human, emotional aspect of experiencing products and services.

- *Embracing the power of the five senses.* According to Michlewski, designers have a 'fondness' for using their aesthetic sense and judgement while interacting with the environment. As a third dimension of design attitude, this is not only about 'making things visible', or about crafting beautiful designs, but about merging form and function in ways that work well for people, drawing on all five human senses. Michlewski (2015, p 84) characterises it as the ability to 'appreciate and use the feedback provided by multiple senses to assess the efficacy of the solutions they are developing'. Designers recognise the significance of a range if sensory stimuli and are more likely than other professionals engage consciously with multiple senses in their work.

- *Playfully bringing to life.* To Michlewski this attitude concerns the ability to create 'traction' and direction in an innovative process or dialogue. In his research Michlewski finds that designers believe in the power of humour, playfulness and bringing ideas to life. At the heart of design practice, he finds, is an attitude that embraces unexpected experimentation and exploration. This dimension is closely related to designers' affinity for creating things, for creatively bringing new ideas to fruition. One designer in Michlewski's research describes this as the process of visualisation and rapid prototyping – a core activity of many, if not all, designers. From a management perspective one could view this as the desire to effect change and create value; to see that new ideas about strategy or organisation are realised.

- *Creating new meaning from complexity.* Michlewski argues that what is at the heart of designers' ways of doing things is the ability to reconcile multiple, often contradicting points of view into something valuable that works – they use empathy as the gauge. This describes the designer as a person who

49

'consolidates various meanings and "reconciles" contradicting objectives' (Michlewski 2008, p 5). This reflects an ability to view a situation from a wide variety of perspectives, essentially creating a landscape for exploring further problems. Michlewski defines this process, essentially of consolidating multidimensional meanings, as the manager's ability to operate in an analytical-synthetical loop in order to achieve a balance between the cohesion of the organisation, on the one hand, and external constraints, on the other.

These five dimensions were empirically derived through ethnographic research within the design consultancy community; a significant number of the interviewees were themselves trained designers. Most public managers have a professional and experiential background that is vastly different; and their personal characteristics and attitudes are, one should think, unlikely to be similar to those of designers. However, design attitude is an interesting interpretative prism. Some of the more intriguing questions might be: Are managers who choose to engage with design practice (for instance by hiring service designers to develop a particular service or policy) somehow inclined to display something akin to the attitude of professional designers? And further, does the concrete unfolding of a design project catalyse more of a design attitude on the part of the manager, essentially enabling the emergence of some degree of stronger design sensibility, or confidence?

Design defined

Through the sections above I have shown how design is a profession undergoing change and that is now lending itself to a very broad range of applications, increasingly also in the public and social sector. Design is becoming not only more socially oriented but also more collaborative, open and engaging. For the purpose of this book, I suggest the following definition of design as an approach or process:

> Design is a systematic, creative process that combines different elements to achieve a particular commercial

or societal purpose. The process is visual and experimental, with human experience and behaviour at its core. The results can be graphics, products, services, systems and new organisation and governance models.

This definition can be useful to keep in mind as I unfold how public managers have used design in practice, in Part Two of the book.

How to do it: raising the organisation's design awareness

This chapter has explored what design is and what it could mean in a management and policy context, and how the discipline is undergoing significant transformations. I have discussed the emerging, if perhaps still somewhat marginal, practices of co-design, service design and related approaches as a distinct branch of the design profession. Further, I have relayed the relatively novel phenomenon – rising over the last decade or so – of applying design to public services. Finally, I have considered the tentative discussions and perspectives on the relationship between management and design, or managers and designers, which still seem to be relatively unexplored. A key point here is how the use of design signifies a fundamentally different approach to leading change.

As a public manager who is curious to engage with design, your starting point could be:

- **Understanding the value designers and design approaches can bring** to your organisation, beyond graphic design and visual communication, but as a strategic and socially oriented and collaborative approach to innovation.
- Recognising that **much design work in the public sector is not about novelty or invention**, but about re-design of current solutions and systems. This entails dealing with the 'thrownness' of everyday life as a manager, carving out the time and opportunity to ask what the need for change really is.
- **Reflecting on what a design attitude to management might mean** for your own leadership practice. Not least,

51

what would it mean if new projects were really addressed more often as opportunities for re-invention and re-design?

- **Being willing to invest in design**, either by commissioning outside consultancy services or by recruiting designers into development and innovation roles in public sector organisations, perhaps organised in innovation teams or labs.

The following chapter charts the emergence of a new paradigm of public management and analyses the surprisingly similar kinds of changes that are taking place within that profession.

Notes

[1] The following sections build on Bason (2014b).

[2] First relayed by Sabine Junginger at a paper presentation at the DMI research conference in London, September 2014.

[3] This section builds on Bason (2014a).

[4] The original (Michlewski, 2008) terminology on design attitudes was a little less straightforward, which perhaps reflects that Michlewski's recent work (2015) is intended for a wider and also non-academic audience: (1) embracing discontinuity and open-endedness; (2) engaging polysensorial aesthetics; (3) engaging personal and commercial empathy; (4) creating, bringing to life; (5) consolidating multi-dimensional meanings.

[5] Based on e-mail correspondence with author (February–March 2014) and subsequent cross-referencing with his new book (Michlewski, 2015).

FOUR

In search of the next
governance model

It is both misguided and remarkably premature to
announce the death of the ethos of bureaucratic office.
(Paul du Gay, *In Praise of Bureaucracy*, 2000, p 146)

Often, when I have been involved in conversations on the
future of government, the term 'bureaucracy' has been invoked
as the ultimate threat to innovation and change in public
organisations. However, the daily reality of almost every
manager and employee in the public sector is that bureaucratic
management is a fundamental part of how they work. As new
forms of innovative ways of working are introduced, they must
thus come somehow to co-exist with the existing paradigm. In
one public organisation that I have worked with, the staff chose
to embrace the interplay between bureaucracy and innovation
by coining the term 'innocracy'. They recognised that in their
work (taxation services), there might be a need for fresh thinking
and innovation, but some of the core bureaucratic ground rules
were probably sound enough.

Certainly, the presence of bureaucratic governance cannot be
ignored. Peters (2010, p 147) suggests that 'Despite numerous
changes in the public sector, Max Weber's conceptions
of bureaucracy still constitute the starting point for most
discussions'; and so will they for discussion in this book. My
sense is that without an honest recognition of our bureaucratic
legacy and its strengths and weaknesses, much work to bring
design into play in public organisations will remain unrealistic,
out of touch with reality and naïve.

I thus start this chapter by providing a classic typology of three eras of public management: traditional public administration, new public management and networked governance. I characterise the two first approaches before expanding on the nature and properties associated with networked governance. I consider whether – as some now claim – public management theory and practice might be undergoing transformations that (roughly) follow a trajectory that mirrors the evolution of the design profession. What are the principles and patterns within the chorus of voices arguing for new approaches to public management?

I conclude the chapter by examining an intriguing question: Is some degree of convergence taking place between design and public management? To what extent are recent developments in the two fields somewhat similar? What does that tell us about the potential of design approaches to catalyse the next public governance model?

The quest for a new paradigm

In a recent analysis of the future of the state Yves Doz, a strategy professor, and Mikko Koskonen, a Finnish senior government official, point out that the complexity of the policy environment has developed dramatically at the same time (especially since the 2008 global financial crisis) that the availability of resources has declined. Government organisations find themselves under conditions of technological, environmental, social and political turbulence at the same time as their access to funding and resources is constrained. Part of the austerity has perhaps to some extent been self-imposed, but none the less, the current situation seems to present three major challenges that put the current model of public governance under strain (Doz and Koskonen, 2014, pp 6–8): *strategic atrophy, the imprisonment of resources*, and *diverging commitments*. Doz and Koskonen argue that 'many policies need to incorporate a far wider array of contingencies and interrelated factors in their search for solutions – decision-makers need to dig deeper in their search for solutions, seek input from farther afield, and execute as a "single, unified government" rather than from their traditional bureaucratic silos' (2014, p 6). As Ansell and Torfing (2014) argue, this kind of collaborative approach to public sector innovation calls not for less management, but for a *different* kind of management and governance.

Not least, the siloed nature of organisations and knowledge domains is a key legacy of public institutions. Professional disciplines such as economics, law and health work in distinct organisational and professional domains have a tendency to impede communication, thus creating a culture of hyper-specialisation. Each discipline or agency looks at the world through its perceptual lens and operates within the rules of the silo, creating biases. This is particularly problematic, given that the types of scaled challenges discussed above are interlaced, with interdependencies that do not respect disciplinary silos. The central planning culture and political aversion to real experimentation work against modalities of innovation that are focused on fundamentally rethinking solutions and systems (Doz and Koskonen, 2014; Banerjee, 2014).

The need for better alignment between public organisations, their objectives and their changing context has certainly not gone unnoticed among public management practitioners and scholars. So, what are the discussions within public management, how is the existing legacy being challenged and to what extent might the changes occurring even be somehow aligned with the innovations taking place within the design profession?

The next governance model: searching for a new balance

The search is on among public management practitioners, scholars and consultants for a new form of public governance. That search is best understood in the frame of the governance models we have inherited. These matters have been discussed in the public management literature intensely for the last two decades. My purpose here is to highlight some of the key themes from this vast literature. One of the most-quoted contributions to the public management literature is Benington and Hartley's (2001) distinction between bureaucracy or 'traditional' public administration, the 'new' public management and 'networked governance' (Table 4.1).

Table 4.1: Competing paradigms: changing ideological conceptions of governance and public management

	Traditional public administration	New public management	Networked governance
Context	Stable	Competitive	Continuously changing
Population	Homogeneous	Atomised	Diverse
Needs/problems	Straightforward, defined by professionals	Wants, expressed through the market	Complex, volatile and prone to risk
Strategy	State and producer centred	Market and customer centred	Shaped by civil society
Governance through actors	Hierarchies Public servants	Markets Purchasers and providers Clients and contractors	Networks and partnerships Civic leadership
Key concepts	Public goods	Public choice	Public value

Source: Benington and Hartley (2001)

These three ideal types of public governance are in many ways artificial distinctions, since one would be hard pressed to find any contemporary Western public sector organisation that did not display some form of hybrid, or mix them all. Before exploring the current search for the next paradigm I will briefly characterise the key tenets of traditional public administration and the new public management, respectively.

Traditional public administration: the Weberian legacy

By some accounts, bureaucracy 'appears to be responsible for most of the troubles of our times' (du Gay, 2000, p 1). Certainly, judging not just from everyday media stories or personal anecdotes but from a very large proportion of recent public management literature, bureaucratic organisations are blamed for many dysfunctions of the public sector (Osborne and Gaebler, 1992; Pollitt, 2003). Indeed, Osborne and Gaebler (1992), among others, have called for the 'reinvention' of public organisations. Likewise, in this book I argue in favour of more innovation in government. However, as du Gay (2000, p 146) asserts towards the end of his contrastingly titled book, *In Praise of Bureaucracy*, when it comes to principles of bureaucracy, 'Many of its key features as they came into existence a century or so ago remain as or more essential to the provision of good government today as they did then (…)'. What are these key factors, then?

Max Weber was the German economist, sociologist and scholar who founded the modern notion of bureaucracy. He addressed concerns about despotism by formalising organisational offices and roles and insisting that these be based on competencies explicitly underpinned by rules, laws and administrative regulations. The scope of power, the capacity to coerce others, was to be defined and limited by regulation, and the selection of people to assume positions of power ws to be determined in accordance with certifiable qualifications. Weber translated these broad ideas into specific principles; according to Wren and Bedeian (2009, pp 231–2), Weberian bureaucracy is based on the following principles.

- *Division of labour:* Labour is divided so that authority and responsibilities are clearly defined.
- *Managerial hierarchy:* Offices or positions are organised in a hierarchy of authority.
- *Formal selection:* All employees are selected on the basis of technical qualifications demonstrated by formal examination, education or training.
- *Career orientation:* Employees are career professionals rather than 'politicians'. They work for fixed salaries and pursue careers within their respective fields.
- *Formal rules:* All employees are subject to formal rules regarding the performance of their duties.
- *Impersonality:* Rules and other controls are impersonal and uniformly applied in all cases.

Certainly, to Max Weber, bureaucracy not only leads to a number of positive outcomes but is a necessity for the functioning of modern capitalist societies. As a modern organisational necessity, the Weberian bureaucracy allegedly leads to at least four positive results (Weber, 1964; du Gay, 2000):

- efficiency
- predictability and reliability

- procedural fairness
- equality and democracy.

A key point to note here is that the production of public *outcomes*, understood as changes in the experience or behaviour of people, business, communities and societies, does not seem to be considered by Weber as an important result in its own right. In other words, the ability of bureaucratic governance to lead to better health, learning, growth or a better environment is not considered very clearly in Weber's writing.

According to Weber, the establishment of a bureaucracy does lead to one potentially important societal outcome, in that it 'favours the levelling of social classes'. He describes this as a virtuous circle where the levelling of social classes in turn positively affects the development of bureaucracy by eliminating class privileges, which makes it less likely that 'occupation of offices' happens based on belonging to a certain class or the size of personal means. This process 'inevitably foreshadows the development of mass democracy' (Weber, 1964, p 340). The efficiency of bureaucracy, in other words, is a prerequisite for effective democracy.

However, as I discussed in Chapter Two and will develop further below, the critique of the ability of bureaucratic organisations to cope with emergence and change has been rising. As I documented in my previous book, *Leading Public Sector Innovation*, the bureaucratic model of governance leads to a range of significant barriers or constraints to innovation in government at numerous levels: the political context (which means that objectives are usually politically given and prone to significant change outside of the public manager's control); the lack of regular market competition and multiple value types, making it difficult to measure and assess the success or failure of government initiatives (Wilson, 1989); limited ability to make and shape long-term strategy (Mulgan, 2009; Doz and Koskonen, 2014); hierarchical and bureaucratic organisational structures; limited and often inefficient leveraging of new information technology; and (too) homogenous a composition of managers and staff, to name just a few (Osborne and Brown, 2005; van Wart, 2008; Bason, 2010; Doz and Koskonen, 2014).

Current government systems, drawing on their bureaucratic legacy, have largely been built to ensure efficiency, predictability, objectivity and stability – and mass delivery – over adaptation, flexibility, dynamism and more individualised approaches. However, the issue of identifying different and more effective models of governance may not be a question of abandoning existing models and institutions without having anything to place instead. In Marco Steinberg's perspective (2014, p 99), the challenge is that

> to manage a shift towards new competencies, cultures, incentives, and resource allocation models, cannot happen at the expense of the current delivery needs and long-term stability. As such the core issue is to design coherent transitions whereby current obligations can be fulfilled while simultaneously building necessary future ones.

What Steinberg proposes here, in line with Agranoff (2014), is that the introduction of different or new approaches within a government context never happens on a blank canvas. Managers must take account of context, of what is already there, in order to enable sustainable change. A potential problematic part of our current public management legacy is, then, that we may not truly possess the strategies, tools and processes allowing us to make such 'coherent transitions'. As Bourgon (2008, p 390) points out, in spite of the emergence of new articulations of what governance is or could be, 'Public sector organisations are not yet aligned in theory and in practice with the new global context or with the problems they have for their mission to solve'.

The new public management: a call for reinvention

The new public management, which emerged in the 1980s and 1990s, offered a compelling set of principles that set off what has arguably been a world-wide public sector reform movement that has continued to this day (Hood, 1991; Osborne and Gaebler, 1992). The British academic Christopher Hood first coined the term in his seminal article 'A public management for all seasons' (Hood, 1991). However, probably the most central work driving this movement was Osborne and Gaebler's seminal work of 1992, *Reinventing Government: How the Entrepreneurial Spirit is Transforming the Public Sector*. It is worth noting that the 'burning platform', or hopes for change formulated by Osborne and Gaebler, was strikingly similar to the arguments made today by proponents of the emerging management paradigms. For instance, consider this quote (Osborne and Gaebler, 1992, p 15):

> Today's environment demands institutions that are extremely flexible and adaptable. It demands institutions that deliver high-quality goods and services, squeezing ever more bang out of every buck. It demands institutions that are responsive to their customers, offering choices of non-standardized services; that lead by persuasion and incentives rather than commands; that give their employees a sense of meaning and control, even ownership. It demands institutions that empower citizens rather than simply serving them.

In *Reinventing Government*, Osborne and Gaebler introduced 10 principles for new public management that they felt described some of the most innovative and forward-thinking public organisations of their contemporary society. In other words, they offered not so much ideas about what should be done to 'reinvent' the state; they showed what was already happening. Among the principles, there was a strong emphasis on learning from the private sector and benefiting from the introduction of market mechanisms and principles into public service provision. The promotion of competition between service providers and the reframing of citizens as customers, who should be given a range of choices, were each devoted significant treatment in the book. In essence, the market mechanism, according to Osborne and Gaebler (1992, pp 19–20), should replace bureaucratic mechanisms. They even suggest that public organisations should get into the business of 'earning money' rather than only spending it. Additionally, public organisations should measure their performance not on the basis of their expenditures (inputs) or activities but on the basis of the results and outcomes they generate.

As we shall see below, the market-oriented tenets of the new public management have been extensively criticised in the context of the current debate on the next governance paradigm. For the most comprehensive critique to date, Christopher Hood and Ruth Dixon's evaluation of 30 years of new public management reforms in the UK is a key resource (Hood and Dixon, 2015). What is perhaps less well recognised is that Osborne and Gaebler also posited some of the same principles as are being discussed and promoted by the 'next' governance school. For instance, they argued for more mission-driven goals, prevention, and decentralisation of authority. And with a suggestion that resonates with today's discussions on networks, co-production and collective impact, Osborne and Gaebler highlighted the need for government organisations to catalyse a wide span of sectors (public, private, civic) to address problems and create lasting impact.

Rediscovering the state

Different ways of framing the next paradigm that could replace or supplement bureaucracy and the new public management abound, and go beyond the title provided originally by Benington and Hartley: 'governing by network' (Goldsmith and Eggers, 2004); 'co-production' (Alford, 2009); 'collaborative governance' (Paquet, 2009); 'a new synthesis' (Bourgon, 2011); 'collaborative innovation' (Ansell and Torfing, 2014); and 'strategic agility' (Doz and Koskonen, 2014). As Peters (2010, p 145) asserts:

> If bureaucracy has declined as a paradigm for the public sector, however, it has not been replaced with any single model that can provide descriptive and prescriptive certainty. Neither scholars attempting to capture the reality of contemporary public administration, nor politicians and managers attempting to make the system work on a day to day basis, have any simple model of what the contemporary reality is.

Rather than a simple or single model for the next governance approach, a number of different models are currently in play. Christensen (2012) suggests that the organisational forms of public management have become increasingly complex and multifunctional. In a paper titled 'Ideas in Public Management Reform for the 2010s', Carsten Greve (2015) describes three self-styled conceptual alternatives from the literature on public management. 'Self-styled' refers to the fact that these are all explicitly describing themselves as alternatives to the new public management. It is useful, for the purpose of this book, to expand a bit on these conceptual alternatives, as to some degree they make up the playing field onto which new approaches catalysed by design processes would necessarily enter. The next governance model is not a blank space, it is already full of ideas, suggestions, frameworks and approaches – some based on empirical practice, others perhaps still more theoretically informed. Greve (2015) proposes the following alternatives of what might be termed 'emergent public management':

- *Digital-era governance*, which has mainly been formulated by Patrick Dunleavy (Dunleavy et al, 2006). Key components in this governance thinking are obviously the opportunities raised by digital (e-government) services, including issues of transparency, social media and shared service centres. Dunleavy et al characterized digital-era governance as being composed of three elements (Dunleavy et al, 2006). First, the roll-back of agencies, joined-up governance, re-governmentalisation, reinstating central processes, radically squeezing production costs, re-engineering back-office functions, procurement concentration and specialisation and network simplification. Second, a needs-based holism, including client-based or need-based reorganisation, one-stop provision, interactive and ask-once information seeking, data warehousing, end-to-end service re-engineering, agile government processes. And third, 'digitisation' processes among others including electronic service delivery, new forms of automated processes, active channel streaming, facilitating co-production, moving toward open-book government.

- *Public value management*, which has been suggested by Benington and Moore (2011). Here the key themes include strategy making, performance governance and innovation and strategic human resource management. This strand of governance thinking builds in part on Mark Moore's earlier work on public value (Moore, 1995). In terms of strategy making for public value creation, according to Greve, Benington and Moore place public managers in 'a strategic triangle' between a legitimising and authorising environment, an organising environment in their focus and an environment of results; that is, efforts to produce results that are, in effect, a value-creation process. Greve (2015, pp 55–6) suggests (also referencing Alford and O'Flynn) that the public value management framework has something different to offer than new public management. Whereas new public management is competitive government, public value management is post-competitive; it focuses more on relationships, sees collective preferences as expressed, sees how multiple objectives are pursued, including service outputs, satisfaction, outcomes, trust and legitimacy, sees multiple accountability systems. Whereas the preferred system of service delivery under the new public management paradigm is the private sector or tightly defined arm's-length public agencies, public value management's delivery system 'is a menu of alternatives selected pragmatically'. New public value management also expands on the notion of 'performance governance' as an integrated, institutional framework that includes use of data for managing not only performance but also transparency. Finally, according to Greve (2015, p 56), 'The innovation agenda can be accommodated in the discussion of public value management as Moore emphasized the strategic and innovative aspects of public management in his writings.'
- *Collaborative governance, or new public governance.* Here it is scholars such as O'Leary and Bingham (2009), Osborne (2010), Donahue and Zeckhauser (2011) and Ansell and Torfing (2014) who formulate the paradigm. Some of the central concepts here are networks and collaboration, public-private partnerships and new ways of engaging active citizens. Greve (2015, p 58) points out that new public governance

can be viewed as an overarching theory of institutionalised relationships within society, not least when it comes to relations between public organisations and the for- and not-for-profit sectors. New public governance hereby focuses attention on partnerships, networks, joined-up services and new ways to work together. The numerous ways that citizens can become active and enter into co-producing relationships are key (Alford, 2009; Newman and Clarke, 2009). In this paradigm, the strategic orchestration of public-private partnerships, allowing sharing of risk or leveraging of resources, is also a key theme. Finally, when it comes to citizen engagement, new public governance suggests that efforts can be stepped up and become more systematic.

Needed: a governance road map

Carsten Greve's account of the state of the art indicates that the search for the next governance paradigm is still very much on-going. However, some patterns seem to stand out across the three alternatives described above. In a summary of 'post-new public management' reform efforts, Tom Christensen (2012) argues that new governance elements and networks are supplementing hierarchy and market as coordination mechanisms. Organisational forms such as partnerships and collegial bodies spanning organisational boundaries are being used more intensively. Networks have been introduced in most Western democracies as a way to increase the capacity of the public sector to deliver services (Klijn and Skelcher, 2008). Christensen further suggests that there is a state-centric approach to governance in which public-public networks are a main component (Peters and Pierre, 2003). Here civil servants have networking and boundary-spanning competences allowing them to act as go-betweens and brokers across organisational boundaries both vertically and horizontally. Additionally, public-public networks bring together civil servants from different policy areas to trump hierarchy (Hood and Lodge, 2006), that is, they are facilitators, negotiators and diplomats rather than exercising only hierarchical authority, which may be especially important in tackling 'wicked issues' that transcend traditional sectors and policy areas.

The avenue certainly seems open for an exploration of what design approaches really involve, when it comes to implications for the future of public governance. The critical implication is that public managers may need to *discover* for themselves what is the contemporary reality they need to relate to, and govern in, and then make their own judgements as to the right approach.

That being said, the distinction between different governance paradigms allows us to characterise different structures, processes and organising principles that we may find in our public institutions; and it also allows us to ask what a more 'modern', or perhaps 'postmodern' or 're-enchanted', organisation based to a higher degree on networked governance might actually look like. Since 2000, if not earlier, the public management debate not only in academic but also in practitioners' circles began to shift towards the 'networked governance' paradigm. From Goldsmith and Eggers' volume on *Governing by Network* (2004) to Bruno Latour's dry observation that it is time to lay new public management's implicit attack on the state behind us,

> It is amazing that such a dispute could have passed for so long as a serious intellectual endeavour, so obvious is it for us now, that there is no alternative to the State – on condition of rediscovering its realistic cognitive equipment. (Latour, 2007, p 3, original emphasis)

It is exactly this question of 'rediscovering the state', perhaps even more so than 'reinventing it', that this book explores. The question becomes one of how to accommodate the need for a broader and perhaps different vocabulary and, dare one say it, concrete practices for problem solving and for navigating the process towards some different model of governance.

The convergence of design and public management?

I opened this book by suggesting that the worlds and cultures of public management and design were akin to two waves crashing against each other, as if these two different domains of knowledge and professional practice could not fruitfully co-exist. However, I believe this account demonstrates that perhaps the most powerful crash is not necessarily between public management and design per se, but between the 'scientific', bureaucratic and decision-making foundations of public management, on the one hand, and the societal context in which we now live, on the other hand. Is it, rather, a clash between a globalised, fast-paced, 21st-century world infused with technology being governed by institutions designed at the dawn of the 20th-century? Is it the widening gap between the nature of our world and the design 'blueprint' of government that is the real challenge? Is the problem that – to paraphrase Colander and Kupers (2014) – using ever-more refined tools, we have climbed to the top of the mountain of bureaucratic management, only to discover from the top of the pinnacle a very different mountain? Is the issue, as we are beginning to explore a different kind of governance paradigm, that it is an entirely different mountain that must be climbed? And does this particular mountain have more in common with the collaborative design approaches toward which the pendulum is swinging today?

My point is this: as regards the *emerging* forms of governance and design, there are signs of convergence. Building on this chapter and the previous one, what kind of agendas are emerging at the intersection between design and public management?

Design seems to be moving closer to public organisations, and public organisations are, perhaps, opening up to design. Whereas public management may need to begin an ascent of an entirely new mountain, based on something different than bureaucratic governance and rational decision making, design may have to ascend a similarly different mountain, characterised by the new roles of designers as stewards, co-creators and social innovators.

Table 4.2 summarises some of the key shifts happening within public management and design, as discussed here and in the previous chapter, and proposes how they relate.

First, we have seen that public management is opening up: management practice and theory are becoming increasingly receptive to the messiness, complexity and unpredictability of the policy environment. As Peters (2010) argues, that ambiguity may not be a bad thing. There may be advantages, not least 'that the

Table 4.2: Convergence of public management and design

	Emerging public management	Emerging design
Opening up	Recognising the need to deal more proactively with emergence, turbulence, complexity, austerity, increased reflection on the limitations of current governance models	Embracing new social and policy contexts; adopting other disciplines such as anthropology into design practice; building experience base in public service design
Focus shift	Shift from focusing on political and systems level to (also) engaging and differentiating user-level experience, wider stakeholders and focusing on outcomes and public value	Shift from supporting industrial mass production to increased individualisation, tailoring of designed services and products to (co-create) value
Transforming discipline	Search for new tools to achieve change and innovation; recognising that new processes, skills may be needed	Offering new tools for role of designers in relation to stakeholder engagement and collaboration; changing organisations and users
Implications	More systematic innovation in governance and focus on interactions/relations with citizens	Move to strategically position design to support innovation processes in public organisations

latitude for action by the individual is enhanced' (2010, p 156). Recognising the widening gap between the policy levers and tools currently available to managers, in particular within the context of the call for 'innovation' in times of turbulence and austerity, public organisations and their managers are becoming receptive to new ways of doing things, even if they do not know exactly what they are searching for (Goldsmith and Eggers, 2004; Bourgon, 2012; Ansell and Torfing, 2014). As Peters (2010) suggests, they may also be granted, or be increasingly able to grab, the agency needed to engage in that search. As discussed above, the missing link between the current governance paradigms and a future one seems to be the approaches, methodologies and ways of thinking that can drive the *process* and make the transition towards a different future state. This opening up happens as the design discipline is also opening to making a contribution in the policy and social sectors – taking a 'social turn' in terms of context and interest.

Second, public management may already be becoming more balanced, in search of a 'new synthesis' that accommodates more complex and individualised user (citizen, business) needs and adopts structures, processes and technologies to support this shift (Goldsmith and Eggers, 2004; Bourgon, 2012). Focusing on outcomes for citizens, or public value (Moore, 1995; Cole and Parston, 2006), has become increasingly the 'new black' in many public organisations. Similarly, we saw a shift in design's role in industrial society, in part driven by digitisation, to facilitate much more tailor-made and individually oriented 'co-creation of value'. The professional design community itself would certainly argue, as Angela Meyer does (2011, p 188), that 'design is fundamentally about value creation'. Of course, this does not entail, that all is good just by focusing on 'value', or outcomes, understood as the results flowing from public interventions, as both Moore and Cole and Parston would argue. As we saw in the analysis of Weber's principles of bureaucratic organisation, there are other aspects of public organisations that are at stake and that may be at odds with a strong emphasis on outcomes. What happens, for instance, with principles of equality or, for that matter, with efficiency?

Third, as public organisations and their managers are on the search for new process tools, design is transforming: it is taking new forms and is beginning, as a practice and profession, to lend itself to new applications, contexts and roles, also in the domain of public service and policy design (Meyer, 2011; Ansell and Torfing, 2014; Sanders, 2014). The 'social and political turn' in design is happening in sync with a 'collaboration turn' towards increased co-design with stakeholders and users. So, designers, as professionals, are finding themselves increasingly in the role of process designers, facilitators, stewards and orchestrators. Meanwhile, public managers find themselves cast into increasingly complex circumstances in which they are expected to find effective courses of action. In these circumstances, managers are searching for the tools, approaches and perhaps even paradigms that can help them achieve their stated goals.

Fourth, whereas the term 'innovation' has helped to open up and perhaps legitimise the search for 'new public futures' (Christiansen, 2014), managers need to somehow give form, substance and direction to this search. To some extent, this type of search for methodologies and tools to support a paradigm shift has happened before, but in a different context. With the evaluation and performance management movement in the 1990s and 2000s, public managers increasingly accessed tools that could increase transparency, accountability and organisational learning under the overall guise of the new public management. Later, with the lean management 'toolbox' that became strong in the 2000s in the public sector, managers gained access to efficiency- and error-reducing methodologies (essentially, process-innovation tools) that were suited to certain contexts and problems as well. Both of these broad domains of management techniques seem to have fitted quite well with the dominant new public management paradigm, along with Weber's bureaucratic principles of rationality, efficiency and predictability. But what kinds of approaches and methodologies are set to accompany, or perhaps to help realise, an emergent networked 'new' public governance paradigm? Just as the arc of design practice has come round to a more individual and tailored understanding of consumption, interaction and use, so is Benington and Hartley's concept of networked governance – and the other forms of 'new' approaches discussed in contemporary academic circles – also associated with increased 'citizen-centricity' and differentiation as one-size-fits-all approaches begin to give way to more customised and flexible modes of service production (Goldsmith and Eggers, 2004; Alford, 2009; Greve, 2015).

How to do it: exploring the next public governance

This chapter has charted the evolution of public management from Weberian times until today and has characterised the current debate on alternative directions for the next governance model. I have also discussed how there are some surprising similarities between the developments taking place within the design profession and the emergence of new ideas about public governance.

Ultimately, my argument is that public managers are now in confusing territory. There is no blueprint, no broad consensus, as to what governance model should, or will, replace the new public management. In this situation, multiple models are being floated and offered to public organisations all the time, while our legacy model, bureaucratic governance, inherited from over a century ago, is still very much around. Can we expect that a clearer picture of the appropriate governance approach will emerge, or can we expect more 'overlays' of different models?

As a public manager, it could be relevant to reflect on the following.

- **What characterises the governance set-up that your organisation is currently part of?** How would you place it in relation to the three ideal-types of governance models – bureaucratic, new public management or networked governance (or the like)? What is the balance? Do you experience one of the models as more prevalent than the others? What are the factors (chains of command, measurement systems and data, contracts, financial arrangements, etc) by which you judge the kind of governance model that dominates your organisation?
- **In what ways is your current governance model positively contributing** to your ability to carry out your mission and solve and address the challenges you face? To what extent is your current governance set-up part of the problem? What would have to change to make your governance approach more fit for purpose? If something needs to change, what key questions should you start with?
- **How would you hope to benefit** by transforming your current governance model? What opportunities might you realise, and what would be the risks involved? At a personal level, what could motivate you to experiment with a different way of governing?

PART TWO

LEADING DESIGN FOR
PUBLIC INNOVATION

FIVE

Design practice in government

A distinctive approach to 'service design', which seeks to shape service organisations around the experiences and interactions of their users, presents a major opportunity for the next stages of public service reform: a route to get there. (Sophia Parker and Joe Heapy, *The Journey to the Interface*, 2006, p 9)

In Part One of the book I provided a conceptual framework through three chapters: the character of public problems; the evolution of the design profession; and the search for the next governance paradigm. The questions I raised were what approaches may *contribute to the journey towards a new practice of public management and governance* – and what role design might play.

A small but increasing number of public managers are now experimenting with using design to make the transition towards a different way of governing. It is their efforts and experiences – documented via a range of case studies – that form the heart of this book.

This chapter kicks off Part Two of the book. First, I provide a brief overview of the case studies on which this book is based. Second, I describe and discuss how the public managers studied came to commission design work in the first place: what were their entry points into drawing on design skills and expertise? What motivated them? What were their expectations as to how design will assist them? Third, as an extension of this, I provide a typology of the design approaches found across the cases: what are the kinds of concrete methods and activities associated with 'design approaches'? Fourth, I share an overview of the key issue in this book: how does the exposure to design matter to public managers? How do they engage with design? This model, which integrates design methods with leadership behaviour, forms the conceptual framework for the following three chapters.

Case overview: management narratives on design

The empirical foundation of this book is 15 carefully selected cases that in various ways illustrate the scope and depth of what design approaches might mean to public organisations, and how those approaches can be managed and led. Table 5.1 displays the primary respondents involved in the cases. In terms of sample, they represent a balance between service and policy design, geographical distribution and content topics (public policy domains). However, it is important to underline that this sample is by no means statistically representative; rather, it is a set of strategically selected cases, from which it is possible to identify patterns and findings.

The table shows that the cases cover a balance of both service and policy focus, and a quite wide span of policy domains, ranging from health and social services to business and labour market policy. In the following I will explore what motivated these public managers to engage with design methods and design.

Commissioning design

Within public sector organisations, how does the application of design approaches come about? Why do public managers look to and commission design, and what tools, techniques, processes and methods are brought into play?

Public managers continuously face difficult problems and dilemmas that spur them to seek methods and approaches that might help to overcome them. That is also the case for the managers included in this book. This situation fits rather well with the 'wickedness' of public problems that I described in Chapter Two. The types of pressure and motivations that the managers face, however, vary somewhat from case to case. It is

Table 5.1: Case studies overview

Case	Title of manager	Organization	Country	Design focus	Domain/ theme
1	Director	National Board of Industrial Injuries	DK	Policy	Labour market (industrial injuries)
2	Director	City of Adelaide / The Australian Centre for Social Innovation (TACSI)	AUS	Service	Social (family services)
3	Development Director	Borough of Lewisham	UK	Service and policy	Social (homelessness)
4	Special Advisor	Suffolk County Council	UK	Service	Health (youth engagement)
5	Manager	'Camillagaarden' workplace for adult mentally disabled	DK	Service	Social (mentally handicapped)
6	Head of Division	Danish Business Agency	DK	Service	Business (registering new business)
7	Special Advisor	City of Helsinki Economic and Planning Centre	Finland	Service and policy	Business (obtaining city permits)
8	Head of Division	Ministry of Taxation	DK	Service and policy	Administration (compliance with tax code)
9	Head Nurse	Rigshospitalet (National Hospital of Denmark), Heart Clinic	DK	Service	Health (patient involvement)
10	Vice Chancellor	Stenhus Community College	DK	Service	Education (course development)
11	Director, former Principal	New York City Department of Education	USA	Service and policy	Education (new learning environment)
12	Head of Secretariat and Visitation	Holstebro Municipality	DK	Service	Social (meals on wheels)
13	Director of Strategic Planning	New York City Department of Housing Preservation and Development	USA	Service and policy	Urban (citizen/ resident engagement)
14	Head of Division	Kolding Municipality	DK	Service	Social (quality of life for handicapped)
15	Special Advisor	Danish Competition and Consumer Authority	DK	Service and policy	Consumer policy (children's online behaviour)

from slightly different starting points that the managers come to engage with design approaches. What seems clear is that it is necessary to have multiple strong reasons for engaging with design – in many ways a foreign and strange approach to draw into a public sector setting. As one manager said, "It was a very, very long learning process to procure service design because we didn't know what it was." Another commented that "no one [in our municipality] knew about service design." Commissioning a largely unknown methodology for transforming the service or policy for which one is responsible is no small thing in a system that is characterised by its resistance to uncertainty. As one manager asked, "how do you buy service design when you don't know what is in it?"

Other risks come into play as well. For instance, one manager worried that the design project would be met with jealousy by the wider organisation because it would cast a particular spotlight on her unit. Another commented, somewhat in the same vein, that she was keeping knowledge about the project 'under the radar' for the top management, because if they started paying attention to it, it would put too much pressure on the staff and might put the positive, if tentative, results in jeopardy.

Rationales for bringing design in play

Across the cases in this book, a wide variety of rationales for commissioning and engaging with design approaches can be identified. Usually it is not a single 'trigger' or opportunity, but a set of interdependent conditions that in combination lead to the decision to obtain the assistance of designers. However, these three motivations are the most prevalent:

- *Reacting to performance pressure.* Public organisations are under pressure to cut costs or to produce different or better outcomes without additional resources. Design approaches are seen as a novel, fresh approach to achieving better results and outcomes.
- *Vision-driven change.* Here, there are organisational strategies or visions in place, or particular problems arise, that prompt the need for change. Design is commissioned as a contribution to realising the vision.

- *Opportunity to access design skills.* In a number of cases design is commissioned with some degree of financial support, or there are design skills available within the organisation's ecosystem – for instance in the form of access to innovation teams or centres. The use of design is more opportunistic and managers don't necessarily know what to expect from using the methods.

Across all three motivations there is an underlying ambition to realise value from bringing design into the organisation. Ultimately, the creation of public value through organisational change is the aim. Table 5.2 exemplifies the kinds of changes that are at stake for the managers in the cases. It displays the types of public value that I suggested in Chapter One, and which are also espoused by, among others, Moore (1995), NAO (2006) and myself (Bason, 2007, 2009, 2010). Here, public value includes the desire to achieve better *service experiences* for citizens and business; higher *government productivity*; better *outcomes* (changes in concrete behaviour); or enhanced *democracy* (transparency, accessibility, accountability, etc).

Table 5.2: Ambitions, expectations and hopes for the creation of value through design

Ambition for public value	Better service experience (How end-users experience the public service)	Higher productivity (Cost savings at similar output or increased output at same budget level)	Better outcomes (Changes in actions and behaviours by citizens)	Enhanced democracy and regulation (Improvements in accountability, legality, transparency, participation)
Example	"We do not want to be second-rate, we want to deliver the best service." (Hostebro, meals on wheels)	"We could manage a few more rounds of savings, but then it would hurt quality. So we need inspiration." (Rigshospitalet, healthcare)	"Permanent housing is the ultimate outcome that we aim for." (Lewisham Borough, homelessness services)	"The last step before regulation meets the business users was simply not designed in an understandable way." (Branchekode. dk, business services)

The table illustrates quotes from four different cases, showing how public managers articulate their ambition to create change that makes a difference in terms the four types of public value.

Creating change: a personal ambition?

On analysing the interviews with managers, and looking at their professional and personal backgrounds, certain characteristics seem to stand out. This does not tell us whether these managers are particularly "atypical" or "outliers" or, as the academic Sandford Borins (2000) has called public management innovators, "rule-breakers" and "loose cannons". But it does seem that these particular managers have a quite well-developed appetite for change and development, and that this may be something that has characterised their careers beyond the particular cases examined here. Consider some of the backgrounds of the managers involved in the study.

- One manager was originally trained as a TV repairer, but put himself through business school and then applied for and won a public management position.
- Another got involved in sustainability issues as a UK policy maker and decided to stop driving a car herself but to run and bike to workplaces; then she took up running half marathons; later she became head of development in a local council.
- One is a trained psychiatrist who worked in a hospital context but realised that to truly help patients, municipalities need to do a better preventative job; so she changed position to work in the local government context, ultimately driving change towards stronger rehabilitation efforts in social care.
- A development director works mostly among engineers in a city business development unit, but has a PhD in education and has worked extensively abroad: "when you have worked in Iraq you are not scared of a powerful city director".
- A centre manager working with severely handicapped people was trained first to work as a forest manager, was later trained as an educator and held numerous other positions, working with a broad range of user groups, before becoming a manager in the particular institution.

- A manager with a business education decided to enter a teaching fellows programme, worked as a maths teacher, then joined a government innovation initiative and was asked to run a New York City transfer school.

This is not to say that there are not also a handful of managers with rather 'classic' careers and professional public sector backgrounds; one was a manager in the same position for 15 years in the same high school; another had worked at the tax agency for several decades. Whether these personal traits of public managers matter to how they engage, and lead, design is an open question. Asked directly, one manager says that coming into the organisation from a different setting was significant: "I think I was able to see the challenges in a new way", and adds: "I think it is great fun. But I might have done that before and maybe I have actually done that all my life."

Finally, there may well be a role of 'the manager's manager' in catalysing the opportunity for using design approaches. For instance, as the initial story about Carolyn Curtis in Chapter One illustrates, the significant space and time she was given to conduct the long and resource-intensive exploratory process with families at risk was necessarily enabled by her top management. While this factor is, interestingly, not touched on explicitly by very many of the respondents, it is probably a latent, underlying condition that is not at all unimportant.

Towards a typology of design: three design dimensions[1]

We have now seen some of the rationales, motives and incentives for managers who choose to commission design work. But what are the particular types of contributions of design approach to a development process, whether in high-level policy making or in the more specific reshaping of public services? As I discussed in Chapter Three, design is a discipline and practice undergoing significant changes, in both the academic and operational sense, and so this makes it difficult to pinpoint the boundaries of design methods and processes (Moggridge, 2007, p 648). Meanwhile, the potential significance of design is worth exploring. Bruno Latour has pointed out that 'Every change in our conception of knowledge creation instruments must have huge effects on what we can expect from the state to envision and foresee' (2007, p 3). The question becomes what kind of 'knowledge creation instrument' is design in a public sector context, and what are its effects?

When looking for design approaches applied in a public sector setting some pragmatism has been warranted. The question then is: if I have been able to identify a range of instances where design has been an entry point, what are the concrete methods and processes (what I in this book characterise as *design approaches*) that have been put into play? In the next section I provide an overview of the approaches; the introductory sections of the chapters that follow will provide a detailed account of the key methodologies that are brought into play.

We now have a rough sense of the design approaches that have been applied in the research context of this book. We have seen how some might claim that design knows no boundaries, and also that one can list a rather wide range of methods or approaches. But the individual approaches do not provide a particularly clear overview of what design implies in the context of public sector change processes. What is the direction provided by the design approaches, what is their significance?

In a public sector context how might one place some kind of boundaries or frame around the application of design? One way to view the role of design methodologies is from a sequential perspective: ranging from efforts to understand the nature of problems, to 'tinkering' and exploring the world of possible responses, to the decisions and articulations leading to the organisational adoption of one or more new solutions (Boyer et al, 2011; Bason, 2014b).

Exploring the problem space

First, design offers a distinctive set of approaches to the task of *exploring the problem space*. Design provides an array of highly concrete research tools, ranging from ethnographic, qualitative, user-centred research, to probing and experimentation via rapid prototyping, to visualising data. Drawing on elements of systems thinking, design research claims to be able to help policy makers better understand the root causes of problems and their underlying interdependencies – the 'architecture of problems' (Boyer et al, 2011; Mulgan, 2014). In the collaborative, human-centred design approaches studied in this book, it seems that in particular the qualitative research tools play an important role in this dimension of the design process. Here, the focus of the research to enable empathy with end-users' experience with public services is key.

Generating alternative scenarios

Second, the emergent and more collaborative aspects of design discussed earlier suggest that policy options could be increasingly co-designed through an interplay between policy makers at different levels of the governance system, interest and lobby groups, external experts and, not least, end-users such as citizens or business representatives themselves. Graphic facilitation and the use of tangible models, prompt cards, design games and other visual tools for service and use scenarios can provide the means for cross-cutting dialogue, joint idea-generation, mutual understanding and collective ownership of new ideas and concepts. Design, as a creative discipline, seems to be ripe with ways and means of stimulating individual and group creativity, and might thus facilitate a wide divergence of views and ideas, enabling selection, then synthesising them by generating alternative future scenarios (Halse et al, 2010; Michlewski, 2015).

Enacting new practices

Third, design offers the devices – concepts, identities, graphics, products, service templates, system maps – that can help to give form and shape to policies and services in practice: professional design skills are used to create the tangible artefacts or 'design outputs' that humans can engage with physically and emotionally. The ability to create deliberate user experiences and to make visual expressions, services and products desirable and attractive is in this sense at the heart of design practice. Beyond the most visual results there is also, of course, the question of whether design approaches help to catalyse wider changes in systems, such as in governance, that facilitate particular kinds of behaviours and outcomes. One might call this *enacting new practices* (Winhall and Maschi, 2014).

Figure 5.1 illustrates this mapping of design approaches across the three overall dimensions. In line with Halse's argument, it is important to underline that the individual design approaches do not necessarily fit neatly into the three overall dimensions. For instance, prototypes and testing are approaches that are not only apparently useful for generating new policy or service options for decision makers; they are also partly vehicles for providing a better understanding of the problem at hand; and partly they are vehicles that pave the way for subsequent implementation by key stakeholders. In other words, there is a very dynamic and intimate relationship between the approaches across the somewhat artificial sequence of design dimensions. For purposes of clarity and structure, however, it seems useful to organise the approaches and actions accordingly.

Figure 5.1: Three design dimensions and related methods

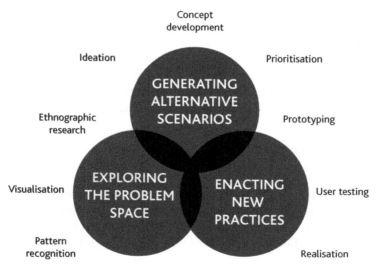

My research indicates that in practice these three dimensions are not necessarily sequential at all, but are intertwined in a complex interplay that mixes different methods across timescales, and where there is an on-going conversation between design research (ethnography, field-work), developing ideas and concepts for policies and services, and the articulation of those ideas in tangible and implementable ways that engage the wider organisation. As Halse et al (2010, p 38) remind us, 'it is reminiscent of a rationalistic distinction between knowing and doing to seek this closure of the existing before the imagination of new opportunities is encouraged'. Instead, 'knowing' and 'doing' is in practice intimately intertwined in complex connections between understanding and intervention, as a form of reflection in action (Schön, 1983; Halse et al, 2010; Michlewski, 2015).

Six management engagements with design

What is the interplay between the manager's perhaps more latent approaches to problem solving and the methods and tools associated with the three dimensions of design that we saw above: exploring problems, generating scenarios and enacting new futures? As discussed earlier, one might ask whether managers themselves display a design attitude as discussed by Boland and Collopy (2004) and Michlewski (2008, 2015). However, it is too early to know whether managers really approach policy and public service problems as designers would approach a design problem. In line with my methodological approach, I simply start out with a curiosity as to how managers engage with design, and whether there are some common patterns in that engagement across the processes I have studied.

In this study of managers, it is important to note that some management behaviour that might be termed 'designerly' has perhaps not always much to do with the managers' experience of design methods. Rather, these are managers who simply are always searching for ways of enacting change. There might therefore be some selection bias in terms of which kind of managers choose to engage with design in the first place, as is also discussed above.

My empirical research, which will be analysed in depth in the following chapters, has revealed six distinctive but closely interrelated patterns in how public managers engage with design practice. These patterns, or dimensions, are shown in Figure 5.2

Figure 5.2: Management engagement with design

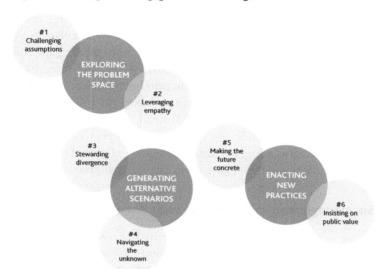

These patterns are tentatively described as *themes* or *dimensions*, not as causalities: in other words, it is not necessarily the case that a particular dimension of design approach (say, 'exploring the problem space') prompts a certain reaction by managers (say, the management engagement of 'challenging assumptions'). It is also not the case that the themes present a particular linearity, although I have chosen to describe and analyse them in a flow from left to right in Figure 4.2. However, my claim is that there seems to be a particular dialogue, or interaction, taking place between the manager as an agent within the organisation and the design approaches as they unfold in his/her immediate organisational context (Bason, 2012). The question, ultimately, becomes whether design processes catalyse certain sensibilities and perhaps strengthen latent inclinations in the manager. Do design approaches open up certain opportunities for leading change – perhaps with implications for the wider organisation – that might not otherwise have been available?

My research does indicate that there are some relatively similar ways in which the sampled public managers address the challenges and opportunities they face. Even though they have different vantage points and are situated in very different national, cultural and organisational contexts, it is striking how they use quite similar language and terms in describing their approaches to innovation and change as they engage with design practice. I have characterised these ways as 'management engagements with design', or simply 'design engagements'.

The connections between specific design methods, the three dimensions of design and types of design engagements are shown in Table 5.3.

Table 5.3: Management engagements, design dimensions and design approaches

MANAGEMENT ENGAGEMENTS	#1 Questioning assumptions #2 Leveraging empathy			#3 Stewarding divergence #4 Navigating discomfort			#5 Making the future concrete #6 Insisting on public value		
Design dimensions	Exploring the problem space			Generating alternative scenarios			Enacting new practices		
Design approaches	Ethnographic research	Visualisation	Pattern recognition	Ideation	Concept development	Prioritisation	Prototyping	User testing	Business cases, evaluation

The table shows how different types of management engagement relate to the three overall dimensions of design that I described above – and, in turn, how they connect back to the approaches and methodologies applied. The next three chapters of Part Two will explore in detail how each of the three design dimensions relate to the management engagements. Each chapter first puts the design dimension into context, followed by analysis of the empirical findings and insights with regard to management engagements with design, before turning to a theoretically informed discussion of the implications.

How to do it: getting started with design approaches

This chapter has demonstrated how public managers come to engage with design approaches and laid out the range of concrete methods involved. It has also presented the overall framework for management engagement with design, which constitutes the core of this part of the book.

For public managers, getting started to collaborate with designers is the first critical step on the journey towards a different mode of governing. But what are the key 'to dos' in getting started? In this chapter, and in all the following chapters in this section, I conclude with a bit of advice.

- Start out by **reflecting on your change agenda:** What motivates you to seek out a different approach to creating change? What are the challenges you hope to overcome or the opportunities you hope to capture? Why does design as an approach appeal to you? What are the kinds of changes you would hope for? Use these reflections to draft the design brief.
- **Commission a design team:** If you are fortunate to have access to an in-house innovation team or lab that can provide the methodological expertise, processes and resources you need, then the choice should be easy. However, most public managers today would usually have to commission outside designers to work with them in a consulting role. If that is the case, it goes without saying that there are classic public procurement rules and procedures to follow. However, the challenge is first to provide the designers with a brief that is sufficiently open ended, as well as ambitious, to really provide scope for innovation; be careful not to over-specify the brief; rather, spend more time on characterising the challenges you see and your expectations of the value the designers should bring to your organisation. Remember to insist that people on your staff come to work, for real, as part of the design team, either as pure observers or as domain (policy) experts so that they will come to internalise the methods and findings and can bring their learning back into your organisation.
- Finally, be careful to invite only **the best and most qualified design team**. When trying out a new approach to innovation,

everything is hard and you don't need design rookies who feel just as lost as you and your staff do. Look for firms that focus on service design, co-design or design-driven innovation and that have some degree of public or social sector track record. Ask around for references. Request the advice of national or regional design bodies, if one is accessible to you (such as the UK Design Council, AIGA (US) or the Danish Design Centre) to scan the market and identify the top firms that can help you. Since design work is often intensive and challenging, be sure to meet and interview the design team and ensure that there is positive chemistry and rapport between yourself, your staff and the team. Finally, make sure to get a competitive government rate for the work!

Note

[1]   This section builds in part on Bason (2010; 2014b).

SIX

Exploring the problem space

The first step in any problem–solving episode is representing the problem, and to a large extent, that representation has the solution hidden inside it. (Richard Boland and Fred Collopy, *Managing as Designing*, 2004, p 9)

This chapter shows the role of design in catalysing an exploration of the problem space. First, I share and discuss how design approaches can be used to explore how public interventions are experienced by citizens and business, drawing on highly qualitative research methods from ethnography and anthropology.

Second, the chapter considers how managers, through various types of interplay with the design approaches, reflect about the challenges they are facing, and the types of questions they ask themselves and their staff. This I call *questioning assumptions*. I consider two central themes: how do these managers think about the problem space from the outset – sometimes before they choose to engage with design? Further, as they begin to collaborate with designers, how do design approaches influence their thinking?

Third, I analyse the extent to which the managers draw actively on the design research, typically field-work among end–users (citizens) or among staff at the 'front-stage' interaction level, to *leverage empathy*. Again, I build the analysis from the patterns emerging from the empirical material I have collected. What is the role of design practices, including highly qualitative 'emphatic' data, as well as visualisation tools? How do the design approaches bring citizens' experiences into play, and how do managers consciously, strategically use this knowledge to start to catalyse organisational change? In this analysis I consider the interplay between the exploration of user interactions, on the one hand, and the ensuing challenging of pre-existing assumptions across the wider organisation, on the other hand.

Fourth, I interpret and discuss the findings concerning management engagements by drawing on theoretical perspectives from design and governance research, respectively. This leads to an analysis of the kinds of activities associated with design approaches in the public sector, focusing on problem exploration.

I conclude, fifth, by summing up this empirically grounded account of how design is applied, across the cases studied, as a set of distinct methodologies and tools for exploring the problems faced by public managers and their organisations.

Methods: design research as enquiry

The French sociologist Bruno Latour, whose work I mentioned in Chapter Two, has proposed that the type of knowledge obtained and used by governments matters greatly to the kinds of decisions that can be made:

> there is nothing more complex, nothing more susceptible of mistakes, nothing in greater need of specific and constantly refreshed inquiries than to detect what, at any point, is the public's problem. (Latour, 2007, p 4)

Latour proposes that it is really an on-going endeavour to 'detect' the character of the problem faced by the public, and thus by the state. The ways in which we come to know public problems are critically important for the ways in which we might address them. Design processes seem to influence the ways in which public managers come to know and, in various ways, leverage a new understanding of public problems in their quest for organisational change.

In the following I will present and discuss what characterises the design methods typically associated with researching user experience and public problems.

Exploratory enquiry

Halse et al (2010, p 27) suggest that design research can be characterised as 'exploratory inquiry', in that it is research without a hypothesis to be tested. This type of approach offers a break with traditional modes of research as it is often applied in the public sector, such as the use of statistical data or the conduct of statistically representative quantitative surveys, for instance among users of a particular public service. Instead, Halse et al argue that design research understood as a process of enquiry is both more and less than the typical data-collection methodologies:

> It is less, because it does not search for testable facts.
> It is more, because it aims for an understanding that
> is profoundly concerned with purpose and intent:
> why, for whom and for what is this understanding
> directed? (2010, p 27)

What Halse et al point out here is that as designers conduct research that is concerned with observing and documenting the present, they are simultaneously exploring that which does not yet exist. Likewise Junginger (2014) suggests that policy making as designing would differ from 'traditional' development of policies or public services by adding the ability (1) to enquire into *situations* and (2) to explore what makes them problematic for people. In Junginger's view, 'In other words, policymaking as designing begins with an inquiry, not a problem' (2014, p 62)

Rowe (1987, p 3) describes this approach, which is typical of designers and architects, as drawing as much on 'hunches' as on highly structured information gathering. As discussed earlier, Halse et al (2010) maintain that design research essentially provides a more complex connection between processes of understanding (empirical research of the present state) and intervention (proposing possible new futures). Taking this approach, the data material becomes essentially incomplete, by not offering a full 'true' account through empirical research, but also not proposing final solutions. This opens up the design process to allow for other stakeholders to engage with it, and, in Halse's words, it 'avoids premature closure of the design space'. Donald Schön, in a similar vein, describes the act of designing as 'a conversation with the materials of a situation' (1983, p 78). As this conversation unfolds and the designer reflects upon it, the design space is kept open and fluid.

As I will discuss in the next chapter, this avoidance of closing the problem or design space becomes a crucial element in what appears to differentiate design approaches from other innovation and change techniques.

As illustrated in the previous chapter, design provides an array of highly concrete research tools, ranging from ethnographic, qualitative and user-centred research methods, to probing and experimentation via rapid prototyping, to graphically visualising large quantities of data and information. Drawing on elements of systems thinking, design research claims to help policy makers better understand the root causes of problems and their underlying interdependencies – the 'architecture of problems' (Boyer et al, 2011; Mulgan, 2014). The assumption appears to be that it is possible to discover root causes and underlying causalities that have hitherto escaped the managers' or decision makers' attention. Or, as Meroni and Sangiorgi (2011, p 37) propose, 'Investigating how a service occurs and how it is perceived individually and collectively helps to evaluate the quality and the very nature of the service itself.'

The kinds of design work considered here thereby also cast citizens into different roles. Bate and Robert (2007, p 10) propose that this type of investigation, which may also be called a process of co-designing for understanding and (re)shaping citizens' experience of a service or policy, can be understood at the far end of a continuum. The continuum, which represents different ways of engaging with citizens, ranges from only listening to complaints to co-designing for better experiences, as shown in Figure 6.1

In the collaborative, human-centred design approaches discussed in this book, it seems that in particular the qualitative research methodologies play an important role at this stage of the design or co-design process. As was shown in the previous chapter, some form of user research was conducted in all of the cases.

Figure 6.1: Citizens' roles in shaping public services

Complaining ➔ Giving information ➔ Listening and responding ➔ Consulting and advising ➔ Experience-based co-design

Returning to Latour's argument, the proposition here seems to be that 'It is never the case that you first know and then act, you first act tentatively and then begin to know a bit more before attempting again' (2007, p 4). This approach to the exploration of problems is linked to an appreciation of the complexity of many of the problem spaces encountered by public managers, which was discussed earlier. As Bourgon (2012) suggests, attempting to understand complex phenomena by taking them apart and studying their constituent parts is pointless, since emergent situations cannot be understood or addressed only through analysis. In fact, it is the complexity that calls for designers' professional contribution, since they 'value originality over predictability and standardisation' (Michlewski, 2015, p 54). Or, as Schön puts it, because the process of making within a certain situation is often complex, it is not possible in advance to know what will be the outcome of the design process: 'Because of this complexity, designers' moves tend, happily or unhappily, to produce consequences other than those intended' (1983, p 79). It is not difficult to see why design work is often equated with innovation.

What characterises the particular methodologies involved in this dimension of design as I have explored them through the empirical research presented here? There seem to be two broad sets of methodological approaches involved in this dimension: field research and visualisation of the current situation.

Field research

All of the cases studied, except one, involve some form of field research. The use of field research – using text, photo, audio or video as documentation tools – refers to ethnographically inspired research practices and methodologies. Madsbjerg and Rasmussen define ethnography as 'the process of observing, documenting and analysing behaviour' (2014, p 90). Ethnographic research focuses on understanding the world from the perspective of the study objects. A variation of this is to take the broader team (also non-designers) into the context of the users. Polaine et al (2013) call this version of the methodology a *service safari*, in which key team members get to experience and see a service or life context personally, at first hand. The process can be extremely *open*, such as 'documenting a day in a person's life'; or more *focused*, such as 'mapping the citizen's journey through a specific public service'; and finally it can be *challenging*, by testing explicit hypotheses about what is perceived to be the problem. This on-going dynamic interplay between opening, closing and challenging is part of what makes ethnographic research such a good fit with the iterative process of co-designing.

The approach becomes an active learning process; a process with the purpose to change the researcher's perspective and understanding of the different contexts and to create new grounds for reflection (Hasse, 2003; Halse et al, 2010). As Polaine et al (2013) emphasise, however, designers who engage in such activity only rarely conduct what might be termed 'proper' ethnography in its own right. For instance, many who conduct design research are not trained ethnographers, and the time horizons and resources allowed for the empirical observation, interviewing and other data-gathering activities will rarely match the criteria applied by ethnographic researchers. That is certainly also the case in the present set of cases, where – with a few exceptions – the research is much more focused and conducted in short bursts of activity rather than through a prolonged, week- or month-long field study. For some designers, this is really a strength, since, as Halse et al (2010) point out, the objective is to keep the design space open, not to attempt to reach conclusive insights: 'Ethnographers take a disciplinary pride in the integrity of their accounts of everyday use. Often this integrity is the biggest obstacle for creating new openings for design' (2010, p 39). From Halse's point of view, 'pure' ethnography is overly focused on the documentation aspect and not sufficiently receptive to discovery and insights that may lead to new solutions. Leonard and Rayport (1997) suggest that the role of the ideal design researcher may, rather, be characterised as 'emphatic design'. They describe emphatic design as essentially multidisciplinary, since it combines the visualisation expertise of designers with the sensitivity to context and culture characteristic of the anthropologist. Michlewski discusses how professionally trained designers are particularly skilled at 'engaging deep empathy' and suggests that their relation to empathy is a fundamental 'way of doing things by groups of people and organisations' (2015, p 67). Generating, and working systematically with, empathy takes more than tools and methods. It is part of designers' professional culture.

Another perspective on the role of design research in coming up close to the concrete experiences of citizens is to view the process as one of collecting 'stories' (Wetter-Edman, 2014). As Quesenbery and Brooks argue, in a volume on the role of storytelling in user experience design, developing and activating stories from users 'not only describe actions, but also explain them and set them into a context that help you understand why they happened' (2010, p 17). Bate and Robert propose that in design research:

> The role of users (and the value and justification for being there) is to bring the knowledge of their experience to the table so that the designers can work with them to translate and build that knowledge into new and future designs. (2006, p 31)

It thus becomes a key issue to capture users'/citizens' experience in ways that allow for this type of translation into future designs. Understanding design research as the building of stories, Quesenbery and Brooks (2010, p 29) highlight four key roles of the stories: (1) to explain research and ideas; (2) to engage the imagination and spark new ideas; (3) to create a shared understanding; and (4) to persuade an audience. The issue of 'persuading' is similarly emphasised by Michlewski, who compares design to rhetoric, in the sense that designers are concerned with constructing an argument of a particular kind of solution (2015, p 35).

These roles, or contributions, of design research, understood as the collection and sharing of stories (about use, about context, about actions, solutions, and so on), indicate that the research process is not only about gathering new knowledge or insight. It is already at this – often early – stage in a design project focused on initiating new ideas and possibilities that may be turned into concrete solutions that create change.

Visualisation of the current situation

The other main dimension of design research is the use of visual representation. A key contribution of (graphic) design is to visualise people, groups, systems, interactions, flows and processes, helping decision makers to see citizens and services in context and facilitating collaboration across agency and professional boundaries. Some of these visualisations were shown throughout the empirical sections above. Use of visuals to drive and document research as well as to facilitate the creative process is widespread in connection with design approaches (Leonard and Rayport, 1997; Michlewski, 2015). In fact, the argument may be that 'engaging in a constructive, often visually led, dialogue is part of what makes a designer a designer' (Michlewski, 2015, p 78). Visualising people can be done by building *personas* out of the individual data material that has been harvested, where possible combining it with quantitative data from existing databases or from surveys (Pruitt and Tamara, 2006; Bason, 2010). Another key visualisation tool that also emphasises citizen-centric processes and is quite widespread in design research practice is the mapping of users' *service journeys*. A service journey is a visual map, or blueprint, of service interactions with government over time, with users' actions and experiences at the centre (Parker and Heapy, 2006; Bason, 2010; Meroni and Sangiorgi 2011, Polaine, Lövlie and Reason, 2013). Often, such visualisation can include end-user perspective (processes, flows and behaviours on the part of citizens or businesses) or the internal user perspective, mapping the roles, interactions and handovers among staff and other stakeholders. For instance, when the City of Helsinki project mapped service journeys for businesses wanting to register for outdoor events, it found that they were required to obtain, on average, somewhere between 10 and 14 permits from different sections and departments across the city. A majority of the cases studied include some form of visualisation of processes, often emphasising the outside-in (citizen/business) perspective. Often the designers will take such as user journey-mapping process and create clearer and more precise visualisations.

The use of infographics and the visualisation of large quantities of data is also a key design activity, understood as 'the use of abstract, non-representational pictures to display numbers' (Tufte, 1983, p 9). Data visualisation is increasingly associated with design research and with the facilitation of design-led change processes. The notion is that, in order for designers, clients, users and other stakeholders to build a shared understanding, visualisation can, just like stories and narrative, be a powerful contribution.

> At their best, graphics are instruments for reasoning about quantitative information. Often the most effective way to describe, explore, and summarise a set of numbers – even a very large set – is to look at pictures of those numbers. (Tufte, 1983, p 9)

This statement by Tufte, perhaps the scholar most closely associated with the art and practice of visual display of quantitative information, sounds almost prophetic in light of the more recent advent of 'big data' and emphasis on 'mining' data for insights and patterns within it. However, this kind of design practice has not been used in any major way in the cases.

A final form of visualisation that is relatively prevalent across the cases studied is the creation of prototypes – sketches or models that are created for the purpose of illustration, engagement, feedback and learning. Prototypes can be considered a key design research tool, for instance through what Halse (2014) calls 'evocative sketching', whereby preliminary ideas for solutions are presented to users, and their feedback and reactions are registered. The research approach thus comes to engage actively with the field, to suggest potentialities and to iteratively understand the present state as well the possible actions that, in Simon's (1996) words, could lead to a preferred outcome. Halse et al (2010) drive this point home when they say that: 'The challenge of fieldwork in design is not so much to collect data, as it is one of sensing the other's (user's, client's, stakeholder's) competence and willingness to change and innovate.' As Polaine, Lövlie and Reason (2013) point out, and as I have previously discussed in detail in Chapter Three, the key to collaborative forms of design is that every dimension of the design process, including the exploration of problems, involves end-users. However, prototypes are more than a research tool: they are also vehicles for facilitating and directing the enactment of new futures. Because designers don't necessarily distinguish between researching the present state and evoking new possible futures, prototyping can very well take place early in the process, and thus the dimension of 'exploring problem space' becomes intermingled with the exploration and generation of 'future scenarios'. A case in point is relayed by Jesper Wiese, the manager at the Skansebakken institution, who tells the following about the designers' research approach as they explored relationships between staff and handicapped users:

> "It was questions, interviews, but also just observations. They took a lot of pictures. They also jumped the gun and started with some prototypes. Or actually there were not really prototypes, because we hadn't been involved, but they were more like tests of theories: when unpopular issues occur, will it be less unpopular if we bring some cake?"

In other words, prototyping, probing and testing is used by the designers as an integral part of the research process. Wiese, the manager, feels it is not "really" prototyping in his understanding of the term, since it did not involve his staff in the trial, but for sure it is to the designers.

Engagement #1: questioning assumptions

Among the public managers interviewed, there seems to be a pattern, that in various ways they tend to question the assumptions on which they base their decisions. This manifests itself in a range of different ways, but partly it concerns what might be called the managers' ability to confront their understanding of the problem space. By understanding the problem space I refer to the process of exploring the characteristics, dynamics and boundaries of the problem at hand; and making those dimensions explicit: 'Formulating the mess' (Ackoff et al, 2006, p 44).

It appears in the research that some managers engage with the problems in ways not directly related to the use of design methods. Rather, they seem to have an inclination to challenge their own assumptions that prompts them to be open and curious to what design might have to offer; they see the option of working with designers as an opportunity to catalyse change, even if they do not know exactly what this might entail. Subsequently the design research (field-work, visualisation) lends itself to generating new questions and thus further catalyses the managers' ability to question their assumptions.

I will consider these two perspectives – first, the a priori questioning of assumptions, and second, the catalysing of new questioning through the insights generated by design research – in the following.

A priori questioning: managers' propensity to challenge their own assumptions

Before the prospect of leveraging design approaches enters the picture, some of the public managers appear to have a pre-existing inclination to be reflective, curious and critical of what they already know (or *think* they already know). This issue is thus related to the discussion in the previous chapter of the personal traits or make-up of these managers. By their very choice to apply design methods in their organisation, are they already displaying a particular attitude towards problem solving? Are they already inclined to be open to a process of enquiry and discovery?

In defining this notion of 'questioning assumptions' I will examine a couple of ways in which the managers do this, before they even encounter design approaches in practice, starting with Mette Kynemund, Vice Chancellor at Stenhus Community College in Denmark.

"[A few years ago], our schedule planner and I could see that there is something in the way students choose subjects on the General Study Preparation, which is inconsistent with the goal. So either we have completely misinterpreted what is happening, or there is something wrong with the target."

Mette Kynemund considers two very different perspectives on the problem space: the first is the students' concrete behaviour in choosing the two subjects (such as a combination of maths and history). Here, she wonders if she and her colleagues really understand what is driving the choices the students make, and how this 'wrong' behaviour has come about. The second is the policy goal or target for the General Study Preparation course, which is set by the Danish Ministry of Education. Her curiosity thus starts with discovering user (student) behaviour that is inconsistent with what is expected and desired. This in turn prompts her to ask new questions about what 'really' is going on, and about the objective of the public provision – in this case a certain study programme that is designed to prepare upper secondary school children for advanced study. By asking these questions, Kynemund essentially opens up the problem space for further exploration.

A similar theme arises in the case of Holstebro, the meals on wheels project, which focused on redesigning food services for ageing citizens. During a meeting where Head of Secretariat and Visitation Poula Sangill has just presented the service design project for her staff of mid-level managers, they complain about how little time is allocated for food services (nominally 10 minutes). However, Sangill challenges what kinds of service interactions could take place within that time span. The staff explain that in the time span they typically must assist the citizen with using the bathroom and simultaneously prepare the food. Insisting that they need to focus on end-user experience, Sangill initiates a role play to understand and challenge the detailed processes that the staff go through to serve the citizen. She plays the role of a staff member, pretends to walk through the door to meet an imaginary "Ms Sorensen" and questions whether or not the specific interactions could be ever so slightly redesigned so that the citizen has a better service experience. Sangill keeps insisting that the staff should revisit their assumptions about the service they are shaping: "Are we speaking about how we want citizens to experience our work? (…) Are we concerned with what they say to their loved ones when they call them after the meal?" are the rhetorical questions she poses. As she seeks to challenge her staff's assumptions about what is possible, she also challenges her own. One might say that this personal enactment of concrete practices is a display of a sensitivity, and an ambition, about the design of the service for which Ms Sangill is ultimately responsible.

Another example is Mette Rosendal Darmer, Head Nurse at the Danish National Hospital's heart clinic, who initiated a design project to create more meaningful patient experiences. In her approach to managing her own assumptions she uses measurement: "[I also make it a priority] to measure all the time, because you are deceived by your own preconceptions of what people think works if you do not measure." In this quote, Mette Rosendal Darmer reflects on how she can use systematic measurement of performance as a way to continuously challenge her own preconceptions.

Consider also how Anne Lind, Director of a mid-sized state agency, the Board of Industrial Injuries in Denmark, reflects on the mission of her organisation. She notes that some years ago the agency was transferred from the Ministry of Social Affairs to the Ministry of Employment, as part of a wider change in Danish labour market policy. She notes, "Something didn't fit. Because the idea of that reform was to engage people a lot more in terms of their work potential. But in the work injury system, we just threw insurance settlements at people." In part, her subsequent interest in the design project was to explore and deal with this mismatch, as she saw it, between the intent of the reform and her agency's practices.

The above examples all address the issue, and the propensity, of challenging and (re)framing the problem as it is understood by the public manager.

The Vice Chancellor is prepared to embrace some troubling questions about the current performance of the General Study Preparation course. The Head Nurse uses measurement to cut through her own preconceptions. The Director reflects on the mismatch, the incongruity, between the purpose of the labour market reform and how her agency works.

The key point here is that none of these examples seems to relate very directly to the commissioning and use of design approaches. They happened before design was brought into play by the managers. However, the propensity to be prepared to challenge one's own assumptions may be part of the reason why the managers, when given the opportunity, look to design. However, something more and different appears to happen when design research is brought into play. It appears that the managers' ability to challenge their own assumptions, and thus their possibilities for developing a different understanding of the problem space, becomes catalysed in different ways by design research. I will take a closer look at this in the following.

The eye-opener: design as catalyst of challenging assumptions

Let me return to Anne Lind, who was until the end of 2012 the Director of the Board of Industrial Injuries (BII) in Denmark. As mentioned earlier in this chapter, the BII undertook a range of design research and co-design activities. One of the key insights, emerging from video films with end-users, was that the injured citizens felt confused and burdened by the virtual barrage of information letters they received concerning their case process – an average of 23 letters per case. In one interview, a citizen expressed that one had to be healthy to be able to manage having an industrial injury case. Anne Lind, the Director, explains how she had the sense that something in her organisation needed to change, although she could not be precise about what it was:

> "It is an eye opener ... it is more concrete. [The design process] has made me aware that there are some things we have to look at. ... So far we have been describing a service to citizens, not giving them one."

Anne Lind – who, as we saw earlier, was prepared to challenge her own assumptions – starts reflecting on what this insight could mean to her organisation:

"What has happened throughout the years is that we have had lots of user satisfaction surveys, lots of dialogue meetings with users, with our stakeholders. When we have had a user survey we have made a nice action plan to follow up and what then happens is that as the users' requests become more and more detailed, the system becomes more complex. What has happened in terms of the wishes the users and stakeholders had … was that we piled information onto users. We thought that was good, because then they could follow their case. But fortunately, we are smarter now."

Under Anne Lind's leadership, a range of seminars and conferences were held where various insights and results from the design projects were shared internally among staff and externally among stakeholders such as local government, trade unions, insurance firms, healthcare organisations and so on. The purpose was to understand the significance of the users' insights and to begin to leverage them to create more system–wide change (Figure 6.2). How that change could unfold is something I will explore further later in this chapter.

Figure 6.2: User journey mapping of an industrial injury process from a citizen perspective

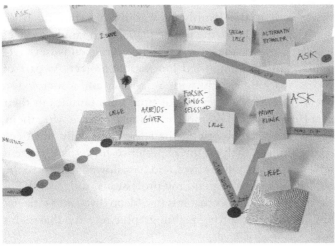

Source: MindLab

In the UK, Development Director Peter Gadsdon managed a design project in the Homelessness Services Division of Lewisham Borough Council in Greater London. The project was supported by funding from the Business, Industry and Skills Department (BIS) and the UK Design Council and with concrete methodologies delivered by the design consultancy ThinkPublic. Staff in Homelessness Services were trained by the designers in basic video filming and were then asked to record their colleagues' interactions with citizens applying for housing. Peter Gadsdon was responsible for bringing the design team in to work with Homelessness Services. Reflecting on the process where staff filmed video of their interactions with homeless users, he says:

> "... it is so powerful. You were showing it on the screen and listening to the single parent talking about their situation and it could be violent. When you are watching that, it is quite an emotional journey, it makes it personal, does it not. It is really good to get people's minds open to change. Using visuals is very powerful."

Gadsdon recognises how the tools employed by the design team have a different kind of impact on staff than other, typical management approaches.

Another case is the Family by Family programme from Australia. Carolyn Curtis, the public manager in family services in Adelaide, conveys the process of involving end-users (at-risk families) in the design-led innovation project. As part of the process, working closely with a designer and a sociologist, Carolyn spent extended periods of time with families in their homes, at barbeques, in fast-food restaurants, interviewing them, speaking with them, observing their lives and daily practices. To her, the project "helped me experience how these citizens themselves experience their lives, and has allowed me to see the barriers. I have had to suspend my professional judgement." In this case Carolyn indicates that it is the "deep dive" into citizens' (families') experience through ethnographic research that seems to allow her to shift her professional knowledge and experience to the background, and to suspend judgement.

Mette Rosendal Darmer, the Head Nurse at Rigshospitalet, reflects on the implications of the observation and documentation of how patients experienced her ward's services: "Well, it meant that there were scratches in the paint all over our own cool picture – our self-image that we are so good." This reflection is probably difficult to overstate in terms of its importance; as the self-image of the professional staff in the country's foremost heart clinic is challenged, what kinds of changes might this lead to?

Andrew Eickmann, the strategy advisor overseeing a design project to improve New York City's (NYC) Housing and Preservation Department's (HPD) service to citizens, says that, compared to previous development work, "the designer focusing on the experience and perspective of the end-user, of everyday people", was significantly different. He gives the example that, as part of the project, the existing website used by marketing division, called NYC Housing Connect, was evaluated from a design perspective. One of the "design fellows" carrying out the project brought the concrete functioning of the portal into play by allowing Eickmann to watch how people used the service, screen by screen. According to Andrew Eickmann this process was "very powerful, as it gave arguments for changes that otherwise would not have happened".

In Helsinki, the city administration commissioned designers to develop visual mapping of local businesses' 'service' journey for obtaining a city permit. As it turned out, they needed to register with anywhere between 10 and 14 different places within the city administration in order to be granted a permit for outdoor events. Marja-Leena Vaittinen explains the impression:

> "It was our responsibility and it was our processes and we believed we were customer oriented. But if you see the whole customer journey you open your eyes and look: Ow! So many [contact points] … So the customer journey as a concept is a very eye-opening approach in a cross-sectional public service context."

It almost seems as if the insight into the painful business registration process physically hurt Vaittinen, and possibly her colleagues too.

Sune Knudsen, who led the development of a new digital registration tool for new businesses, describes the significance, in terms of challenging assumptions, of one particular ethnographic interview (with a business owner) like this:

> "There was this amazing, 'golden' interview that really put it bluntly, that we have a problem here. This entrepreneur had to choose an industry code, which is, we must remember, a tiny little procedure that we expect to be done very quickly … but for this person, something that should not take longer than, say, 10 minutes, ended up taking the entire day. He was so unsure of which code to choose that he had taken his car and driven around to three different authorities to try to get an answer. This gap between our assumption about how long it should take to register the code and the reality of this particular case just made us all sit and think: well, if we had any doubts before about what the trouble is, we don't anymore."

An important point concerning the role of representing the problem is that, as this manager points out, the design methodology appears to trigger an on-going dialogue between insight into problem space and tentative ideas about possible new answers or solutions: "It was such a holistic design process, where you also thought of solutions while you were uncovering the problem," says the manager of the Branchekode.dk project, Sune Knudsen. To exemplify, a key insight was that the written information provided to businesses – including online – did not make sense to them; the connection from this insight to new solutions and, ultimately, the production of value, is rather straightforward, as stated by Knudsen:

> "Some of that which generates the complaints is that they simply do not understand what is on public websites. They do not understand the letters they

receive. The letters come at the wrong time. So, it is not synchronised with the businesses´ daily practice. And if we succeed with it, thus creating something that is understandable and synchronised with the day-to-day operations, the daily practice, I am pretty sure we will achieve greater user satisfaction."

Avenues for solutions, including 'understandable the letters' and 'synchronisation with businesses' daily practices' hereby become opportunities for influencing business owners' behaviour (thereby enhancing compliance and reducing error) and increasing satisfaction.

A final perspective on the issue of challenging assumptions is that, in some cases, the designers do not just let the empirical, 'emphatic' material speak for itself. They actively interpret and communicate to the managers and staff what they make of the findings. The design team, in other words, seeks to challenge the managers' assumptions. This role is a reflection of the design attitude, to quote Michlewski (2015, p 104), to 'challenge and subvert the status quo'. Managers, thereby, have to deal with being challenged, sometimes explicitly, by the designers in terms of the implications of the research. This puts them on the spot, in a sense as stewards of the current situation, but also as dialogue partners and explorers of a possible future state. As Jesper Wiese, the manager at Skansebakken, says, this is a difficult balance to strike:

"… it is a balancing act between, on the one hand, to be challenged, but also to stand against it and say 'Well it might be you see it that way, but we do not think it should be seen in that way'. I think that is a challenge that we must learn to deal with."

Engaging with design as a catalyst for challenging assumptions thereby also becomes a learning journey, and a question of difficult choices on behalf of the manager.

Engagement #2: leveraging empathy

A closely related engagement with design has to do with the notion that, ultimately, public services are not valuable in their own right, but only if they make a positive difference for citizens and other users. Various values and perspectives are at stake here: attitudes towards the role of government and the nature of the relationship with citizens, and the notion of 'empathy' with citizens' experience. Several of the examples discussed in the previous section contain such elements, such as when Ms Curtis says she experiences how citizens experience their own lives, or when Mr Knudsen refers to a "golden" moment when his team really understood what was at stake for entrepreneurs engaging with the agency's services.

Sometimes this stance has been articulated as taking an 'outside-in' perspective on the organisation. Boland and Collopy write that this concerns the fundamental question of 'what are we trying to do?' (2004, p 7). Underlying much design research is the idea that the systematic generation of empathy with end-users will help to catalyse not only insight but curiosity and a desire for change among managers and staff. In a volume written by design and innovation practitioners focusing on the intersection between design and empathy, the authors suggest that:

> The most basic tool in any people-centred innovation process is our congenial curiosity ... the most important tools we have are the questions we carefully and humbly articulate and ask, what we learn from the answers, and the new questions that emerge on the go. (Wildewuur et al, 2013, p 190)

Across the cases, two processes or dimensions seem to matter in terms of the generation of empathy, which in turn can be utilised by managers to initiate change. The first, which was discussed in the previous section, is the ability of design research to be an 'eye-opener' that catalyses the challenging of assumptions about the problem space. The second, which I will consider in the following, is the strategic use by managers of design-research insights to set in motion processes of organisational change. In other words, the leveraging of data about citizen experiences, behaviours and outcomes to engage staff to begin to change their behaviour.

Citizen-first perspective

In order to understand how the public managers work actively to leverage the empathy and eye-openers from design research so as to generate change, it seems important to note that the managers tend to place a higher priority on citizens' experiences and on *outcomes for citizens* than on staff satisfaction.

Christina Pawsø who was the Manager of Camillagaarden, a workplace for mentally handicapped adults in the city of Odense in Denmark, is an example of this. She engaged with consultants from Local Government Denmark, an interest organisation, and with an experienced external design team to develop her organisation and to rethink the relationship between staff and employees. The following quote illustrates how she thinks about outcomes:

> "... my job is primarily to give the users what they want because they have nowhere else to go.... [the staff] can find other jobs, but our users cannot. They have no other options. My greatest obligation is to them. Some of my staff obviously disagree and say, well, a leader is first and foremost leader of her staff. But I think in the public sector, we have two obligations as a leader, and sometimes you must determine what to put first."

To Ms Pawsø, when it comes to a choice, outcomes for citizens (such as thriving by having a meaningful daily experience) are more important than satisfaction among her staff. She goes on to clarify how focusing on outcomes means that input variables, such as money and staff, lose importance relative to the quality of the experience of citizen-users: "The focus is on experiences rather than services, and I think really it has been very clear that it is the [citizens'] experience that it is all about."

Consider another example from Mette Kynemund, the Vice Chancellor who sought to improve the General Study Preparatory course in her school. As part of the design project she organised a workshop with a small task force of nine teachers who were asked to analyse the results of a survey that had been conducted among all of the school's teaching staff. As a tool in the workshop, Kynemund used a graphical template that helped to structure ideas and concepts across two dimensions: value to the organisation on one axis, and ease of implementation on the other. Commenting on the dialogue unfolding at this workshop she says:

> "it was very obvious that the first priority in the group's response to the survey results was about the teachers themselves. The second priority was about the concept of professionalism – which really also is about the teachers. Only the third priority was about the students.... and then it appeared, I would almost say fortunately, that the teacher group said, well, we really don't know what the students think about this, we can only guess. So, every time the group discussed what the students would get out of the General Study Preparatory course, I would say, well, how do we know this?"

Just like Pawsø, Kynemund draws attention to the experience of the end-users (students) and to how outcomes (in this case, learning) are ultimately shaped, or carried, by them. She addresses the problem that the group of teachers simply does not know well enough what is going on from the perspective of their users. The quote here also illustrates that there is an intimate link between focusing on end-users or outcomes and the ability to question assumptions. "How do we know this?" is a very powerful question to ask. Interestingly, a similar search process, driven by that question, was characteristic of Poula Sangill in the Holstebro cases I discussed above. In Sangill's case she challenged her staff by almost forcing an enactment to find out what was assumed and what was known.

This engagement with design that emerges from the interviews with public managers concerns their insistence to focus on empathy with end-users and outcomes of the services and policies for which they are responsible. One might also have called it an inherent 'user centredness' or 'citizen centredness', but this perhaps misses the point slightly. Leveraging empathy and centring on outcomes calls our attention more precisely to the intended change in the world that the managers wish to achieve. It addresses Boland and Collopy's point that design attitude concerns the desire to leave the world a better place than we found it (Boland and Collopy, 2004, p 9), or Herbert Simon's definition of design as an activity focused on changing an existing situation into a preferred one.

Just like their a priori tendency to be prepared to challenge their own assumptions, the managers seem to be also, at a rather fundamental level, a priori attuned to concern themselves with their organisation's impact and meaning for citizens. This implies that when design research then delivers 'emphatic data' into their hands, they are prepared to use it actively.

Strategically leveraging empathy for staff engagement

In the following I consider the leveraging of empathy as a sort of galvanising tool, a change tool that managers use to set in motion processes of organisational innovation.

In the design project carried out at the Danish national hospital, Rigshospitalet, substantial ethnographic work was carried out, including observation studies in the ward, interviews and the production of edited audio recordings. The recordings were shared with a team of doctors, nurses and administrative staff to facilitate a process of improving the patient experience. Head Nurse Mette Rosendal Darmer reflects as follows on the patient experience as she sees it:

> "We usually lift the patient's shirt to see if the electrode is properly fixed, if it does not work. So, we have no such boundaries as to what we do with patients. But of course the patients have boundaries. And then I had a sudden insight. I have thought a

lot about how the patients leave their dignity outside the door when they enter the hospital, to the point where they go to the public lunch buffet in their underpants. And we must say to them, in this place we wear a gown. But it is we who foster this kind of behaviour, because we ourselves overstep their personal limits all the time."

Here, Darmer highlights how the user research puts the spotlight on something her organisation needs to do differently, and how she and her staff must be the initiators of change. Part of the design process was thus to run workshops where the patient experiences were listened to by the staff and where they had the opportunity to start developing new ideas for solutions. Considering how the use of patients' voices helped to galvanise the staff to change behaviour. Darmer reflects that "We have to grab people's feelings, because it is their emotions that make the staff motivated to think they must do something different."

This consideration, which is essentially strategic, is that she recognises the need to engage her staff emotionally in the patient experience in order to initiate change. She describes her staff's reactions when listening to some rather critical patient statements, such as about an extremely high noise level at night in the ward, or rude treatment by a doctor, or dirty bathrooms as "puzzlement" and "a little embarrassment". She explains that by listening to the patients' stories, the staff became so disturbed, but also ambitious, that they took a range of change initiatives upon themselves. The patients' voices challenged their view of their own professionalism. Mette Rosendal Darmer explains that her management colleague, the Head Doctor with whom she co-manages the ward, was also challenged personally and as a leader. She describes how it "hurt" him to hear patients express their dissatisfaction with the service experience. The dilemma is that while patients are happy and relieved that they are treated extremely professionally from a purely medical-technical point of view, their subjective, personal, human experience is not very good. Says Darmer: "... patients are happy that we are very academically proficient at what we do, but they actually expect that we should master the other [experiential] aspects as well".

But Darmer goes further than more or less passively observing how the staff are disturbed by the patients' voices. She consciously orchestrates settings for the purpose of challenging the staff:

> "We decided not to do what we usually do. Usually we would tell the staff that we have these challenges, and here are the actions and milestones you must undertake. But we didn't do that at all. I stood up in front of all the doctors and nurses and secretaries and service workers, etc, I think there were 40 people present, and I told them that the project they had heard about ... we would not tell how we should proceed further. They were briefly told this. What we wanted from this was to disturb them."

Darmer then went on to play the challenging and uncomfortable sounds clips from interviews with patients. Darmer is thus extremely strategic about how she uses this empathy-creating data. She finds that already, at this stage (design dimension) of insight and engagement with patient's stories, change has started to take root in the department. For instance, she shares the story of one of the staff, in a service function, who could not let go of her impressions from experiencing what the patients experienced. "And it had certainly started a reflection with her. Because now, she tells me that when she goes down there with food trolley or is serving food, then she hears the patient´s voice."

Figure 6.3 is an illustration from field research carried out in one of the study's cases at Rigshospitalet. The photo was taken during the week-long observation study, combined with interviewing of approximately 20 patients.

As discussed earlier, in Lewisham the manager, Peter Gadsdon, oversaw a project where staff learned to video record each other's interactions with 'customers' in homelessness Services (Figure 6.4). The result was three films, edited with support from the designers, that illustrated how citizens experienced the service process. In a public commentary on the creation of the film, Sean Miller, the project's lead design facilitator, stated that the visual was hugely enlightening to both front-line staff and management. It demonstrated in particular that clients often wrongly remember or misinterpret what they've just been told in a meeting. "You wouldn't find this out with traditional questionnaires. It's incredibly raw and real ... It's the first time they'd received a form of insight that wasn't written," said Miller (*Guardian*, 2012).

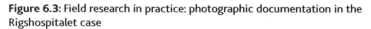

Figure 6.3: Field research in practice: photographic documentation in the Rigshospitalet case

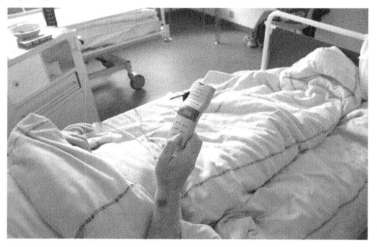

Source: MindLab

Peter Gadsdon, the manager, reflects on the power of this approach: "In a big area of policy impact these things are quite useful, I think, for senior decision makers because they really get to see the real situations." What Gadsdon points to here is that it was an eye-opener for the management team across Homelessness Services to view the recordings of how their staff dealt in practice with citizens. To Gadsdon, "seeing the real situations" was important because it made otherwise abstract management conversations about concepts like "service transformation" very concrete and tangible. Through a series of workshops, managers and staff could collaboratively interpret findings from the qualitative video material and develop ideas about how they might improve the service. However, the process went beyond the notion of new ideas, and influenced the view of the service and, almost immediately, the staff's behaviour as they interacted with citizens.

> "It had a profound effect on them, because it changed their view of the service they were providing. Because, if you had asked them before, they had said they were doing a good job, and they were working hard, and there were satisfied customers. I think, if you asked them afterwards they probably would be reflecting differently. You have got them to think differently. Maybe we could do different things differently. It was opening them up for changes, because you know, if they are the ones taking ownership, they will also in a different setting talk to people."

Figure 6.4: Field research in practice: video-filming the interactions between homeless citizens and case managers in the Lewisham case

Source: UK Design Council

For Gadsdon, the issue of 'ownership' through the deep engagement of staff was hereby quite critical for the achievement of change.

In New York's Housing and Preservation department, Andrew Eickmann, a strategy advisor, comments that what was really significant in the process (which explored the service experience of residents in the city's public housing) was "the designer focusing on the experience and perspective of end-users, of everyday people". Having worked with a range of classic management consultants, this was methodologically a very different approach to Eickmann.

To Anne Lind, the Director of the BII, leveraging design approaches to better see how her organization's services impact on citizens was "a shift in perspective". This reflects a questioning by Lind: what is the ultimate contribution of an organisation such as the BII? Is it to efficiently handle the case process to settle insurance claims and payment in accordance with legal standards, or is it to produce some kind of longer-term outcome for citizens and society? Seeing how outcomes are concretely manifested from the point of view of citizens was a key starting point, and an emotional driver of this change. Some of the first interviews with citizens, which were video-filmed in their own homes, were, according to Lind, of great significance. To staff, it was almost shocking to learn that although their case management was perhaps legally correct, citizens experienced it as confusing, bureaucratic and sometimes nearly meaningless. A universal finding seemed to be that the overwhelming amount of paperwork tended to get people caught up in the work injury process to the extent that they felt they *were* the work injury. As a result, the case management process in some instances made people more ill than they were already. "It has been good, but it has been tough", is how Anne Lind characterises the process. At first, the staff needed a lot of attention from her, simply because of the emotional challenge of realising that their work was in some cases doing more harm than good. This challenged their world-view. It also initiated significant processes of change within the agency. Ms Lind was very aware that it was her role to facilitate or catalyse that change in a positive way.

A similar shift in perspective took place at the Skansebakken institution for mentally and physically handicapped users. Centre manager Jesper Wiese explains how the insight came that the role of staff is not only to have good relations with the users, it is to foster positive and nurturing human relations between users and people (relatives, local citizens, school students, other visitors) from *outside* the institution:

> "Well there were some key employees who at one point said, 'Oh, so if *we* are not the relationships, we need to *facilitate* them?' Others said, 'Yes. I had even thought about it, but I had not been able to express it.' This is something that happens when you are together. So, I thought – damn, this is it! This is what it is about! ... And then it set off an avalanche of events, because it happened among some of the educationists who have a voice in the matter."

Wiese here describes that the ensuing 'avalanche' of events – of a series of changes within the institution to foster new relationships between users and the outside world – was carried by key people, the educational staff, who were role models for the others. He thus saw his own role in supporting and strengthening the voices of these staff members, who had the ability to bring everyone else along on the journey. In the Skansebakken project, the staff was involved in mapping user journeys. Figure 6.5 shows a workshop with staff, managed by designers from the Kolding School of Design.

Figure 6.5: User journey development by staff at Skansebakken

Source: Skansebakken and Kolding School of Design

Reflection: exploring new avenues for change

Rita Gunther McGrath has suggested that the first step in a process of innovation is to build mechanisms that cause you to re-examine your assumptions (Cliffe, 2011). The research tools employed by designers – ethnographically inspired field-work and visualisation of user journeys and *touchpoints* – are intended to help generate *insights* that in turn may challenge current perceptions of user needs, organisational effectiveness, which users and stakeholders are most important and so forth. What emerges from the empirical findings above seems to support this view that design approaches associated with problem exploration lead to various forms of insight, literally *seeing* the world in a new light. As Mette Rosendal Darmer of Rigshospitalet reflects, "It is like your bathroom tiles which are crooked and you will never get jointed, because you have stopped seeing them." Design research, in essence, casts fresh light on those crooked tiles.

In particular, the design methodologies seem to lead to new or revised understandings of citizens and how they experience their interactions with public service systems. The ensuing shifts in assumptions become ways of initiating new avenues for change, sparking emerging ideas on the parts of the manager.

However, the sections above indicates that more than insight is at play when design research unfolds. Rather than merely the gaining of new knowledge, it seems that the revisiting of assumptions and the empathy with citizen experience function as *prompts* for the managers: it is almost as if the kernel of possible futures lies embedded within the eye-openers created through user research. Almost immediately, as the frustrations and sometimes humiliations of citizens come to the fore through narratives, stories and visualisations, the managers begin to consider what to do about it. What might be the actions, interventions, services, regulations that could ameliorate the situation? What could be different ways (perhaps *very* different ways) of governing the service provision? Perhaps the exact solution is still far off, but there is a beginning, an early receptiveness to *what the solution should address*. An avenue, or perhaps several avenues, towards change is opened up. Some might call this the beginning of 'insight-led innovation'.

Jesper Wiese, the manager at Skansebakken (who is a trained social educator), suggests that design and educational practice have something in common, since design helps to drive learning; new insights rather immediately generate motivation for action: "We have talked about [some of the insights] with the staff and they said, 'when we observe something that could be done smarter, are we allowed to change it, or should we wait until we have been through it all?'"

Similarly, Marja-Lena Vaittinen explains that as the user insights were driven home, this energised the staff to take on the challenges of beginning to redesign the service processes.

> "If we here understand the customer situation and we really want to improve our services it's our duty to do so. There are obstacles – there are practical obstacles here in the city administration – but we can overcome them. It needs discussions and decision making but it's possible. You just have to try."

This quote indicates how new ideas about how to 'try' begin to flow simultaneously as the problem is represented through the research into the user's situation. Exploring problems becomes intertwined with considering new opportunities.

How to do it: leveraging insight and empathy

This chapter has illustrated various ways in which public managers insist on being curious about how their organisations' efforts actually could influence the experiences of the citizens they serve. In particular, they focus on engaging the public employees – both as individuals and collectively – who will need to change work practices and procedures as a consequence of the design work.

To work successfully with this dimension of design approaches, public managers could benefit from the following practices.

- **Ensure the legitimacy of the research.** Insist that the design team conducts deep, nuanced qualitative research in order to really obtain fine-grained data about the subjective, human experience of the citizens the organisation seeks to serve. Make sure that the sample of respondents or interviewees they involve in the research is strategically relevant and meaningful to the organisation. The quality of data collected at this stage is foundational for the further work, so it is important that it is perceived as solid and as legitimate by the wider organisation. This can sometimes entail conducting a few more field studies or interviews than the design team think is necessary; a number of, say, ten case subjects might resonate more strongly among critics than only five – even if that had been enough to reach saturation of data.
- **Be the guardian of the organisation's involvement.** As it is an explorative process, it is important to ensure that key employees, and perhaps other stakeholders, are part of the design research work. Make sure that internal people with relevant expertise and decision-making power are closely involved, so that the process becomes a journey of discovery for them as well.
- **Stay curious.** Maintain openness as to what might ultimately be the challenge for the organisation. As the chapter has illustrated, the design process is at this stage still very open ended, and it is important to avoid too-early closure. Instead of viewing design research only as problem discovery, it can be useful to see it as an open inquiry that may uncover problems but that may equally well lead to surprising opportunities for innovation.

As managers gain a richer understanding, through design research, of problems as well as opportunities, the time becomes ripe for generating new ideas and potential solutions. That is the topic of the next chapter.

SEVEN

Generating alternative scenarios

Transforming the system means passing through zones of uncertainty. (Donald Schön, *Beyond the Stable State*, 1971, p 12)

If there is one word that sits at odds with government, it is probably 'creativity'. However, for new, powerful ideas to emerge and become available for further development, scrutiny and testing, creativity is needed. The ability to embrace a divergence of possible solutions, and to keep those options in play for an extended period of time, is one of the characteristics that distinguishes truly innovative organisations from mediocre ones. However, as I have often suggested, public organisations and staff are sometimes decidedly afraid of 'the Post-It': worried that wild and unruly creativity, especially when it involves other actors outside the organisation, will unleash chaos and lack of control, and perhaps lead to political liabilities.

The previous chapter analysed how design methodologies, in part inspired by ethnographic research, contributed to making particular representations of the problem space for public managers and to bringing 'empathic data' into play. Approaches such as field research, generating emotional and empathic data, and visualisation of user journeys were key in this process.

The second dimension of design concerns the processes of identifying which possible actions to take – sometimes with the starting point in the input generated through user research, sometimes simply starting with an ambition, vision or inspiration to create change. This can be perceived as even more challenging than the research work, since the process now becomes more future oriented. Even though managers in government routinely are called on for their advice and suggestions, the practice of systematically generating new scenarios for the future is often not well developed. It can sometimes seem that where new ideas 'really' come from is somewhat of a black box.

The research behind this book offers insight into the idea-generating activities and experiences of public managers. In this chapter I first present and discuss the design methods associated with creating alternative future scenarios through a range of creative methods, user involvement and collaboration. What is the role of creative workshops (ideation processes) and systematic development of new concepts for solutions?

Second, I explore how the public managers in the cases experience the process of generating new solutions under conditions that are often complex, uncertain and open ended. How do they lead, or *steward* divergence: processes that are essentially concerned with broadening the available set of solutions, and thus decisions, available to them?

Third, I discuss the role of the managers in 'navigating the unknown', in particular when it concerns their own personal experience of losing control and certainty with the process. How do the managers deal with the fact that they are sometimes just as confused about where the design process will take them as their staff are?

Finally, I reflect on the wider implications of these two management engagements, before turning to a range of 'how to' recommendations.

An important qualification to the seemingly neat process (organised by this chapter structure) of shifting from the design dimension of exploring problems to that of generating alternative scenarios, which cannot be stated clearly enough, is Halse's point that 'we must acknowledge that design problems and their solutions emerge in parallel' (2010, p 40). The reader should keep this in mind, since the processes described in this chapter will thereby, naturally, mesh with some of the processes discussed in the previous one and in the next.

Methods: design as facilitator of divergence

In analysing the empirical cases in this book, designing visual tools for exploration can further be broken down into three types of situations – each stage roughly corresponding (but not fully, as they tend to blur) to the three dimensions of design: visualisation for understanding the current situation (for instance, service journeys, personas, which were discussed in the previous chapter); visualisation to stimulate collaboration for ideation (creativity-facilitating visuals, including idea mapping and concept design, which will be expanded below); and visualisation to propose possible solutions (prototypes, which are covered in the next chapter). Among the concrete methodologies applied in the cases studied, the following stand out as the most commonly used.

Ideation

Workshops, brainstorming processes, creative sessions and design games are very frequently part of the portfolio of activities connected with design approaches. That is also the case for the processes that were researched for the present book. Idea generation, or ideation, is among the activities most closely associated with innovation and design methodologies: developing new creative ideas, applying imagination and energy to describe possible futures. Most often, this endeavour is highly collaborative, reflecting the recognition that 'No design team will possess all the relevant knowledge by itself. To accomplish innovation, a network of stakeholders must be set in motion' (Halse et al, 2010, p 27).

Even if collaborative idea generation is by no means an exact science, it certainly is a discipline, and it can be done in quite systematic ways (Kelley, 2005; Michlewski, 2015). Karl Ulrich, Professor of Operations and Information Management at the Wharton School at the University of Pennsylvania, has conducted research that shows that 'diminishing returns to scale' of more new ideas don't kick in until after 150–200 ideas (Terwiesch and Ulrich, 2009). In other words, to be sure that the quality of ideas is as high as possible, as judged by the innovation team itself, the group has to develop at least 150 distinct ideas.

In nearly all of the cases studied, some form of ideation process, usually involving staff and sometimes also users, is carried out. Often the starting point of the process is in material from the design research phase, such as photos, audio recordings, films, service journey-mappings and so forth. In other cases ideation and brainstorming are stimulated by the use of visuals simply to unleash the imagination of the workshop participants.

For instance, in the Lewisham homelessness project, ideas were generated on the basis of the three films recorded by staff of their interactions with service users. As part of the design of relationships project at Skansebakken, visual 'prompt cards' were deployed to facilitate creative idea generation.

What is interesting here is how the very process of bringing designers into the public organisation seems to create allowance for more divergence, or creativity. Commenting on his experience of working closely with designers, strategy advisor Andrew Eickmann from New York City's Department for Housing Preservation and Development, recognises the contribution of the design process in creating divergence: "The design process is allowed to breathe, bring more life to ideas in their pure form before they are subject to typical analysis." Eickmann reflects that many of the consultants he otherwise encounters are more "Trained to think like a public agency. This makes them more conversing, but also not disruptive." Andrew Eickmann observes that because of their title and identity, designers are by default being asked to be creative, to pitch ideas, to iterate – "that is their job". He suggests that a parallel job done by a consultancy like McKinsey and Co would, by way of expectations, have more risk calculation built in, such as thinking about funding, about legal implications etc.

Michlewski (2015, p 104) observes that 'Designers are seen as creative types, giving them more scope and cultural permission to behave and think differently.' Eickmann observes that the creativity of designers is thereby "less bounded by the limitations we otherwise have in place". He acknowledges that the elements can be imitated, but professional designers also think about things differently, are hard to mimic. "It is easy to acknowledge that end-user perspective has value but not easy in practice, it takes someone with that mission and training and perspective to collect it, show it in a convincing way," says Andrew Eickmann. One might say that by allowing designers to focus strongly and clearly on the end-user's role, with the skills to do it, the citizen's perspective is suddenly placed front and centre in the organisation – at least for a while.

Concept development

Growing ideas from simple, individual words or short one-liners to mature, well-described and valuable solutions can be termed concept development. A concept is a coherent set of solutions, activities and benefits that are based on one particular 'pitch' or fundamental idea. It is usually tightly connected to findings generated, for example, by design research, and to key insights (Bason, 2010).

Getting to concept development requires that the range of ideas generated via ideation processes be narrowed down. This can be done in various ways, ranging from a quite closed 'elite' selection taking place within the design team or among a group of managers, or even by the responsible manager him- or herself. Most often, however, in the context of the cases studied here, there is some form of collaborative, almost democratic process, where staff (and sometimes users) are invited to examine the ideas and make judgements about which ones to develop further. This examination, and judgement process, often involves frameworks (for instance matrixes or axes upon which to assess the viability and cost of potential solutions) and selection mechanisms (such as 'dot voting', where workshop participants indicate their preferences for certain solutions).

For instance, in the Lewisham case, around 40 ideas emerged from the design research; a series of staff workshops then narrowed the range of ideas down to 10 that could be developed further as concepts and subsequently prototyped. One concept was called a 'What Next?' document that was intended to show citizens their place in the case management process, thus providing overview, ownership and transparency for them (*Guardian*, 2010).

An interesting aspect that is highlighted across many of the cases, and that seemed to take many managers by surprise, was the degree of precision and focus that was involved in the various workshops conducted in the course of the design work. Mette Rosendal Darmer at Rigshospitalet, for instance, says that the process being handled and facilitated by the design team was important: "The fact that you are placed in a different setting I think is important, because it is not themselves who decide."

Additionally, and perhaps also significant in terms of the dynamics of change unfolding in the projects, is that a substantial number of the managers express that they were energised by the workshop activity. Consider Marja-Leena Vaittinen, the city manager in Helsinki, who says: "From my experience in those three workshops I was awfully tired when I went there but when I came out I was so full of energy," or Mette Rosendal Darmer from Rigshospitalet, who states that, compared to the design workshops, a recent lean management project "didn't have the same energy".

Engagement #3: stewarding divergence

As the design approaches of ideation and concept development are brought into play, managers and employees – and in some cases users – find themselves in a territory of openness, exploration and flux. The design engagement of 'stewarding divergence' concerns how managers deal with these processes. Marco Steinberg (2014, p 97) describes the concept of 'stewardship' in the context of designing in public organisations as follows:

> Stewardship is the art of aligning decisions with impact when many minds are involved in making a plan and many hands enacting it. As such, design stewardship is about the craft of navigating forces outside of one's control. In the case of public sector innovation these include organizational incentives, prevailing investment logic and political mood swings.

Steinberg hints that as managers engage with the process of generating potential new ideas, they must deal with a range of actors and influences that determine which solutions are brought into play, which are considered and which are (or should be) given momentum, shape and form as the design process unfolds.

Throughout this process, managers are allowing, to the best of their ability, for divergence, meaning the capacity to let a broad range of ideas and possible solutions grow and expand.

Michlewski (2015) characterises this as the challenge of dealing with ambiguity, something that sits uncomfortably with much management practice, which strives to control all factors and facets of a process in the belief that such control contributes to the success of the project. Meanwhile, 'designers believe that the chances of success increase by actually letting go' (Michlewski, 2015, p 54).

Even though some managers may well embrace the open-endedness of the design process, they cannot allow it to be guided by blind faith. Somehow they must be close enough to the process to know when it should start to converge towards more certainty and, ultimately, to decision making about which solutions to take forward.

This is, in the truest sense of the phrase, a delicate balancing act.

Jesper Wiese of Skansebakken reflects on the perils of managing the uncertainty of the process and expresses some regret that he and his fellow management colleagues did not articulate a bit more precisely where they thought the design work would lead:

"At that time we did not communicate very much. Retrospectively it was very stupid. We started out by saying, 'Now we are going to create a design process. We will be working on relationships. And, by the way, we don't know quite what it is.' There were many who asked, 'please, tell us what you expect us to do'. No, not really. We will participate; we must be happy and cheer at the right moment. But in addition to that we don't really know what is expected of us. I think – this is at least some of what I have learned from it and that can be used next time: becoming a little more exact in creating the idea of where we want to end."

Figure 7.1: Using visuals to stimulate creativity and engage staff

Source: Kolding School of Design; Skansebakken project

Vaittinen, the manager in Helsinki, observes that as the mapping of the user journey opened up the ideation process to a wide range of actors, challenges arose:

> "We don't know each other [across city agencies and units]. We have never worked together. It was the first time. The staff were sceptical, but this is also important. There's a need for patience and time to adjust different experts to different mind-sets and languages, because in that administrative unit you speak a different language or your culture is quite different from ours here and you haven't met those people, you don't know them, who are you, what you are doing, what is your organisation doing? So – we don't know. We are about 40,000 people here."

To steward the openness of the opportunity space in the spirit of a design attitude is not without organisational and personal challenges. In the following I explore how managers reflect on the issue of 'navigating the unknown' for prolonged periods of time.

Engagement #4: navigating the unknown

This management engagement concerns how managers lead, govern or navigate the design process as it increasingly challenges the organisation and staff. In the previous chapter we saw that in governing the collaborative process some of the managers took active responsibility for disturbing or challenging their staff, for instance by initiating various forms of experimentation or by putting them in situations beyond their usual comfort zones. Often this happened through the ability of design research to call to the fore the concrete situations and experiences citizens had with the public services. I called this 'leveraging empathy' to engage the organisation.

Leveraging empathy, as it turns out, is a double-edged sword. As the design process leads to a divergence of ideas and options, staff look to managers for control, for reassurance and for closure – something that, given the nature of the process, managers often cannot provide. So, paradoxically, the public managers facilitate disruptions and allow for collaboration to unfold in an uncertain space, at least for a while. This provides engagement and ownership, and perhaps even energy among staff, but also discomfort. So, while they are largely responsible for the creation of discomfort, the managers must also navigate it and ameliorate it, make it 'OK' to be in a situation that is characterised by open-endedness and ambiguity.

A further complication of this stage, and a further paradox perhaps, is that some of the managers are in fact uncomfortable themselves. Often they are nearly as uncertain as their staff about where the design process will end. They have to try to deal with this personal emotional state, to manage it, so to speak, in ways that it do not affect the staff too adversely. While there is an outer journey happening in the organisation, the managers go through an inner journey too.

Let me consider these two perspectives in turn: how managers help their staff to navigate the discomfort of the open-ended design process; and how managers themselves reflect on their personal feelings and experience of dealing with divergence, open-endedness and ambiguity.

Helping staff to navigate discomfort

There seems to be a rather clear pattern that managers find different ways of helping their staff to deal with the inherent discomfort of not knowing where the design processes will lead. Consider for example how Poula Sangill, manager of the 'meals on wheels' project to improve municipal food service for the elderly in the city of Holstebro expresses this perspective:

> "I tell them that if it all becomes too uncertain, then they shouldn't doubt that we [the management] will back them up. We're all in the same boat, so when it's uncertain for you, then it's uncertain for Anne Marie and me."

In this quote, Sangill essentially displays solidarity with her staff and underlines how important it is for her that they know that the management – she and the section chief, Anne Marie – are on the same page. Sangill goes on to explain:

> "Yes, it is to dare to show that you are uncertain, that it doesn't matter so much. When we were going into this project I said to them, I don't how this is going to end up. It may end up in all sorts of places, we don't know. But we have taken a decision, we will not be grey and municipal."

What Sangill expresses here is that she is trying to create a space, a frame, where it is OK for the staff to feel uncertain about where the project will end up. She shares her own uncertainty and honestly conveys that nor does she does know where it will end. However – and this is a key theme for many of the cases – she insists that change *will* happen. Because her vision is that "we will not be grey and municipal".

In the Lewisham case, which focused on redesigning services for the homeless, Development Director Peter Gadsdon explains how the relationship with staff was somewhat contentious. In this quote he discusses what happened as the staff were working on the insights gathered from video-filming their own interactions with homeless clients:

> "Even though they had captured the information on film themselves, they were looking a bit uncomfortable, because it is their service."

Much is at stake here. In some cases employees are not prepared to deal with the temporality of the processes, or with the emerging shifts in underlying governance models. In a few extreme situations this even leads to people becoming stressed, or in other cases being made redundant. Consider this quote, which I have kept anonymous due to the sensitivity of the matter. A manager speaks about a key employee in the organisation and her relation to the design project:

> "She also had stress, and was sick with stress, but I actually think that what gave her stress was this transformation thing. Not necessarily what we were going to do, but the unknown situation in itself."

In another case a manager describes how she had to make a new hire redundant because the design work showed that the person's competencies were not required or needed by the users. Jesper Wiese from Skansebakken similarly reflects on the insecurity of staff.

> "You know, there was insecurity in the most basic way; do I lose my job, but also insecurity coming out like 'what the hell are we going to do?'"

A key challenge in these processes is that, as the design projects unfold, and potential new ideas and avenues for change emerge, they represent breaks or disruptions from the past. Managers find themselves placed in between, having to manage the shaping of the new future while not making the past look as if everything the staff did was wrong. This is an immensely delicate balance, really one of change leadership. Consider these passages where Jesper Wiese at Skansebakken reflects that "it is a huge challenge to navigate in this, for instance [when employees say] 'Well, were we doing it the wrong way before?'" Wiese goes on to reflect that "You must find a way to navigate your way through this story without accusing people of having been wrong."

> "Well, you emphasise, of course, that no one will be sacked. That was not the case, so there was no reason to say anything other than that nobody will be sacked. I was also very careful in saying that even though we did not know what we were doing, we would do it together. Nobody would be forcing it on us."

As the insight emerged at Skansebakken that the institution and its staff needed to shift towards a much more relational and emphatic model for engaging with users, the need to navigate became difficult. Wiese says:

> "We have balance between saying 'Yes, maybe it is a criticism' of what we have done. We have done a lot to, say, culture and system and we have learned from our predecessors. But we have once in a while said, 'Yes, we have actually done something that was stupid, we probably have'. It is a well-known story in Denmark that in the old days the parents of mentally disabled children came here, dropped the child at the institution and were told that they should forget this child and go home and have a new one. We have used this story to tell the employees that it's not you who are here now who did wrong. This is a heritage that we carry with us, that has been a wrong path to follow. It has also been necessary to say yes, there is probably something that we should change significantly."

The managers thus clearly have a role in navigating and dealing with these types of staffing and organisational challenges.

Managers handling their own discomfort and uncertainty

At the same time as the managers help the staff to deal with
uncertainty and complexity they also have to manage their own
expectations and relation to the design work. Jesper Wiese at
Skansebakken explains how this was a personal journey as well:

> "But I must say it took me quite a long time before I
> realised [what the project was about]. Actually, it also
> took some time before I grasped how much energy
> we were supposed to put into it before it succeeded.
> And it took me even longer to completely capture
> how big it was going to be. ... [Managing the design
> process] is really difficult. And to draw a new future,
> because it is such an interaction ... It's like groping
> for something."

In the New York City case on housing preservation and
development, Andrew Eickmann reflects on the attributes of
the design methodologies: "The design process is somehow
allowed to breathe, and brings more life to ideas in their pure
form before they are subject to analysis." Eickmann describes
how some of the ideas that were generated by the design team
were "valuable, but also made people nervous". He describes how
one solution proposed a digital application, a type of 'Yelp' for
housing quality.[1] The proposal was an open source platform for
residents to review the quality of housing in their own building
(star rating) and bring transparency to the issue of housing quality
by way of user experience. This idea is in many ways counter to
a regulatory, compliance-driven approach, which would typically
be employed by public agencies, including by the Agency for
Housing Development and Preservation. In Eickmann's view the
service idea was exciting because it could be a powerful tool, but
would also be very challenging. As a manager he recognised the
risk. Since it would "put all the power in the hands of residents,
it could maybe be misused".

Other managers too seem to be acutely aware of how
challenging some of the design processes are for their staff. In

most cases, they actively seek to manage or steward this. Peter Gadsdon from Lewisham, for instance, says:

> "So it is about not blaming, it is about encouraging improvement. That is the environment we try to have. ... To create the environment for people to deliver, you know, rather than me delivering."

Gadsdon does not see challenging the staff in Homelessness Services as an objective in itself; rather, it is a tool for driving motivation and, ultimately, improvement and change. And throughout the process he saw his role as important in terms of visibly supporting the process and encouraging the shifts in behaviours and culture: "One of the important things is that they see the management engagement in this stuff. ... So I always made the point of being involved."

Elspeth Gibson was the Senior Strategy Manager for Public Health in Suffolk in the UK, where she collaborated with designers on improving the health of young people in the city. Elspeth Gibson emphasises that conducting field-work was not just about creating discomfort; there should also be something motivational about the experience. As she says about spending a day interviewing young people around the university campus: "Let us just learn, and bring the data back, make it fun, enjoy it."

As I also discussed in the previous chapter, in the case of Anne Lind of the Danish BII, she felt that she had to almost nurse her entire staff following some particularly direct video footage of citizen interviews relaying how work-injury victims were not really helped by the case managers – sometimes to the contrary – so that they became even more ill due to the way the authorities handled their case. Ms Lind explains how, as a result, the staff were shocked and needed her attention due to the clarity with which the citizens' experiences were presented:

> "We might have been clear that something needed to change, but we had not been precise enough about what it was. And we had no sense that things were so bad as some of the statements we have received here."

As a response, she involved her staff heavily in interpreting and presenting the results and findings of the design project. She then fed the results into the organisational structure and delegated responsibility to mid-level managers for follow-up. In this sense, even as this manager is taking control of dealing with uncertainty, she herself initiates a loss of control through delegation. By doing so, however, she motivates people more broadly in her organisation to find meaningful ways of dealing with the challenging insights and coming up with new solutions.

Pawsø, the manager of Camillagaarden, is slightly less comfortable with her role as a steward of the unknown. When relaying how the innovation project she commissioned unfolded, she says, "So there was surely a period where you were a bit without identity and did not really know what to do. I could recognise it for myself at the beginning of this project, where I could easily see, well, I can't keep doing what I used to do, but I didn't really know what to do in instead. And it's frustrating to feel a bit paralysed." Pawsø recognises that being in a state of uncertainty is by no means any more comfortable for her as a manager.

In Suffolk, where designers worked on the youth health improvement project, the manager Elspeth Gibbons describes her experience that:

> "Most of the time it was about having the enthusiasm for something that you could not define, having to explain the value in something, with the value having yet to be realised. Yes, that was very tough, using some sort of incentive to motivate people to be part of something. Saying, we are going meet in the dance house today, and we might have an hour´s dance, you know, free dance, being in a nice space, a nice lunch. Make it attractive. And give people permission just to take a bit of time away from what they are doing and say, let's see where it leads, I can't tell you where we are going to go with it."

In a similar vein, school principal Mette Kynemund says:

"The other thing is my personal perspective, because I have always ... as a leader I have always known where we had to go. Some of the teachers asked me after 20 January [the date of the first project workshop], where is it we are going to end up with this? I answered that I don't know, because I don't know what the students are going to say. 'Well, you must know', they said. And there was actually one teacher who then asked me in May [after the project ended], 'did you really not know how you would control us?' No, I really didn't know. It has been a loss of control for me, and it's been a positive loss of control."

Kynemund's reflection that to her, the loss of control over the process was positive, is interesting. It indicates that 'stewarding the unknown' is a fruitful process, whereas in public management, risk and lack of control is usually characterised as a negative thing. But here it is experienced as positive.

Figure 7.2: Selecting ideas and developing concepts in the Stenhus Community College project

Source: MindLab; Gower Publishing

It appears that the managers, as they seek to achieve direction in their navigation, draw on the underlying intent or meaning of the process in which they are engaging their staff. One could say that they establish certain constructs in order to sustain the process. Let me give some examples.In the Skansebakken case, Jesper Wiese refers continuously to the central construct of 'relationships' and the (quite early) insight that it was a redesign, or reconfiguration, of the relationships between the handicapped users and the outside world that was at stake. He also connects the issue to empathy with users. For instance, using the construct enabled him to identify which people (resources) among the staff would be critical to engage and support in order for the shift in practice to take place.

> "I can see from what we are doing now, the use of empathy is important. It is still the same things we want to do, but we will do it in a better way for some users – we want to deal with the unknown. Maybe we don't know how, but we know what the big target is."

At Camillagaarden, the construct of 'citizen-driven innovation' becomes key as Christina Pawsø navigates the ways in which her staff question and challenge the range of sometimes slightly crazy activities, including organising wheel-chair races along the building's central corridor.

Reflection: managing divergence under complexity

Within innovation literature, it is almost a truism that in order to identify the best possible ideas, a much wider set of options have to be generated (Kelley, 2005; Brown, 2009). However, it is also a point made extensively by Boland and Collopy (2004) and Michlewski (2015) that traditional managers' tendency to adopt a 'decision attitude' involves the risk of closing down opportunities for invention too early, and thereby the risk of making ill-informed choices.The design dimension of generating alternative scenarios has to do with the opening up of possible futures, with acts of 'future making'.

Boland and Collopy emphasise that managers should consider, as designers, that the ability to create great ideas under conditions of uncertainty depends on the ability to adopt a particular stance, a design attitude, that 'assumes that it is difficult to design a good alternative, but that once you have developed a truly great one, the decision about which alternative to select becomes trivial' (2004, p 4).

Additionally, the emergent and more collaborative design approaches discussed earlier suggest that policy options could (or maybe even should) be developed through an interplay between policy makers at different levels of the governance system, interest and lobby groups, external experts and, not least, end-users such as citizens or business representatives themselves. As Polaine, Lövlie and Reason (2013, p 44) point out:

> Service design is about designing *with* people, not *for* them ... 'People' does not just mean customers or users, it also means the people working to provide the service, often called frontline, front-of-house, or customer-facing staff.

The authors underline that there are two main reasons for involving staff in the design process: engagement and buy-in to the ideas and solutions that are developed; and (not least) the recognition that staff have unique knowledge and insight about what it will take to make a new service or process work in practice in their interactions with end-users.

A key part of this interplay with users and staff is, then, the creation of ideas – ensuring that a wide-enough range of options are available for the manager(s) to ultimately decide upon.

Design vs creativity?

There is no shortage of books and publications on processes of creativity for generating innovative ideas (Kelley, 2005). However, the issue for the present book is whether there are particular 'designerly' approaches to engaging and stimulating people's creative abilities to develop ideas. Boland and Collopy emphasise that in speaking of design as a vehicle for problem solving they are speaking about something beyond creativity, even though creativity is 'necessary for the improvement of all our human endeavours' (2004, p 15). Rather:

> creativity is not sufficient for a design attitude to problem solving ... the questions really should be: Creativity in what problem space? And creativity towards what end?

One might say that the issue of 'creativity' in the context of design approaches is embedded. It is embedded in the problem space – the context of current use, of the situation of the organisation, of the manager, the staff and wider stakeholders. And it is embedded in the *intent*, the overall purpose and motivation for running the project in the first place (Body and Terrey, 2014). Perhaps one could say that one way to characterise design is as applied creativity.

This being said, design, as we have seen, is rather ripe with ways and means of stimulating individual and group creativity. Design might thus facilitate a wide divergence of views and ideas, enabling selection, then synthesising them by generating alternative future scenarios. Michlewski highlights the ability of designers to act playfully and to create playful environments and processes to stimulate individual and group creativity. According to Michlewski, 'playfulness encourages unexpected experimentation and exploration' (2015, p 105). His study of designers' professional culture shows that by invoking the label of 'creatives' designers are given more scope and permission to stage and orchestrate playful experimentation and to use unorthodox and ungrounded methods.

Because they feel more comfortable than most with ambiguity and open-endedness, they feel natural and at home with processes of creation. In the cases studied in the book, it is certainly the case that it is the design teams that plan and execute the various workshops, creative sessions and seminars that are intended to stimulate creativity. Perhaps diverging from Michlewski's understanding of the role of the 'playful' designer, designing with his or her own team, in most of the cases studied the designers go to great lengths to facilitate processes that involve the manager and staff in the client organisation. A key part of this involvement is to bring visual tools into play.

Dealing with complexity and ambiguity in the neutral zone

This chapter has illustrated how, in different ways, managers seek to deal with what William Bridges (1980) calls the 'neutral zone' in any transition process. According to Bridges, in dealing constructively with transitions from one state of affairs to another, one needs first to 'surrender', that is, to give in to emptiness and stop struggling to escape it. However, as Bridges also warns, being in the transition or, as he calls it, the 'neutral zone' does not mean that 'anything goes'. 'This is a time for doing things you wouldn't normally do, but it is not a time to hurt yourself' (1980, p 128). In other words, the period of unknownness, or the neutral zone, is not a place to tread lightly. Things, including one's personal world-view, become unstable. Donald Schön, discussing the illusion of a 'stable state' world, proposes that as people experience significant transitions or challenges in their lives – professional or personal – central elements of the self come into question: 'They provoke a transformation of the system of the self, in which a new zone of stability can be attained only by passing through a zone of instability' (1971, p 12). This recognition is in line with the point I made earlier, that processes in organisations do not only change the organisation, they also influence the subjects who may have initiated the change. The managers, as subjects, attach meaning to the process and are 'shaped by the process in turn' (Hernes, 2008, p 51).

As my research has indicated, the managers seek to balance simultaneously between proactively making their staff uncomfortable, dealing with their own personal uncertainty and creating motivation and energy for people to keep going. Throughout this they search for what the design insights mean and what appropriate changes must be made. As transitionary processes, design projects challenge the managers to articulate something while it still is a mystery to them. They must deal, unconsciously or consciously, with a process of making, of emergence. The wider point, which is made by Whitehead, is that 'no innovation, firm or institution – is a final state; rather, everything is merely a stage forming (potentially) other processes' (Hernes, 2008, p 50).

Another way of interpreting this style of thinking and questioning assumptions is to draw on Michlewski's design attitude of embracing ambiguity, uncertainty and disruption. This stance reflects managers 'keeping an open mind while working on a practically focused solution' (Michlewski, 2008, p 381). It is really, as Michlewski puts it, to embrace discontinuity (a break from the past) and open-endedness (not knowing where the future will lead you).

Similarly, Boland and Collopy underline that 'Designers relish the lack of predetermined outcome' (2004, p 9). In Michlewski's recent refinement of his 2008 work, he conducts a survey to explore the differences between designers and non-designers in their approach to problem solving and innovation, and finds that designers, to a significantly higher degree than non-designers, appreciate experimentation, openness and ambiguity (2015, p 53)

How to do it: enabling the creative process

This chapter has illustrated the management engagements of *stewarding divergence* and *navigating the unknown*. These leadership practices attract our attention to the real delicacy of managing innovation. They may also point to a significant difference between managing change, on the one hand, and leading innovation, or design, on the other hand. In managing change, it is 'just' about getting to a well-defined state of affairs, while in leading design much of the focus is on exploring the problem space and searching for as yet unknown solutions. In this sense, managers who successfully pull this off 'manage as designers' because, as Boland and Collopy (2004) state, designers relish the lack of predetermined outcomes.

For the public manager desiring to successfully navigate the divergent, creative process of generating alternative scenarios, the following practical advice might be worth considering.

- **Keep the ideation process open.** As you enter the divergent, creative phases of the design project, be aware of how important it is to let new ideas develop and mature –

avoid too-early closure. For some managers it works well to keep some distance from the ideation activities, simply in order not to influence the process too much at this delicate stage but, rather, let staff take real ownership of the ideas and let other voices and actors make a contribution.

- **Maintain that ideas need to be anchored in insights.** One of the strengths of design-led innovation processes is that the ideas that are generated are based on qualitative research and user insights. As ideas are developed by the design team, by staff, by users and by other stakeholders, continue to reflect back to the insights that were gained during exploration of the problem: do the ideas link back to the directions that were indicated by the design research? Would the ideas truly address the issues that were uncovered? Would they really make a difference to end-users?

- **Be sensitive as to when to close.** If you leave the creative process open for too long, it costs time and resources and quite possibly frustration. If you shut it down too early, the opportunity for real innovation and transformation might be in jeopardy. The best advice is to follow your instinct and let your judgement be the guide as to when to insist that the team moves on, turning ideas and concepts into concrete prototypes – the theme of the next chapter.

Note
[1] Yelp is a smartphone application with descriptions and user ratings of cafes, restaurants and other services.

EIGHT

Enacting new practices

Design is an exploration about people and their future
ways of living. (Elizabeth Sanders, 2014, p 133)

Design is often understood by lay people as an end result: as
the forms, visuals and expressions that we see as products and
graphics, and that we call things and signs. Design approaches are
perhaps most powerful when used to finally give form, to create
the tangible artefacts that humans can engage with physically and
emotionally. The ability to deliberately create user experiences
and to make services and products desirable and attractive is,
in this sense, at the heart of design. One might call this *enacting
new practices*.

However, when it comes to design for service, for the creation of
new experiences for users, the end result is highly contingent on
changes in organisational processes and behaviours within public
institutions. This turns our attention, again, to the experience
of the public managers, and their staff and stakeholders, as they
are involved in the design processes. How are they able to turn
alternative scenarios into tangible changes that can ultimately
be felt and experienced by someone outside the organisation?

This chapter first explores the role of prototyping as a key
process whereby design proposals are developed, refined,
described, given form, shape and expression. How are prototypes
significant in the processes of organisational engagement and of
asserting what might work best in terms of achieving intended
outcomes? Second, I explore and characterise the leadership
engagement with design I call 'Making the future concrete': how

do managers work with designers and their methods to enact change? How do they relate to the power of prototyping and experimentation? Third, I discuss the final of the six management engagements with design, the tendency to insist on public value. Fourth, I reflect on the particular nature of design approaches to bring tangibility and 'life' into public change efforts. The chapter concludes with a number of suggestions on how to get started using design for enacting new practices.

Methods: tools for creating tangible futures

The professional role of designers is, ultimately, to make things concrete. As Michlewski (2015, p 112) suggests, 'Creating models (of absolutely anything) is absolutely essential in a successful design process.' In his view, as mentioned earlier, such models are what enables playfulness and exploration. In the language of designers, models and other graphical and physical expressions, as part of a development process, are called prototypes.

Prototyping

Moggridge (2007, p 685) defines prototypes as 'A representation of a design, made before the final solution exists'. Applying the process of prototyping to public sector development projects can be viewed as a practical way of exploring future solutions at an early stage and of shaping them in ways that allow fast, small-scale testing, iteration and learning. Polaine, Løvlie and Reason (2013, p 139) argue that prototypes are essential in designing services, as:

> When developing a service you can save the organisation large amounts of time and money if you design and test the experience before resources are spent on designing the processes and technology needed to eventually run the service. Therefore, it is important to create an environment where you can involve real people with trying the service as early as possible in the development process.

Michlewski (2015, p 112) states that 'prototyping enables dialogue which focuses on the iterative process around a solution rather than the abstracted planning phase up front'. Similarly, Halse et al (2010, p 37) elaborate that the notion of incompleteness is critical here, since incompleteness as 'work-in-progress ... provides for a flexibility of interpretations that is crucial for continuous engagement and participation'.

In the public sector, prototypes can potentially be models of 'absolutely anything', be it new administrative processes, new citizen service journeys or a visualisation of the mechanisms or resulting processes of a policy initiative (Bason, 2010). What characterises prototypes is that they are highly tangible, either as graphical illustrations or as virtual or physical models or spaces, and that they are intended to explore the experience of use (Parker and Heapy, 2006; Bate and Robert, 2007; Halse et al, 2010; Polaine, Lövlie and Reason, 2013; Halse, 2014; Sanders, 2014).

For instance, service journeys that are created not to show the current situation but to suggest a future process are essentially service prototypes. They are often made visible through graphically showing steps, interactions, relations, events and experiences that make up a service. Another approach is to illustrate the future service not as a diagram but as a story. The story could simply be a text describing what happens and how it feels, using the tools of science fiction literature to create a 'story from the future' (scenario planning is often associated with such stories). Or the story could be turned into a role play or an audio narrative or a film about the future – such as in the case of the iZone project described in this book (see below). Digital services can also be prototyped. Graphical sketches or mock-ups of websites or apps can be drawn by hand, illustrating the layout and specific functions. More advanced drafts can be drawn using graphical software. Physical models, sometimes small and sometimes at full scale, can function as prototypes as well.

Prototypes do not have to look or feel anything like the solution or design output that may ultimately result from the process. They may, while still being graphical or physical, be abstractions or symbols of dimensions of a service or even a policy, or they may provide tools that make up a design game (Kimbell, 2014; Sanders, 2014).

Prototypes versus pilots

Many public organisations do not work explicitly with prototypes, but rather with experimental programmes or pilots. However, it is important to understand that a prototype is a different thing than a pilot programme. With prototypes it is at least as important to fail and learn as it is to achieve success. With pilot programmes the exercise should ideally (roughly speaking) prove that the right solution has been found, and should thereby be a direct pathway to implementation at scale. One could say that whereas prototypes are also successful when they show an organisation how things should not be done, rarely has a massively failed pilot been viewed as a success.

These are thus very different purposes, and very different dynamics. One should be highly aware whether the need is to develop and test a prototype, or the solution has been developed to a point of maturity and certainty where it makes better sense to run a pilot. Table 8.1 seeks to illustrate some essential differences between prototypes and 'pilots'.

Table 8.1: Prototypes versus pilots

	Prototype	Pilot
Purpose	Feedback, learning, development	Demonstration and evidence
Timing	Early in design process	When solution has been designed
Publicity	None or very limited	Medium to high
Risk profile	Very low	Medium

Table 8.1 shows perhaps the most central point to be that prototypes have their justification at an early stage in the innovation process, where there continues to be a significant degree of uncertainty about what could be the right solution. Pilot programmes are to a higher degree useful as more or less final proof (sometimes supported with randomised controlled

trials, RCTs) that a given service or solution is right and can work at large scale.

Currently, some governments around the world, including in Finland and in the United Arab Emirates, are challenging this clear distinction between prototypes and pilots. Here, public organisations are putting in place larger 'experiments' which have the openness and focus on learning of prototypes, but the scale of pilots. At a time of rapid change, where it can make sense for instance to test self-driving cars in a real-life setting, perhaps we will see more of such blurring between prototypes and pilots, moving towards a new hybrid category called public experiments.

User testing

Either as part of design research or as a separate activity, user testing is often connected intimately to collaborative design approaches. Here, end-users and/or key stakeholders are invited to experience the concepts or prototypes that have been developed and to provide their feedback (Mattelmäki, 2008; Polaine et al, 2013; Sanders, 2014; Halse, 2014). If it takes place during (early) field-work, user testing often has a strong generative purpose (Moggridge, 2007; Halse, 2014), leading to a range of new ideas and directions, whereas it might to a take the form of evaluation to a greater degree when it is conducted at a later stage in the design process.

Design research, workshops, seminars, live testing and prototyping are potentially all ways of engaging public sector staff in a design-led development process. Coaching employees on how to use a video camera, smartphone or 'flip' device, and enabling staff to test on a small scale the solutions they have themselves developed are some of a range of activities that foster employee involvement and, potentially, engagement. As the following sections will show, most of the cases studied involve rather significant and direct involvement of employees and mid-level managers in the design process.

Realisation, business cases, evaluation and assessments of public value

These activities are not directly associated with design approaches, but are mentioned here as part of the portfolio of activities because they are regularly carried out in connection with the cases examined for this book. A business case would typically involve attaching a number of assumptions to one or more design solutions (concepts) and then calculating the costs and benefits of implementing them, normally stating the financial return of investment (ROI). Some business cases may be more qualitative in nature. This would mean considering from a more subjective, experiential viewpoint issues such as expected changes in errors in a service, in user experience and so forth (Polaine et al, 2013).

Business cases are used in some of the cases studied. For instance, in the Branchekode project external consultants were hired to develop a business case to better understand the potential savings in time and cost for business and for the government agencies involved. The same was done in the Lewisham homelessness project, where an external consultancy was commissioned by the UK Design Council to evaluate the project. In the Family by Family and Skansebakken cases, external evaluations were carried out as well. The next chapter, on public value, holds more examples of business cases and measurement approaches.

Engagement #5: making the future concrete

This management engagement is very strongly associated with the processes of prototyping as discussed above. This essentially has to do with taking possible future scenarios and making them sufficiently tangible for managers, staff and end-users to enter into dialogue with them. This engagement for public managers is the connection to making and shaping a future state of affairs so concretely that you can see it and, sometimes, even touch it. Using models and sketches, also stories, media and enactments, to envision a desired future state of affairs, are essentially 'designerly' ways of working. These enactments can essentially flow either from the (bottom-up) findings emerging from ethnographic work and concept development, thus informing potentially effective interventions or from visions or strategies that are then transformed (top-down) into concrete narratives or visuals about what they would be like to experience in practice.

In the following I will therefore consider these two perspectives on how managers engage with what one might call tangible futures.

Designing prototypes to facilitate the creation of new futures

First, managers tend to be enabled, by the contributions of designers, to build on the design dimensions of exploring problem space and generating alternative scenarios and to transform them into something actionable. Often, this takes place not as a result of previous research and ideation work, but in a highly integrated way as design research, as also discussed in Chapter Seven. For instance, in the Family by Family project, prototyping of new solutions was generatively carried out alongside the field-work.

Sune Knudsen, the manager overseeing the Branchekode project, describes the role of prototyping as follows:

> "... all the time designing it in concrete ways, making screen dumps or whatever it is, all the time saying, well, this abstract idea that you have, this problem that the company is in doubt, when making this choice, does it look like this, or could a solution look like this, always anchoring a very abstract point of something very real physically. It has been like this all the way through the solution development, and has made it much stronger, I think."

Another example is Poula Sangill, the manager responsible for the meals on wheels project in Holstebro municipality, who rehearsed the future by role-playing the interaction with elderly citizens while carrying out a conversation with her staff.

Andrew Eickmann, in the New York City Housing and Preservation Department (HPD) project, describes his experience with the visualisation and prototyping of the design work, which included design pin-up sessions, beginning with sketches, obtaining feedback from stakeholders, new iterations of development and so forth.

> "It makes a difference, because designers bring skills in rendering an idea, e.g. through sketches, digital rendering, models etc. Having the time to really show an idea rather than just talk about it is very powerful. Design gives life to things which would otherwise be difficult to support if just text and words. It gives life to things which may otherwise not make it."

It is interesting how Eickmann here invokes some of the exact language about 'giving life' that Kamil Michlewski (2015) uses to characterise design attitude. Jesper Wiese, at Skansebakken says:

> "There is a lot of talk in these projects and in fact, I think, something that probably challenges many employees – how do we come from talk to action? The designers, on the other hand, taught us that we needed to act before we started talking, more or less. You act at least simultaneously, and sometimes you simply act and see where you end up."

In the examples provided here, the connection between field-work and prototyping is rather intimate and interactive – in line with the points made above by Halse et al (2010).

Managers using design to catalyse change

A second and somewhat different approach is to create prototypes on the basis of strong future visions, and transforming them into tangible expressions of the desired new situation. The vision could be something very open and amenable to multiple directions for change, such as 'we want more injured workers to return to the labour market'. Mulgan and Albury (2003) have stated this point, emphasising that methods that work backwards from outcomes rather than forwards from existing policies, practices and institutions tend to generate a wider range of options for decision making. Or the vision could be almost the same as a new solution or governance approach, such as the case I will describe in some detail below.

In New York City, Seth Schoenfeld was Principal of Olympus Academy, a high school in Brooklyn. Students who attend are over-age and under-credited and at least two years behind their peers. The vast majority of the children's parents live below the official poverty level. As part of the city's Innovation Zone (iZone), a design-led programme to drive public school reform, Schoenfeld was engaged with a handful of other principals in a workshop facilitated by the Department of Education and a team of designers. In the workshop, Schoenfeld and his Deputy Principal were invited to create a tangible vision − a storyboard − describing their vision for the future of the school. The two managers chose to create a radically different vision, pushing the boundaries of what a school is considered to be. Seth Schoenfeld describes how they used the opportunity to really stretch their thinking. He remembers saying to his colleague, "Let's go further. Let's go through everything in there, what else would be radically different?" For instance, they imagined a situation where all courses and all curriculum in the school were available online for e-learning, and that each student would have his or her own individual schedule based on their particular learning needs. At first, this was just written as a story. But the Department of Education facilitators then gave each of the school management teams a "goodie bag" with a simple-to-operate video camera, a mini projector and other tools, which they were invited to use to create a more concrete prototype of their vision. Upon returning to the school, Schoenfeld and his deputy involved staff and students in creating a three-minute 'day in the life' video of what a school day would look and feel like, should the vision be turned into practice. Today, nearly all of the radical elements in the video − including an individually tailored schedule for each student and 100% online curriculum content − are a reality, and the school is considered a front-runner in the City's Innovation Zone programme.

Like Seth Schoenfeld, many of the other managers I have interviewed also seem inclined to embrace the creation of drawings, models, stories and images of the future that they wish to see materialised. It can either be that they are themselves producing drawings and storyboards, or that they ask others to craft models of the future. For instance, after Kynemund realised that the current scheduling for the General Study Preparation programme was dysfunctional, she and her scheduler literally started drawing a visual of a possible future schedule.

Or consider Mette Rosendal Darmer, the Head Nurse at the Danish National Hospital, who describes making a physical prototype of a medical journal for patients to use for themselves. The idea and concept for the prototype were triggered by the ideation session in the design project, but the actual creation was a job taken on by Darmer herself.

> "We have made a new product that is to be tested. And also an area for patients' plans, where they could write down what they wanted. They could write, well here I would like to go to the movies, if I am hospitalised for a long period, or I would like to ... so it all is included. And then a part that was about the questions they would like to discuss, where they could write, so they always had a communication tool. Actually it wasn't difficult. I sat there I sat down at the computer, and it's something that I really can, I like to transform ideas into products. And we got it ready, and so we are starting to test it. I don't know yet how it will work."

Darmer, as a top executive, is taking responsibility, hands on, for shaping a product that may be used in an organisation of several hundred people.

Elspeth Gibson, the manager working on youth health in Suffolk in the UK, used YouTube videos of people being active in fun ways, for example on a trampoline, to stimulate ideation. "[It is] a prototype thing, and it was sort of like this, we can do this, and this is good fun, let's indulge ourselves."

At Camillagaarden, before the design project was initiated, services were organised around one-way communication that missed out on feedback loops and that did not appreciate the potential in the everyday interactions between staff and citizens.

In this respect it perpetuated a relationship that was inefficient, even dysfunctional. In manager Christina Pawsø's words, the staff attitude was roughly "We come [to work] and we must pass the time until we go home". The key challenge faced by Christina Pawsø, who stepped in as a new young manager, was how to change such an attitude so as to create a more fruitful relationship between staff and users, and generate better outcomes.

Engagement #6: insisting on public value

As I also discussed briefly in Chapter Four, within public management the notion of 'value' has recently gained prominence, not least spurred by Moore's work (1995). Peter Gadsdon, in Lewisham, says:

> "I see my role as supporting improvement in the council. That is my main role as a manager, looking to improve things. So I'm always looking for ways of doing that, and I will always provide full support to things like this. I just see this as my role, as a part of what I do."

Sune Knudsen is Head of Division at the Danish Business Agency (DBA). Starting in 2010, he led an exploratory design project that aimed at making it easier to register a new business in Denmark. In describing the business case for a new solution that was co-designed with small business owners in a range of industries, Knudsen says:

> "If we succeed with this, thus creating something that's understandable and synchronised with day-to-day operations, the daily practice, I'm pretty sure we'll achieve greater user satisfaction. In addition, you'll see that the public sector will save money because compliance will be higher. So you'll get more of the most basic outcome ... And because companies will make fewer mistakes and understand it better, they won't always come back with incorrect reports or a lot of questions. That means that the businesses will

save a lot of money, they'll be more satisfied, you'll get higher efficiency of regulation, and the public sector will save money."

As discussed in Chapter Seven, Mr Knudsen's project addressed a specific government requirement: the selection of an *industry code*, which is the statistical industry category to which a newly registered business will belong. However, the DBA knew that many business owners become frustrated and spend undue amounts of time figuring out which code to choose. To many of them, selecting a code is not merely a question of statistical categorisation, it is making a choice about their business's public identity. Around a fourth of all new businesses in Denmark end up registering a code that does not accurately match what their business does. This then leads to errors in government systems: because the Food Safety Administration, the Ministry of Taxation, the Work Safety Agency and others use the codes to plan and execute controls on businesses (including on-site visits), the knock-on effects on administrative waste and error are huge.

Sune Knudsen engaged designers to use a range of ethnographic techniques to study how business owners experienced the online registration process, and how various public agencies used the industry codes internally and collaborated around them. Building on insights about user experience outside and inside the system, designers then carried out iterative prototyping of web mock-ups, testing them with end-users. The team, consisting of public servants on Mr Knudsen's own staff, a digital design agency and the innovation unit MindLab, then created a working model for a new website to handle business registration, as well as a knowledge management system for administrative staff, to ensure quick knowledge-sharing across the different public agencies.

Sune Knudsen's comments above highlight a pattern in a number of the instances that are part of the empirical research: that the solutions flowing from design-led approaches, when implemented, hold a potential for significant improvements in public value.

Taking a closer look at the quote from Sune Knudsen above, he expects that his design project will make the industry code registration easier and more satisfactory for business owners.

Meanwhile, he is also determined to ensure better outcomes in the form of more accurate registration (compliance) with the codes, and he expects that the public administrators will spend less time answering questions about the codes and will experience fewer errors in planning and executing controls. An externally produced business case study of the project confirmed that these types of value could be expected, to the extent that the cost of the new web-based solution would deliver a saving in time and money for both businesses and the public administration to the tune of approximately a 1:20 ROI over three years.[1]

The British organisation The Innovation Unit characterises such results, where services are produced at lower cost while being better for people and driving more positive outcomes, as 'radical efficiencies'. It seems that co-design helps managers to realise exactly such opportunities.

Sune Knudsen's comments above highlight a pattern in a number of the instances that are part of the empirical research: that the solutions flowing from design-led approaches, when implemented, hold a potential for significant improvements in public value. According to Cole and Parston (2006), 'public value' is increased when public service organisations are able to improve efficiency (productivity) while at the same time improving outcomes. In my own work (Bason, 2010) I argue that, in addition to productivity and outcomes, the value of innovation in the public sector should also include user (citizen) satisfaction and democratic elements such as participation, empowerment, transparency and accountability. In fact, the engagement of citizens might in itself lead to increased value. As Pestoff (2012) points out,

> Sometimes governments attempt to involve their citizens in the provision of goods and services, either for reasons of improving efficiency of public services, effectiveness of public policies, or to promote other important social goals, such as citizen engagement.

I will discuss the idea of citizens co-producing public outcomes, as a cornerstone of the discussions on a new public governance paradigm, in Chapter Twelve.

Reflection: making, enacting, creating, bringing to life

These managers recognise a certain power in the physical, concrete manifestation of what a solution could look like. Because design is essentially about *making*, whether the object is graphical, physical, procedural or systemic, this concerns Michlewski's design attitude of *creating, bringing to life* – the manager's desire to effect change in the world, 'creatively manifesting the ideas' that will later shape successful products, services or experiences (Michlewski, 2008, p 379). Moreover, the way in which the prototypes are developed in close collaboration with users and staff means that empathy is sustained as part of the new solutions, as the process 'aims to embed emotional reactions into products and services' (Michlewski, 2008, p 384).

In terms of the ability of design approaches to catalyse more paradigmatic breaks from past practices and engage staff and organisations in embracing those breaks, it seems that the tangibility of not only the process but the resulting design proposals, and the tendency to take part in enacting them, is important. Writing about design prototypes, Moggridge (2007) quotes the Chinese philosopher Lao Tse as stating that: 'What I hear, I forget; What I see, I remember; What I do, I understand'. As concrete graphical devices, the prototypes help managers and their staff to gain confidence that a certain design solution can actually be realised. Then, one might say, it is 'just' a matter of doing it. Another way of describing the use of prototypes is that they are a way of making the solution space real and tangible, in the same ways that 'professionally empathic' (ethnographic) methods make the problem space real and tangible to the decision makers. As I will discuss in more detail in Chapter Ten, Karl Weick (2004) also suggests that there is an important difference for managers, as they design, in whether they view the world in a categorical (abstract, conceptual) way or in a perceptual way that is closer to discrete experience.

How to do it: using design to try out new futures

This chapter has discussed how design is essentially an activity of future making that allows managers not just to envisage potential alternative futures but to transform ideas and concepts into concrete, tangible prototypes that end-users and staff can engage with. In many ways, this is how most people would view design work: as activities of creation, making and shaping artefacts that come to life as tangible, visible 'things' in the world. For public organisations, which are often overly focused on data, on analysis and on a problem-solving stance, design offers a different focus on people, on synthesis and on realising new opportunities. This chapter has shown how, when focusing on the innovation of services and organisational processes, the role of visually and physically prototyping potential approaches together with end-users is at the heart of design practice.

As a policy maker or public manager, how can you in practice engage with design to try out new futures? The following are some factors to consider.

- **How can prototyping and testing become a central part of our next development project?** What could prototyping entail in practice? Which ideas could be given concrete form and expression? Consider which resources – such as designers – you need to draw on in order to create tangible prototypes. But also do not be afraid to try something out on your own, beginning to build a culture of early experimentation and testing possible solutions with users.
- **Among your organisation's user groups, who would be the relevant audiences to involve in testing?** And who in your organisation should be part of that process? It is essential to continue the involvement of internal staff in this process, which typically gets focused externally. However, it is internal staff within the organisation who need to hear and see the user feedback, and to reflect on possible consequences for the idea or concept. It will be their role to bring their expertise to bear on integrating the feedback, and making the solution work.

- **Consider how you will assure your organisation that it is OK to test ideas and solutions that are still raw and unfinished.** In particular, how will you deal with potential political risk? How will you handle questions and concerns? The practice of prototyping is possibly the most 'foreign' and challenging to public organisations. In many ways, building a practice of on-going experimentation and testing is a cultural shift. Be aware of this and use every opportunity to explain and share why this shift is important.

Note

[1] MindLab (2012).

NINE

Design for public value

Design is fundamentally about value creation. (Angela
Meyer, 2014, p 188)

The creation of value is somewhat of a holy grail of public sector
innovation. Yes, it is great to explore problems and opportunities,
it is fine to develop new exciting ideas and it is gratifying to
see those ideas tested, refined and eventually implemented. *But
so what?* If, ultimately, new solutions do not make a positive
difference to at least some part of the world, how can all the
effort be worthwhile? As the quote above indicates, and as I also
suggested in Chapter One, proponents of design approaches do
not hesitate to claim that design creates value.

Part Two, which includes the preceding four chapters and
this one, has opened up and explored design approaches as they
unfold within and beyond public organisations. I have mapped
the kinds of processes associated with design work and analysed
how public managers engage with key dimensions of design.
Now it is time to take a bit of a step back from the concrete
developmental processes.

This chapter examines the patterns among the book's cases in
terms of three different perspectives: what appear to have been
the most significant triggers of change and transformation?
What do the results, or outputs, of the design work ultimately
look like? And to what extent are there signs across the cases of
subsequent creation of public value – directly or indirectly – by
applying design methods?

First, I summarise the findings across the previous chapters in terms of how design contributes to change processes in the cases studied. Design work unfolded across three dimensions, including the exploration of problems, generating alternative scenarios and enacting new futures. But did the design approaches nonetheless have some primary, catalysing roles? And if so, how are they distributed across the cases?

Second, I seek to chart the concrete types of *outputs* flowing from the design processes: what characterises the types of design outputs? What was ultimately created and decided by managers in terms of implementation? What form do some of these design outputs take? And to what extent are they not only singular 'stand-alone' 'solutions' but also imply wider-ranging organisational, management and strategic governance changes? To do this, I map the types of outputs (graphics, products, services, governance systems) that result from the individual cases.

Third, I discuss the outcomes, or *value* of the results of the design approaches and the outputs flowing from them. Ultimately, the 'so what?' question must be whether there are any signs, actual or perceived, of positive changes flowing from the design work. Beyond changes within the organisation, such as a new view on its mission and purpose, or a different view of the relation with citizens, are any external changes realised through the implemented solutions? This is an issue of the creation of public value through design approaches (Moore, 1995; Cole and Parston, 2006).

Fourth and finally, I conclude with a discussion of the relationship between design and public value.

Design dimensions: drivers of change

This part of the book has explored in detail, building on the empirical material, how design processes unfold within a range of different organisational and policy contexts. The pattern emerged that there were three dimensions across which managers engaged with design. The first dimension was the exploration of public problems; the second was the generation (ideation) of possible futures; and the third entailed the beginning enactment of those futures into tangible concepts and prototypes, including in some instances business cases and assessments of their potential value. In all of the cases, all the three design dimensions were in play to varying degrees.

However, the role and significance of the different processes varies significantly across the cases. Even though all cases involved some degree of design work across all three dimensions, it therefore seems relevant to ask what were the *main* dynamics and contributions of design approaches.

Table 9.1: Significance of design across cases for catalysing change

Role of design dimension in catalysing change	Example	Exemplary cases	Qualification	Role of manager to facilitate change
Exploring the problem space	Eye-opener that citizens become more sick than they already are, due to case management process*	BII* City of Adelaide Borough of Lewisham Danish Business Agency City of Helsinki Helsinki Ministry of Taxation Rigshospitalet Skansebakken	In some instances the insights generated were surprising or novel to managers; in others they were part of an exploration of problems that managers were already to some extent aware of	Openness to having assumptions challenged; ability to use 'empathic data' to mobilise staff
Generating alternative futures	By engaging mentally handicapped users in systematic, visual idea-generation, the institution was transformed to become citizen-centred and thriving*	Camillagaarden* Suffolk County Council Stenhus Community College NYC Department of Housing Danish Competition and Consumer Authority	In some cases the dominant role of ideation-led processes might be due to lack of rigorous design research; 'empathic data' was simply not sufficiently available	Patience; allowing for open-endedness; ability to 'nurse' staff through uncertainty; readiness to embrace novel ideas
Enacting new practices	Formulating a compelling and ambitious vision for a digital, student-centric high school*	NYC Department of Education iZone* Holstebro	In the iZone case the starting point is a politically mandated vision, taken up by the manager; in Holstebro it is very much driven by the manager herself	Imagination and ambition of manager on behalf of organisation, and possibly on behalf of self

As shown in Table 9.1, in some cases it was the design research that sparked insights that led to new avenues for designing responses to the problems that were identified. In other cases, the main driver was the process of opening up the opportunity space, generating a wide range of ideas for action. And finally, in some cases it was the envisioning of radically new futures that became the main driver of change.

The table also illustrates that the majority of the cases were heavily influenced by the 'empathic' user insight as a key driver of change. This is by no means to say that this would always, or typically, be the case in design projects. There may well be bias in the selection of the projects covered in this book. However, there is the argument, which was expanded in Chapter Seven, that the 'empathic data' associated with insight-led processes tends to create significant momentum among staff in terms of realising changes to the current situation. For instance, just to provide a single example here, Andrew Eickmann of the New York HPD says that "the spirit and ideas from the design process have life and will be implemented". Words like 'life', 'energy' and 'motivation' are very prevalent in the narratives surrounding the dimension of exploring the problem space.

One might therefore distinguish between three ideal-types of role played by design in catalysing the processes of change.

- *Insight-led:* mainly driven by the 'eye-opener' of empathic material from field research. This paradigm, which includes a significant reframing of problems and opportunities, can be found in much of the literature on humanistic, ethnographic and design-anthropological approaches (Bate and Robert, 2007; Bason, 2010; Polaine et al, 2013; Madsbjerg and Rasmussen, 2014), and also partly in user-driven innovation (von Hippel, 2005) and co-design approaches (Halse et al, 2010)
- *Ideation-led:* driven mainly by an idea or concept that was developed during the design process. This perspective is associated with much of the literature on creativity, but also on open innovation and crowdsourcing (Eggers and Singh, 2009; Surowiecki, 2004; Tapscott and Williams, 2006).

- *Future-led:* driven by the establishment of a clear vision of a future state. This could also be called idealised design. This perspective on design and innovation can be found, for instance, in Ackoff (2006), Norman (2007) and Verganti (2009).

It is important to underline that these ideal-types are not mutually exclusive; as discussed extensively, the relationships between insights, ideas and visions for a better future state are highly intermingled and really part of the reflective process of designing and of managers' engaging with design. However, based on the case analysis, it seems fair to say that certain processes take precedence, or dominance, over others. In the cases there is a certain flow, certain punctuations and certain exclamation marks, which accentuate the significance of particular dimensions of design.

Design outputs: from prototypes to implementation

In the previous chapter I discussed the processes surrounding the design dimension of enacting future practices in the form of prototyping and testing solutions as well as validating those solutions against business cases and, in some instances, evaluation. After (or sometimes together with) prototypes and validation comes decision making: which of the proposed design solutions shall we adopt in the organisation? What are our resources and opportunities for actual implementation? Table 9.2 gives examples of the kinds of designed outputs associated with the processes in four of the cases.

It is important to underline that when I suggest that outputs are *associated* with the design activity, this does not necessarily mean that they were directly *caused* by the design activity. As discussed also in previous chapters, as the design processes unfold they are influenced by, and draw on, pre-existing ideas, visions and notions about what would constitute desirable solutions or changes – whether those be in graphical expression, (digital) products, service processes or systems, strategies and governance principles. The ensuing outputs are also influenced by other organisational processes or inspirations flowing to and interacting with the design process.

Table 9.2: Outputs of design processes

	Design outputs			
	New graphical and visual expressions	New physical or digital products or spaces	Redesigned organisation, rules and/ or service processes	Emerging governance systems or principles
Examples	'Communication tree' at Skansebakken (Kolding Municipality); redesigned packaging of meals on wheels (Holstebro Municipality)	New patient space at Rigshospitalet; new digital interface for Branchekode (Danish Business Agency)	Family by Family process for connecting and facilitating seeking and sharing families (City of Adelaide); redesign of service process for obtaining permits (City of Helsinki)	Citizen-led innovation (Camillagaarden); student-centred e-learning model (iZone, NYC Department of Education); shift from compliance to outcomes (BII, Denmark)

The following is a short gallery with a few selected photos from the various cases, seeking to illustrate a few of the design solutions across the dimensions of graphical expression, physical and digital products and spaces, redesigned service processes and new governance models.

Figure 9.1: Graphical and visual expression: the communication tree 'Georg' at Skansebakken

Source: Kolding School of Design

The 'communication tree' at Skansebakken was created by the design team from Kolding school of design in order to visually display interactions between visitors and citizens in the institution (Figure 9.1).

The two sets of images in Figures 9.2 and 9.3 show redesign of physical space at Rigshospitalet (Denmark) and Lewisham's Housing Options service (UK), respectively.

Figure 9.2: Physical space: before/after redesigning public space for patients at Rigshospitalet

Source: Rigshospitalet

Figure 9.3: Physical space: before/after redesigning public space for Homelessness Services in Lewisham

Source: Borough of Lewisham

Figure 9.4: Digital product: new digital solution for registering a business

Source: Virk.dk

Figure 9.5: Service process: connecting 'seeking' and 'sharing' families in Adelaide

Source: The Australian Centre for Social Innovation (TACSI)

Figure 9.6: Governance: citizens empowered to design and sell their own commercial products. Camillagaarden project 'Støt kuglerne' ('Support the balls'), where mentally handicapped users designed, produced and sold bracelets for men (illustrated) in support of prostate cancer

Source: Camillagaarden

The illustrations exemplify the wide range of physical and social manifestations of the design work, as the processes and methodologies led to tangible outputs and changes in behaviour and experience.

Signs of public value

The purpose of this book is not to systematically evaluate and document the resulting outcomes of the design approaches and processes. Arguably, it would be an overstatement to say that the available material produces robust, conclusive 'evidence' of the causal links between design processes, the resulting 'solutions' and public value. The aim of this section is therefore not to 'prove' that design outputs create more or different public value. However, for all of the effort going into commissioning, managing and engaging with design work, a relevant question to pose is 'so what?' Are there any indications that citizens, businesses and other users or stakeholders are better off as a result of the processes? Is the organisation better capable of creating the results for which it is ostensibly accountable? Do the projects lead to cost savings for public organisations? Of course, ultimately, this matters a great deal.

Public value, and in particular policy and service outcomes, are a bit like the holy grail of public administration (Osborne and Gaebler, 1992; Rist and Kusek, 2004; Cole and Parston, 2006; Mulgan, 2009; Alford, 2009; Bourgon, 2012). Ultimately, what is the result of the efforts of political leaders, policy makers, public managers and their staff to enact change in the world?

According to Cole and Parston (2006) 'public value' is increased when public service organisations are able improve efficiency (productivity) while at the same time improving outcomes. In my own work I argue that in addition to productivity and outcomes, the value of innovation in the public sector should also include user (citizen) satisfaction and democratic elements such as participation, empowerment, transparency and accountability (Bason, 2010). In fact, the engagement of citizens might in itself lead to increased value.

The analysis here will nonetheless have to be tentative and based on the documentation immediately available through the empirical research and other sources. I have chosen to term the analysis 'tentative signs' of public value. By 'signs' I imply qualitative (and sometimes quantitative) indications that a change has likely been caused by the design work, and that it has in some way been valuable for citizens, for the organisation and/ or for society.

There are also leadership implications. As the public managers in question see emerging signs, or even tangible evidence, indicating increased public value being produced as a consequence of the new models they are discovering, this may function as a positive feedback loop along the arc of change they are already venturing on.

Let me share a few examples of what these tentative signs of public value production look like.

Signs of better service experience

One of the most common types of public value that seem to result from the design work is a change in how citizens experience the particular public service in question. This might not be very surprising, since, as discussed in the previous chapters, the role of user experience is central to many of the design methodologies and processes.

At Camillagaarden, according to the institution's own figures, user satisfaction grew and the number of users increased by nearly 30% (without additional staffing), to the point that the institution had a waiting list for the first time in its 40-year history.

Another example is the Holstebro (meals on wheels) project, which focused very clearly on improving citizen satisfaction with the local government offering. According to the municipality (Sangill, 2013), the design project led to an improvement in food quality, more and new choices for citizens through a broader menu; new offerings to people with differentiated needs (such as older citizens who eat smaller portions); and a clearer service profile vis-à-vis citizens. As a result of involving citizens in co-designing the offering, the improvements in service and choice, the municipality has strengthened its image and attracted more satisfied users (customers) of the service.

Signs of increase in productivity

In times of austerity, which have characterised the context of much of the public management discourse since the global financial crisis in 2008, to a great extent emphasis has been placed on cost-cutting and increasing the productivity of public services. As shown above, the objectives of concrete savings or productivity increases have not been key in all cases; however, there seems to be no doubt that productivity requirements have been a very important part of the fabric against which many of the cases unfold.

In some instances, the design methodologies are also claimed to have directly or indirectly led to significant savings or increases in productivity. A key example is the Borough of Lewisham, which in official statements and in an external evaluation claimed to have achieved efficiency savings annually of £368,000 against a design project investment of £7,000 (Design Council, 2014).

In other cases, the available documentation has the character of business case research – indicating potential but not demonstrating actual productivity improvements. For instance, in the Branchekode project an externally produced business case study conducted by a consultancy confirmed that significant productivity gains could be expected. Based on an activity-based costing method, including time and money saved for public sector staff as well as for businesses, the report assessed that the cost of the new web-based solution would deliver a saving in time and money for both businesses and the public administration, to the tune of approximately a 1:20 ROI over three years (Danish Commerce and Companies Agency et al, 2012). It should be underlined, however, that the bulk of the reduction of time spent was on behalf of the businesses; the service improvement would, in other, words matter a lot to them, but less to the taxpayers indirectly funding the service.

Going back to the case of Camillagaarden, the institution for the adult mentally handicapped, manager Christina Pawsø similarly noted an actualised gain in productivity that flowed from the changes in the relationship with citizens. Not only has the institution added 30% more users with a fixed number of staff and increased satisfaction. Pawsø gives the example that on average there is one social worker to eight users at Camillagaarden. However, with the right type of user engagement, a staff of two can easily serve the needs of 30 users for a period of several hours. That is approximately a *doubling* of productivity. Pawsø explains how this is made possible by leveraging the resources and motivation of the individual users: "If you are put into a frame where all your resources are being used instead of everything you are having trouble with, then you can also help others. And this also gives value to the individual."

In the Holstebro case, the municipality registered a range of changes on the staff side that can be translated into productivity gains (which also influence the service experience, as discussed above). Among the key changes were the strengthening of employees' competencies and skills, a reduction in sick leave and improvement of motivation and job satisfaction.

At Skansebakken, an external evaluation showed that employees spent more time with half the residents (ranging from an additional 5 to 9.9 hours weekly) and less time with the remaining half (ranging from -5.5 to -17.9 hours per week). According to the evaluation, the total amount of time spent with residents every week decreased by 10.5 hours. This implies a certain, if only rather small, increase in productivity at Skansebakken, while at the same time the number of relationships between handicapped citizens and visitors increased (as discussed below).

Signs of better outcomes

A significant number of the cases show signs of change in citizens' behaviour and actions – what they do, how they act, how they relate to each other or how they relate to their environment.

An example is the Family by Family project in Adelaide, Australia. For the main goals of the programme, which basically focused on creating more thriving families, 80% of families answered that they were 'better' or 'heaps better' following the first coaching session. After subsequent sessions 90% responded positively that the intervention helped them achieve their goals (External evaluation report, p 20).

In Skansebakken, where the design project focused on redesigning and ultimately increasing the number and quality of relationships between handicapped citizens and non-professionals, the centre manager, Jesper Wiese, says of the experience of visiting and being at the Skansebakken institution:

> "It is completely different now to come on a visit. You know, fundamental things have changed. Actually, I was really concerned now that we have moved, whether we would fall back into old habits. But everyone, including some whom I did not ask, has said, 'It's nice to come here'. And of course it's something to do with the physical environment too, but this is also a question of whether it's acceptable to have guests … It's those very specific things. Hanne has had a friend visiting. There is a 4th-grade school class who come and sing. Now there's a big movement to create voluntary relationships. It's working. I think we have more than 35 [new relationships]."

At Skansebakken, in terms of quantitative change, an evaluation carried out by the Municipality of Vejle showed that among six handicapped citizens studied, they had collectively gained 21 new relationships outside the institution. The evaluation report goes on to state that the trend corresponds directly to the goal that 'citizens through the project would achieve new relations to family, friends, acquaintances, civil society, etc.' (Vejle Municipality and Social Service Agency, 2014, p 24). The report goes on to say that the staff at Skansebakken 'to a high degree have succeeded in facilitating new relationships where they are not themselves a key player'. Staff have played an active role in 'setting citizens free' to gain new experiences. The value of this is underlined in the interview with manager Jesper Wiese, who refers to one of the handicapped users:

> "You don't need much. If you can sit down next to Jakob and read aloud from a book, then Jakob is happy for half an hour. And it makes his day better. It's as simple as that."

It is simple, as Jesper Wiese says, but ostensibly, the result of a quite long and intensive design process.

In Holstebro municipality, Poula Sangill contends that the staff have increased their focus on the entire value chain of the service offering and have a stronger focus on the citizens who use the service, in terms both of food quality and service provision. There is an increased focus on communication and interplay with citizens (Liedtka, 2013).

In the Housing and Preservation Department design project in New York City, a highly comprehensive 2014 evaluation report seeks to assess the findings and results from the 'pilot'. Among other data sources, the report used a survey among more than 2,500 citizens who had interacted with the programme. As illustrated in the paragraph below, a range of changes implemented through the design work indicate, as a whole, that better outcomes are likely to have been achieved, understood as the citizens' ability to reach better, more informed decisions about their housing options and the application process.

The evaluation team found that the pilots clearly met the proposals' stated design objectives: to encourage information accessibility and exchange, account for applicants' lived reality, and enable more informed decision-making (although findings were somewhat mixed regarding the first of those objectives). The pilots also achieved their intended short-term outcomes, to create stronger support for community groups that provide applicants with assistance and to generate greater access to information about the process. (Dragoman and Kühl, 2014, p 5)

As the quote from the executive summary of the evaluation report illustrates, the design project has resulted in tools that shape different service interactions, improving not just the experience but the ability to make important decisions. Another outcome, which is tightly linked to the notion of co-production of services, which I will discuss in the next chapter, is the ability of community groups, who are essentially on the delivery and partner side of the City administration, to perform their role more effectively.

A final example of strengthened outcomes is another New York City case, the iZone programme for a student-centric digital high school. The former principal of the school, Olympus Academy, says that there were significant improvements in learning outcomes as a consequence of the design work, which led to a transformation of the school.

Signs of increased democratic engagement

The signs of various kinds of increases in democratic variables, such as stronger democratic engagement, are often found in terms of transparency and insight for citizens into their own cases. One example is the BII, which digitised the case management process and made citizens' individual records available online. This was not directly a result of the design work but part of a larger process of digitising the agency's interaction with citizens.

One could very well also say that the HPD project in New York, also mentioned above, has strong democratic and participatory potential benefits for citizens, since the aim, among others, is to create a clear and understandable basis for understanding one's rights and possibilities for accessing public housing.

How to do it: capturing the value of design

This chapter has illustrated some of the design outputs, as well as a range of tentative documentation of the kinds of public value flowing from design work. The objective of this book is not to conclusively demonstrate or prove that the design approaches lead to public value; however, it seems fair to conclude that there are indications that various kinds of change happen in connection with the design work. In most cases the changes are more or less directly linked to the insights gained from various processes of citizen engagement. As Pestoff (2012) points out, governments can seek better ways of involving their citizens in the provision of goods and services, either for reasons of improving efficiency of public services or the effectiveness of public policies, or to promote other important social goals, such as citizen empowerment, participation and democracy.

For a public manager, there are three elements, which it could be useful to consider in terms of measuring the value creation of design approaches.

- **Be explicit about value creation.** Start the design engagement with some well-founded hypotheses about what kinds of value you aim to achieve: productivity, service improvements, better outcomes or democratic impact? Be as explicit as you can about what success would look like, and consider how you would measure it. Are there measurement and data-collection processes already in place in your organisation, or are there some that you should be establishing?
- **Monitor for potential value.** During the design process it can be very useful to closely monitor the work and reflect on indications or signs of positive change – or of unintended impacts. What are people (end users, staff, other managers, partners and others) saying? Which kinds of metrics begin to change? Which metrics turn out to be relevant?

- **Track implementation and get data.** Once the design work has been carried through with some degree of success, typically there is a decision and some degree of implementation taking place. Consider whether you have established the appropriate means and procedures to be able to capture and document the results flowing from the design work. This can be done both quantitatively (by setting up a survey or other data gathering system) and qualitatively (for instance through observation studies or interviews with staff and users).

This chapter concludes Part Two of the book. In the next part I will explore what implications for public governance the engagement with design approaches might have for public managers.

PART THREE

DISCOVERING HUMAN-CENTRED GOVERNANCE

TEN

Catalysing change in governance by design

> The question of who is the producer is more complex
> than appears at first sight. (John Alford, *Engaging Public
> Sector Clients*, 2009, p 2)

This book explores the interplay between design approaches and
public governance, through the lived experience and perspective
of public managers. Part Two and its five chapters illustrated how
the change processes associated with design work unfold, and
how this matters in numerous ways to public managers and their
organisations. It showed how public managers actively engage
with design processes to leverage them and create change. I
concluded in Chapter Nine by giving examples of the outputs
of the design process and I discussed some signs of the wider
creation of public value. I also highlighted that some of the
contributions of design did not merely concern new graphics,
products or services but, rather, systems. By systems I mean the
elements and interactions between them that together function
to create intended outcomes. In the private sector the principles
guiding such systems would often be called business models. In a
public management perspective, they would be called governance
models. Although no authoritative definition of governance
exists, its origins are a clear indication of its meaning: governance
is derived from the ancient Greek word *kubernáo*, which is also
the origin of the word government and which means steering
of a ship or cart (Wikipedia, 2016). Hufty (2011) has suggested
that governance is the processes of interaction and decision
making among the actors involved in a collective problem that

lead to the creation, reinforcement or reproduction of social norms and institutions. The question of governance models then becomes what are the principles that guide such processes across dimensions, like laws and regulations, financial arrangements, organisational structure, management procedures, public service operations, documentation, evaluation and accountability and so forth.

The starting point for this chapter is that there are several alternative paradigms, ideal-types or models, in which to view and interpret public governance – the alternatives I discussed in Chapter Four.

The intent here is to illustrate the role that design-led approaches play in practice from a governance perspective: how might design approaches influence managers' ability to identify new and different ways of governing that might be better suited to achieving their organisational mission (or, in some cases, to drive change in that mission itself)? How might the governance approach become better geared to produce value for the public service system and for end-users and society? As I stated in Chapter Four, my intent in this book is not so much to formalise a completely new governance model; rather, it is to illustrate how the public manager's journey of engaging with design influences governance in practice (Bourgon, 2012; Agranoff, 2014; Waldorff et al, 2014) and to distill what the emerging characteristics of such governance seem to be. These may be termed *human-centred governance*.

First, this chapter briefly summarises the findings developed across Part Two of the book by posing the question: what appears to be the significance of design approaches for innovation in public organisations?

Second, I turn the attention to the issue of such a potential shift in the governance model itself: based on my empirical research, I explore what broader changes in the underlying models of public service provision are prompted through the processes of applying design approaches. Across the cases, have the design processes opened up wider considerations of the nature of public service provision that are more profound, or more fundamental, beyond the concrete design outputs? If so, what characterises these considerations, and how are they articulated across the cases? Using my empirical findings, I explore a total of four such characteristics.

Finally, I sum up my findings in the form of a case-based overview that shows the patterns I have discussed, and I suggest ways in which public managers can work productively to change their organisation's governance model.

A pathway to human-centred governance

In the previous chapter I sought to characterise the nature of the distinct kinds of designed 'outputs' flowing from the different cases and from the different design processes. However, more is at stake than 'outputs': it is not only the creation of graphical expressions, of new service processes or of various type of products (often digital) that results from design processes as they unfold in public organisations. Underlying many of the expressions, products and services are emerging and, to some extent, novel principles of system design or governance. As Normann and Ramirez (1994) propose, as offerings change, so do institutions that transact them. One might well say that a new or redesigned governance is the larger game of the quest for public sector innovation: rather than identifying stand-alone 'solutions', might there be fundamentally better ways of steering and organising public organisations that could be of consequence for a much broader set of 'solutions' – of how things are done?

Figure 10.1 summarises the findings of the book to this point. It is framed within current and emerging paradigms of public governance; to the left, the paradigms of 'traditional' and 'new' public management; to the right, an emerging new public governance. I designate it *human-centred governance*. The figure seeks to show the different elements of the processes I have studied in the previous section of the book across the design dimensions of 'exploring problem space', 'generating alternative scenarios' and 'enacting new practices'. As I showed in Chapters Seven, Eight and Nine, each of these dimensions is associated with multiple engagements with design by public managers.

Figure 10.1: Pathway to human-centred governance

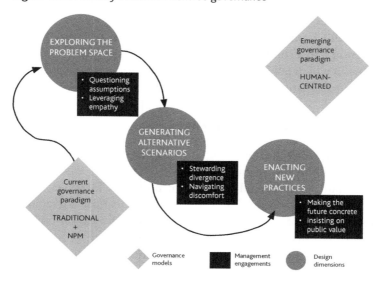

The figure illustrates the pathway and processes involved in catalysing a shift in governance through the use of design approaches. As the key below the figure illustrates, the journey encompasses governance model(s), the engagements of managers with design processes and the design dimensions (which cover the various design approaches). Based on a careful examination of the empirical material in this book, I have attempted to build a somewhat more fine-grained perspective on the nature of this emerging governance model (or perhaps, rather, governance *principles*). The sections below illustrate these principles, or characteristics, in detail. I will this consider each characteristic in turn, discussing its nature and the contributions of design approaches to it.

Relational: reframing purpose around people

First, there is a pattern across many of the cases that the governance principles reflect a more *relational* understanding of the organisation and its role in impacting on users and other actors to create desired outcomes. As Alford (2009, p 206) suggests, this concerns the issue of 'what are we really trying to do here?' In this section (and the following three) I will first consider the empirical findings that I can induct from the case research before turning to literature that can help to interpret them.

Research findings

Consider the powerful relational shifts that are in play in all these cases. At the BII the director, Anne Lind, says in connection with the design project: "The first thing that I see that should be changed is our mission statement." She continues:

> "The perspective I want to change is where we engage the citizen more actively in our case management ... What we are now exploring is whether we can influence – via innovative processes – the entire legislative framework. So that we can carry through this shift in perspective from control to trust."

In the Borough of Lewisham, the shift was towards a new preventative service delivery model that placed the user at the centre and redesigned processes around the needs of the users, starting with initial contact and throughout their service journey. Underpinning this shift was a re-labelling of the Homelessness Services unit to 'Housing Options', signifying a shift from reactive management of the problem of homelessness to proactively attempting to create the outcome of sustainable housing for people and families. Peter Gadsdon in Lewisham remarks, concerning the decision to rename Homelessness Services as Housing Options, that it is about "trying to change people's behaviour around homelessness, and also their expectations about what would happen to someone if they are homeless". So, the emphasis is not only on what people *do* in the course of the case process, managing homelessness cases, but also on how they *think* about the concept of homelessness itself.

The wider issue in the case of Rigshospitalet is whether the entire organisation could be restructured, and processes redesigned, to become much more 'patient-centric'. The Head Nurse, Mette Rosendal Darmer, explains:

> "And our concern is now ... whether we could make the organisation of the entire clinic our innovative purpose. What is needed structurally, managerially, divisionally is that we have good, flexible, fast patient processes, where the patient experience is good. That is, it is the patient's journey that must be the central matter in terms of how we make our structure."

As Darmer speaks of structure, management, divisions, processes of governance, she adds that if the ideas she has developed about reorganising the ward were carried out, they would lead to a significantly more efficient use of resources. The changes would imply that, as an organisation, her unit would "begin to address some of our serious core matters", but that "some of it could very well be possible, because it suddenly becomes the patients' experiences that are so central". In this emerging vision for the hospital ward, human beings are placed as the central factor, rather than professional clinical practice; at the same time, productivity still matters.[1]

In the Family by Family case the shift was from a legally oriented stance, essentially viewing users (families) in a binary way in order to decide whether to remove the children or not, to a much more sophisticated way, probing and exploring what it would take to help families 'thrive', ultimately leading to prevention and to outcomes where fewer children would have to be taken into foster care.

At Skansebakken the shift in relations was almost from the outset at the very heart of the design process – from the moment that the design research made clear that the institution was essentially not hospitable. The notion of 'hospitality' became a key in supporting the relational shift to a situation where staff were successful not just by providing professional care to users; they were successful when increasing the number of non-professional (civic) relations that users had. An example of the concrete expression of this shift was that it became more legitimate among staff to bring users along to a yearly relay race, where staffers would push users in their wheel-chairs in competition with other institutions. The understanding of the importance of social activity, relationships and fun made this more acceptable than in the past. Says the manager, JesperWiese:

> "That is where we really hit on something that we could transform, right? Because at that time, there was a relationship between the educationist and the user ... That is what we do. And we must say that the designers came up with new ideas for thinking and talking about that relationship."

A final example is Camillagaarden, where the relational shift was from providing handicapped users with simple manual work to empowering users to innovate their own daily activities and create new meaning, catalysing thriving and a higher quality of life. In reflecting on the current relationship between government organisations and citizens, Christina Pawsø says that, in her experience, it is designed around top-down decision making and implementation. Citizens, and in particular 'vulnerable' people such as adults with a mental disability, are often perceived, and cast, as passive recipients of public services. Says Pawsø:

> "There is [this image of] a tiled staircase going up a hill, and it is very well constructed. ... And then alongside this fine staircase there is a muddy path that people walk up. And it's a bit like what was happening here. ... it's a really good picture of how our users were actually going by a different path than the one we wanted them to walk along. And so, instead of trying to force them onto our path, we will have to follow them. Having that picture worked well for us."

Using the metaphor of the staircase versus the muddy path, Pawsø explains how public employees and professionals have knowledge about how to operate in the system (bureaucracy, hierarchy, paperwork, procedures, 'helping'), while citizens have knowledge about what motivates and engages them in their everyday life context (relationships, experiences, meaningfulness).

Pawsø points out that both sides of this equation have their own knowledge – but it is a knowledge that isn't necessarily being shared or put into action. Through the use of design in Camillagaarden, Christina Pawsø and her staff built a different kind of relationship with the users, which, as discussed in Chapter Nine, reflected a realisation, and thus a fundamental relational shift, that the professionals were no more experts than the citizens.

Table 10.1 summarises these and the other cases in those instances where a reframing, towards a different relationship with citizens that focuses on different outcomes, is judged to have taken place.

Table 10.1: Reframing the problem towards new relations

Example case	Shift in relations	
	Current framing of problem and users	New framing of problem and users
1 Danish BII	How might we deliver more cost-efficient case management and enhance our legal compliance?	How might we help bring injured citizens back to the labour market?
2 City of Adelaide, Family by Family	How might we reduce the number of children removed from their families?	How might we support families to become thriving families?
3 Borough of Lewisham, Homelessness Services	How can we improve the efficiency of homelessness case management?	How might we provide people with a meaningful journey to new housing options?
4 Suffolk County Council, youth health improvement project	How can we improve our population's health?	What will motivate young people to be more physically active?
5 Camillagaarden, workplace for adult mentally disabled	How can we keep our mentally disabled users occupied during their time here?	How might we empower our users to become the daily innovators of this institution, enabling them to gain a higher quality of life?
6 Danish Business Agency, Branchekode	How can we reduce the number of errors as new businesses register an industry code?	How do we give business owners confidence when choosing a code that is also a signifier of their identity?
7 City of Helsinki, business permits	How might we make it less bureaucratic for businesses to obtain a city permit?	How do we as a city become perceived as a meaningful and professional service provider to business?
8 Ministry of Taxation, Denmark	How do we increase taxpayer compliance?	How do we support a more fruitful [productive?] interplay among key actors to enable citizens to comply in practice?

Example case	Shift in relations	
	Current framing of problem and users	New framing of problem and users
9 Rigshospitalet, Heart Clinic	How can we reduce costs in new ways?	What is a meaningful patient experience?
10 Stenhus Community College	How do we enhance internal collaboration?	How do we create a course that is meaningful to students and that drives learning?
11 NYC Department of Education, iZone	How do we increase the graduation rate from public high schools?	How might we support the public school system to transform itself so as to be based on more personalised learning models?
12 Holstebro Municipality, meals on wheels	How might we create more competitive municipal food delivery for our elderly?	What makes the meal experience attractive?
13 NYC Department of Housing and Preservation	How might we create better service experiences for tenants in public housing?	How might tenants gain more control over their own service experience, and become co-producers of it?
14 Kolding Municipality, Skansebakken institution	How do we keep our residents safe and cared for?	How do we grow the number and quality of relations between our users, their families and non-professionals in the local community?
15 Danish Competition and Consumer Authority	How can consumer protection be increased for children and young people who play or shop online?	N/A

This range of examples illustrate how a large majority of the managers consider the outcomes of the design processes not merely as the creation of particular solutions but as almost paradigmatic shifts, or reframings, of how they view the relationship between their organisation and it users. Consider here Karl Weick (2004, p 77), who suggests in his consideration of design as managing that the potential value of design is to help people 'redecide what matters'.

Discussion: on reframing and co-production

Hilary Cottam, former partner in the social innovation consultancy Participle, argues in her influential paper 'Relational welfare' (Cottam 2012, pp 141–3) that a relational welfare approach to public governance and development is based on five key principles, where the most important in the context of my findings above seem to be: a *focus on the root causes* of deeply embedded social problems; *a developmental approach to achieving change in people lives*; and the seeding and championing of *alternative models of service delivery*. Among the principles Cottam proposes here there are several points that are reflected in the cases studied in this book. In many of the cases, root causes are addressed, understood as the underlying factors that matter in order to shape better outcomes for citizens and society. As public managers take a different perspective on root causes, they start engaging alternative models, or perhaps, rather, they *discover* potential alternative models. Key to these models seems to be, in many of the cases, an emerging reframing of the role of the organisation in achieving outcomes in its relationship with end-users: citizens and businesses (Dorst, 2015).

Paquet (2009, p 120) relates design to public governance as 'a marginal practice', but in doing so hints at this potential of reframing the organisational purpose:

> Effective governance regimes become aware of marginal practices (or alternative ways to re-tool, re-structure, and re-frame their activities according to principles heretofore not regarded as necessarily of central interest) and tend to become involved in lateral thinking: articulating the problem differently, cross-appropriating ways of doing things elsewhere and adjusting them to the task at hand, re-framing the very notion of the business one is in along different lines.

Paquet suggests that this reframing of 'the very notion of the business one is in' can be driven by enquiry based on empathy, on holistic problem setting and on prototyping. Further, he surmises that the kind of reframing would be 'essentially relational, as networks of on-going relations between persons, groups and environment' (2009, p 121). Here, he hints at the networked quality of the shift I have described.

In fact, part of this shift concerns changes in the very understanding of what outcomes the organisation is supposed to contribute to creating, as well as how. In that sense, the relational shift, at least in some cases, also concerns a reframing of the mission of the organisation, as well as the activities needed to accomplish that mission. The notion of reframing the fundamental problem, mission, meaning or effort in the organisation 'from' something 'to' something else is thus quite prevalent across the cases. This reframing is most often articulated via the proposition of a different relationship between the organisation and the citizens (or 'users') that it serves. Dutch professor of design innovation Kees Dorst characterises such reframing as *design abduction*. By this he means 'both a new way of looking at the problem situation and a new way of acting within it' (Dorst, 2015). In Kees Dorst's definition, a 'frame' is a proposal through which one can apply a particular pattern of relationships (or, as Charles Eames would have put it, arrangements of elements) in order to produce a desired outcome. As I also discussed briefly in Chapter Two, designers are skilled at working backwards from a desired outcome (or the problem of producing that outcome) and using abductive thinking to propose a wider set of alternatives to address it.

In the cases studied in this book, the reframing, or redecision, of what matters to managers and their organisation is, to a large extent, centred on the relationship with citizens. John Alford (2009, p 213) suggests that 'client co-production seems to sit most comfortably with a focus on outcomes'. In his consideration of what it means to co-produce public services with citizens, Alford argues that this calls for a recasting of our understanding of how public value is produced. The relationship, and the interactions, between the public organisation and its users comes into play in more complex ways:

> To the question 'What do clients want from our organisation?', a prior question must be added: 'What does our organisation want from its clients?' This in turn calls for a deeper understanding of the value the organisation is seeking to create and the processes by which it produces that value. (Alford, 2009, p 205)

Alford points out that a re-examination not only of how citizens experience and gain value from public services, but also of the means by which organisations produce it, is key when considering the engagement of citizens in the (co-)production of that value. It is a relevant point to keep in mind, given the strong focus on user experience that the design approaches entail, and given the search for new ways of achieving value that drives much of the management engagement with design.

From a theoretical perspective, the relational shift signifies a recognition that citizens to some extent always are 'co-producers' of public value (Hartley, 2005, p 29; Alford, 2009; Bourgon, 2012). Such peer-to-peer production, or co-production, is by no means a new concept. The term was originally coined in the early 1970s; accounts vary on who was the originator of the term, but among its key proponents was Nobel laureate Elinor Ostrom. According to Pestoff (2012, p 16), Ostrom developed the term to describe the 'relationship that could exist between the "regular producer" (such as street-level police officers, social workers or health workers) and their clients, who wanted to be transformed by the service into safer, better-educated or healthier persons'.

Jocelyne Bourgon (2012) characterises co-production as 'the shared and reciprocal activities of public agencies and people to produce results of public value' (2012, p 26). Edgar Cahn defines co-production as a framework and set of techniques used by social service organisations to enlist active client participation in service programming (Cahn, 2004). Building mainly on UK experiences, Boyle and Harris (2009, p 11) describe co-production as:

> Delivering public services in an equal and reciprocal relationship between professionals, people using services, their families and their neighbours. Where activities are co-produced in this way, both services and neighbourhoods become far more effective agents of change.

Normann and Ramirez (1994), in discussing the design of interactive strategy, argue that there are three types of relationships in systems of value-creating actors – such as the system of an institution for adult mentally handicapped, or one for dealing with families at risk, or a school:

- *pooled relationships*, in which each part of a system comes together to form a whole (as when different organisational units work towards a common purpose);
- *sequential relationships* where sections of an organisational system produce outputs to a sequential process (such as in traditional value-chain production processes); and
- *reciprocal relationships*, which are the most complex and which characterise most service-producing organisations.

It seems reasonable to argue that the changes in the perception of the relationship between end users (such as adult mentally disabled persons) and public service organisations can be characterised as a shift toward recognising that, essentially, the relationship is (or should or could be) a reciprocal one. Normann and Ramirez (1994, p 30) state that '*Co-production* is the term we use to describe the "reciprocal" relationships between actors', and they elaborate that this view implies that the customer (or citizen) is not only a passive orderer/buyer/user of the offering but also participates in many other ways in consuming it, for instance in its delivery. John Alford (2009) similarly finds that reciprocity is central to co-production and that it prompts the organisation to truly offer the client, or user, something she wants. This in turn calls for a broader conception of exchange, beyond the traditional transaction of funds or services, to something that may include a range of other human factors such as engagement, dignity, respect, trust and so forth (Alford, 2009, p 38), and even social aesthetic and moral values (Normann and Ramirez, 1994, p 63). It also implies that value can be distributed more over time, so that, for instance, citizens offer their resources in turn for a potential future value.

There seems to be a compelling case that an overarching shift in governance is guided by the notion of a relational and co-productive approach to the creation of value with citizens. In the following I will consider three additional characteristics of a possible change in governance model.

Networked: shift to activating wider resources

The second governance characteristic seems to be the identification and leveraging of a wider set of resources, in a networked fashion, in order to achieve the organisation's (redefined) objectives. Within the same move that citizens, or human beings, and their experiences and behaviours are being repositioned as central to the organisation, there is also a move towards deeper engagement with the actors who are critical for the creation of value for both citizens and society. This in turn increases the number and nature of strategic engagements that the public organisation has – or is conscious of having.

Findings from the case studies

Let us first take a look at how some of the different cases in this book express the role of networks in a governance perspective.

In the case of BII, the design projects helped Anne Lind to see how her organisation could work systematically to re-align a range of actors such as other authorities, healthcare providers and insurers to produce more value with citizens. In the words of Anne Lind:

> "We have a lot of relations. We obtain information from general practitioners, specialist doctors, hospitals, employers, trade unions, municipalities, regions, insurance companies and sometimes the police. So in many cases it is at least 10 – and then the injured citizen – 10 to 11 different actors we obtain information from."

Ultimately, this insight allows for a much more coordinated way of helping citizens back to the labour market, which was reframed as the ultimate outcome of the agency's work. The underlying movement shifts the attention of the BII from focusing on producing processes (correct case management) to producing outcomes (return to labour market). By focusing on the desired outcomes, the Board launched a dialogue with these stakeholders about how to help users to make a better life, based on what best suits their situation.

In the Family by Family case, Carolyn Curtis describes the new families project as a 'resourcing model', which is radically different from how she has worked during her 10-year career as a manager. "It is bottom-up, it has end-user focus, and there is no fixed structure, criteria or categories." The key to the model is to engage 'sharing families' who are 'positive deviants' who display many of the same apparent characteristics in terms of social demographic as the target families, but who, against the odds, are doing fine. While the model was created through a design-led process, it draws on theories about multi-systemic approaches to societal problems and positive deviance (Pascal et al, 2010). The ability to discover and leverage these families, voluntarily, as a resource to help at-risk families thrive is at the heart of the governance model of Family by Family.

In the branchekode.dk case, the design research uncovers the critical roles of other actors such as Statistics Denmark and the Ministry of Taxation across the case process of registering a new business. In the case, the manager, Sune Knudsen, has become aware that without systematic dialogue between his own agency, the Danish Business Agency, and these other actors, it will not be possible to facilitate business registrations that are more accurate. Part of the design concept therefore becomes a 'back office' platform that will enable workers across all three agencies to systematically update their joint definitions of which kinds of businesses belong to which kind of code.

In the taxation case, the manager, Niels Anker Jørgensen, asserts that the ethnographic research project has provided the organisation with "a new perspective on the interplay between companies, bookkeepers and accountants", leading to a reconsideration of the tax authority's means of engaging with them to support better outcomes (higher tax compliance).

As I have already discussed extensively, the Skansebakken case is built on the principle that activating and engaging civic resources outside the boundaries of the institution will contribute to a better quality of life for residents.

The contributions of design to activating wider network resources are thus several in the cases studied. In some instances it is the graphical mapping of systems and networks that has been key; in others it has been to chart citizen service journeys and thereby discover hidden or unrecognised actors, such as when it turned out that the partners living with injured workers were critically positioned to play an active part in rehabilitation processes. In almost all cases there have been instances of designing workshops to engage stakeholders, to identify how they can contribute and why.

On thrownness and networks in governance

As Normann and Ramirez (1994) observe, relationships in co-production are not only more complex but also more multi-directional and simultaneous. The outside-in view of user experience that is provided by various design approaches (and not least the visualisations used to illustrate it) tends to expose the entire network of actors, including citizens who can potentially take part in value creation. As such, the involved partners 'create value together through inventing new relationships' (Normann and Ramirez, 1994, p 43). This discovery, or rediscovery, of outside actors who may be of critical importance to effectively addressing the problems at hand reflects Karl Weick's observation that typically,

> Designing unfolds in a world that is already interpreted where people are already acting, where options are constrained, where control is minimal, and where things and options already matter for reasons that are taken-for-granted. (Weick, 2004, p 76)

Karl Weick draws on the philosopher Heidegger's concept of 'thrownness' in arguing that people (and organisations) are 'already in the middle of something', meaning that designing never takes place on a blank slate. Rather, designing is almost always about redesigning in a given context, full of conditions, constraints, incongruities and dilemmas. Design thus becomes not about novelty but about 're-design, interruption, resumption, continuity, and re-contextualising' (Weick, 2004, p 74). As public managers reflect on and appreciate the nature of the challenges they are addressing from a human-centred view-point, they come to discover other actors, such as agencies and public institutions at various levels, suppliers, industrial partners and businesses, who are 'already acting', in the middle of something.[2] Normann and Ramirez (1994, p 42–3) underline that this is a general characteristic of our contemporary world. It is becoming so interrelated 'that many actors are involved in co-production without consciously realizing that they are working together. This means that many strategic opportunities are seriously undervalued, sometimes dangerously so.' As managers become aware of and begin to engage other external actors in line with the relational perspective discussed above, they are prompted to new forms of behaviour that can ameliorate this gap.

The challenge, as the roles and potential contributions of these actors are brought to the forefront, is that they may need to be engaged more explicitly to align their way of acting with the problem and objectives in question. In other words, through the design process it is not enough to identify actors of importance to the problem, they must be activated in the reframed context that flows from the design work.

The network perspective on governance has been elaborated from a range of sides, not least by Goldsmith and Eggers (2004, p 55), who argue that there is a distinct role for the 'network designer' to identify possible partners, bring the relevant stakeholders to the table, analyse current operations, set expectations for the way the network will operate, assemble and enmesh its various pieces and activate it. This design phase must, according to Goldsmith and Eggers, address issues such as policy objectives, tools used to activate the network, partners to involve, network design and management and governance principles. In terms of on-going governance and management, Goldsmith and Eggers (2004, p 159) emphasise that the roles of senior and mid-level managers include the development of relationships and strategy, understanding customer (user/ citizen) needs and managing projects and outcomes. As such the (mid-level) public manager's role shifts from enforcing rules and monitoring inputs to actively managing the network. Goldsmith and Eggers contend that new job functions and skills that reflect these roles need to be created and filled in public organisations that wish to take a network approach.

Again, the leveraging of wider resources is linked to the notion of co-production. Normann and Ramirez (1994) characterise this as a process of *reconfiguring*, so that actors come together to co-produce value via what they call not a value chain but a 'value constellation'. This constellation, or network, is designed so that its partners end up performing the 'right' activities for them, engendering value creation on both, or rather *all* sides. In particular, in the context of the public sector organisations, which are typically concerned with the production of services and not products, and with highly complex problem spaces, the notion of 'constellation' seems a better fit than the more mechanistic or industrial term 'chain'.

In considering 'a new synthesis' of public management, Jocelyne Bourgon (2012) similarly highlights the ability to focus on outcomes and whole-of-system results as a key driver of innovation. The key, in her perspective, it is the *collective* capacity for creating public results and achieving societal value. This notion is central in many of the cases, where managers, inspired by the design work, recognise that in order to engage the wider network they have to extend a meaningful value proposition to it as well.

Interactive: shaping processes and behaviours

From the enactment of tentative new practices to the creation of graphical, product, service and system 'outputs', the design approaches covered by the cases in this study seem to potentially work to embody such new processes and behaviours across the organisation's engagement with citizens and other actors. What I mean is, the design work is tangible. In Chapter Nine I showed a range of examples of these outputs. What is important to highlight is that in many cases the solutions are not about stand-alone facilitated interactions; rather, they concern understanding how a range of different interactions – physical, virtual, distributed in time and space – are guided by the overarching relational perspective. Interactions in this context thus go beyond what is typically characterised as 'interaction design' (Moggridge, 2007) or user experience design, and are more characteristic of holistic 'service design' (Polaine et al, 2013, p 87) .

Findings from the case studies

For instance, at Skansebakken the design of a 'communication tree' (with the strange name 'Georg') was a device designed to facilitate concrete acts of hospitality, such as a visitor taking a book from the tree and reading it to a resident. Even though the manager, Jesper Wiese, was sceptical of the role of this artefact, he reflects that "maybe it actually has worked, since we now sit and talk about it, because it has been such a visible design thing that constantly reminded the staff that something must change here". However, at Skansebakken, digital media were also a driver of new interactions; for instance the creation of Facebook pages on iPads facilitated new forms of digital meetings between users and outside relations.

In the Branchekode case, it was necessary not only to create a new digital interface mediating interactions between start-up businesses and the Danish Business Agency, but also to build a back-end digital knowledge-sharing system that could, over time, improve accuracy and update the interactions across multiple government agencies.

In the City of Helsinki, a new digital platform for accessing city permits was developed that essentially facilitated the internal interactions across the (hitherto) wide range of city units necessary for obtaining a permit.

For the BII to realise a shift from solely ensuring legally correct case management to *also* managing for outcomes, different devices had to be developed, including an online graphical guide to enable injured citizens to better engage with their case. Part of the solution was also for the organisation to underpin its shift to digital solutions with new services, such as proactively calling new clients by phone to enable them to manage their case online. In the case of BII these new solutions were to be enabled by a new organisational unit, a Citizen Secretariat. As Anne Lind, the director, says: "The idea with the citizen secretariat is to immediately ask the client, do you have access to a computer, do you have one nearby? Would you mind going online now? Then together we can try to see how your case looks right now."

However, it is not only physical or virtual artefacts, or formally redesigned service processes, that can underpin new interactions. The very process of producing insight-led change by creating empathy with citizens can apparently play a powerful role too. An example is an assistant at Rigshospitalet who could not help but hear the citizens' voices replayed in her head as she pushed her trolley around; for her, relations with patients had changed because of the experience of listening to audio recordings of patients' experiences. The 'meaningful patient experience' became a guideline for her in a very concrete sense, as well as for the management (in a very strategic sense) as it started reorganising professional processes around the patient rather than the other way around.

Also, in the Lewisham example, Peter Gadsdon, the development director, reflects on how the design process in itself has generated momentum and a culture of more continuous improvement among staff, not due to a particular 'solution' but because of how staff experienced and were engaged in the process.

> "[The process] sort of gathered its own momentum, and we then set up for the service, because they had lots of ideas, and we only implemented the first in that project. But then we try to get more of the staff to look at new ideas, and take on some more of them, so it continues the way of thinking and gathering insight and always trying to improve. It is like a bit of a culture thing."

One might say that the on-going exploration, or inquiry, by staff into how to continuously develop more productive interactions in support of the organisation's (reframed) objective then becomes the de facto development methodology. This seems to be very much what Cottam (2012) was hinting at in her call for a more 'developmental' approach to identifying alternative public service provision models. Normann and Ramirez (1994, p 78) contend that viewing producer/client relationships as co-productive, and considering the organisation's role in a wider value constellation or network, is a 'useful way' to enable firms to question, redefine and reconfigure interfaces.

Interactions, mediation and the journey to outcomes

For relational, networked models of governance to function, it seems that they must be able, at a visceral level, to facilitate, or mediate, new forms of interactions between units of the public service system, other actors, and end-users. As much as a shift in relationship, a reframing of the problem, might have been identified at a paradigmatic or strategic level, it must be given concrete form to become actionable across the organisation's activities and beyond to engage its network of stakeholders.

We saw above that when we understand an organisation's efforts from a relational perspective, it becomes clear that user engagement is not transactional but, rather, reciprocal – or interactive. As Polaine et al (2013, p 87) underline, 'All experiences of a service are a result of interactions of some kind.' They suggest that interactions have to do not only with concrete touchpoints such as objects, (digital) interfaces and interpersonal dialogue. Alford (2009) similarly argues that a key process in achieving a more co-productive mode of governance is for a public organisation to identify 'key points in the [value] chain to be influenced, and people associated with those points' (2009, p 208). This then entails determining how to influence those people and actors, taking into account a broad range of motivators and facilitators that may impact on experience and behaviour. This necessarily needs to be a rather holistic and broad view: as Polaine et al (2013) remind us, interactions, in the context of service experience, are also between previous experiences or beliefs, such as when a hospital patient's current experience and behaviour are influenced by a traumatic healthcare event in the past.

Designing the organisation's interactions, inside and outside, to intelligently take account of such factors is no little task, contends Alford (2009), but must somehow be made into an operational strategy.

Reflective: different ways of 'knowing' and learning

Parsons (2010) reminds us that public policy is essentially about constructing or framing what we then come to constitute as 'the public's problem' and thus calling for collective action. In doing so, public policy makers are involved in producing, or *discovering* the public's problems, in the same vein as they go about trying to solve it (my emphasis). Importantly, Parsons suggests that:

> The study of public policy involves the study of the policy making process itself, but it is also about the analysis used *in* that process, or the analysis which is produced in the hope of influencing the process. (2010, p 13, original emphasis)

It would not be reasonable to merely characterise the insights generated by design approaches – covering research, ideation and prototyping dimensions – as 'analysis'. The activities used in the process of policy making, drawing on design, are very different than what is normally used within public organisations. As discussed in Chapter Five, for nearly all the managers in question, they were exposed to design work for the first time in their careers. In terms of methodology in particular, for many of the managers studied, using qualitative design research approaches is a major departure from past practice, and one that seems to allow their organisations to design different responses.

Findings from the case studies

For instance, at the BII, the main research method had previously been quantitative satisfaction surveys. "When we did a user survey we made a nice action plan to follow up ... we then piled additional information onto the users", says Anne Lind, the director. One could argue that the previous mode of understanding the world, and thus of problem solving, did not simplify the service-production process but made it even more complex both for the system and for users, without addressing the real question of how better outcomes are created. As a consequence there was a real risk that citizens were cast in a role of passive recipients, while the system was attempting to become ever-more efficient at a process that created dysfunctional outcomes. Ethnographic research therefore became a more prevalent way of 'knowing' users in the BII.

In Lewisham Borough, the Development Director, inspired by the design work within Homelessness Services (now Housing Options), chose to revise policies and procedures so as to embed new ways of working within the organisation. In order to 'cement' a cultural shift among staff as well as users the borough embedded film-making as a tool within its service-transformation methodology so as to capture and use new insight and create buy-in and commitment for change (Gadsdon, 2012).

In the taxation case, Niels Anker Jørgensen contends that:

> "We are discovering how complex the world actually is – through our efforts on planning compliance and control actions, getting feedback by user testing etc. Currently we are not in a position to write the ultimate guide on what works, and how."

In this sense, even in such a relatively data- and technology-driven agency as the tax office, there is a strong sense of humility towards the ability to 'know' the world of taxpayers and compliance, and the actors who influence it.

In Helsinki the manager, Marja-Leena Vaittinen, recognises at a fundamental level how the government staff must know the world they are dealing with:

> "We think that we know and understand their world. But it's not true if you don't go and talk with them and see how they are working and what facilities they have and what their problems are and how can we help them."

As a consequence of the experience in the design project, the City of Helsinki developed a toolbox to support wider design-led work in the organisation.

At Rigshospitalet, Mette Rosendal Darmer highlights that the qualitative way of understanding the patient was not only essential in the design project, but is also something that the organisation needs in the future; in fact she already has plans for where to apply it.

> "The anthropological material is an essential prerequisite. ... it is something we actually think of how to do, because now we have it in our hands, and some of it we can facilitate ourselves. But we need someone to conduct interviews. ... I could well imagine that as the next project, we will map the electrical patient's progress."[3]

In New York City's HPD, Andrew Eickmann says: "If I were to come across another project with focus on the end-user I would advocate for this kind of user experience research." He continues to emphasise that if he had new more openings in his strategy team he would "seriously consider hiring a designer, since there is so much power in the rendering, the graphics and the creative methods". Eickmann explains that the organisation has internalised some of the methods, for instance in terms of making an effort to give real focus and life to the creative act that is part of developing potential solutions to a problem. There is also talk of creating a new position to focus solely on the user experience. Andrew Eickmann further suggests that some approaches to meetings could change, some things could be organised as workshops, for instance the careful curating of development activities, voting mechanisms, feedback sessions with staff and so on.

At Skansebakken, the realisation is that dealing with the lack of knowing presents a continuous challenge and effort. Jesper Wiese says, reflecting on the change:

> "I can see from what we are doing now that the use of empathy is important. It is still the same things we want to do, but we will do it in a better way for our users – we want to deal with the unknown. Maybe we do not know exactly how, but we know what the bigger objective is."

The sense of purpose and "bigger objective" described here by the manager, Jesper Wiese, goes hand in hand with the desire to "deal with the unknown" – to continue to try out solutions, learn from them and try again.

Reflection through an epistemological shift

As a fourth characteristic, the emerging governance model thus entails a reflective dimension that may best be described as an epistemological shift. By this I imply that the design processes seem to trigger changes in how the manager, and perhaps also the wider organisation, gains knowledge of the world and thus, through learning, becomes able to act. One might say, with Latour, that what comes into play is a continuous discovery of the state; or, with Dewey, that public managers are prompted to continuously inquire into what is 'exactly' the public's problem.

This is a question of the degree to which the managers, through the exposure to design work, have been challenged beyond their 'stable state' and are compelled to embrace new ways of working empirically, and thereby also strategically, with their organisation. Part of this has to do with something as concrete as methodology for research and analysis, but part of it is, in a sense, more philosophical.

What are we to make of the reflective dimension of this mode of governance? As Alford (2009) suggests, there seems to be a major role for factors of intuition and (subjective) judgement, rather than certainty and rationality. There seems to be an appreciation, as I also discussed in Chapter Eight, that 'not knowing' and being outside the stable state may be a natural order of things, in all its disorder. Weick (2004) contends that when managers design, it matters whether they adopt a categorically based epistemic mode or a perceptional mode. What this means according to Weick (2004, p 44) is that:

- in a *categorically based epistemic mode*, managers build increasingly abstract concepts about the world, in which they essentially come to know 'less and less about more and more'. The categorically based mode is useful for achieving coordination and control under conditions of increasing social complexity, but risks becoming over-specified and focusing overly heavily on decision making;

- in a *perceptional epistemic mode*, the way of knowing is increasingly concrete and tangible – very much like the kinds of experiences public managers are exposed to via the design processes analysed in this book. Here, managers come to know, according to Weick, 'more and more about less and less', in that they focus on the micro level and on discrete interactions. However, a potential for (macro, or strategic) contribution by this kind of designing arises, recognises Weick, if we understand the focus of this activity as sense making.

As such, public managers must come to terms with perhaps a more 'loose' and essentially less structured way of governing, where they take responsibility for the achievement of outcomes for citizens and society even though they cannot necessarily control them. In this emerging reflective epistemology, the emphasis becomes on sense making of the 'why are we here' question rather than decision making 'because we are here'.

How to do it: making human-centred governance real

This chapter has illustrated four distinct patterns of human-centred governance that seem to arise from using design approaches to innovation in public policies and services. Table 10.2 sums up the main defining characteristics.

Table 10.2: Defining characteristics of human-centred governance

	Emerging governance characteristics			
	Relational: Reframing relationship with users towards outcomes	**Networked:** Activating new or different resources beyond primary users	**Interactive:** New artefacts to mediate and facilitate collaborative governance processes	**Reflective:** Other ways of learning and of 'knowing' the world
Example	Increased and different framing of relations with end-users and the creation of outcomes (user experience, behavioural change), for instance by empowering vulnerable families (City of Adelaide, Family by Family) or shifting to student-centric education (NYC Department of Education, iZone)	Engaging wider stakeholders and resources in contributing to co-producing outcomes, for instance engaging insurance companies to support rehabilitation of injured citizens (BII, Denmark) or opening up relations with service users (Vejle Municipality, Skansebakken)	Using graphical expression physically or online to facilitate new interactions and dialogues with citizens, for example case process map for homeless families (Borough of Lewisham) or among staff (Danish Competition and Consumer Authority, Branchekode)	Embedding more qualitative ways of informing management processes, for instance by continuously using service design or ethnography in elder care services (Holstebro Municipality, meals on wheels); or by observing children playing with iPads (Danish Competition and Consumer Authority)

What are the implications for public managers who wish to work with changing the governance model towards a more human-centred paradigm? The following are some starting points.

- **Reflect on how new design solutions might challenge your organisation's current model.** What governance arrangements may need to change in order to provide a context for new innovative, citizen–centred solutions to actually work? This is obviously best done in a situation where your organisation is already engaged in a design project, where the ensuing results can then be assessed against the governance set-up. However, it could also be that these reflections are what would lead you to choose to start a design process.

- **Examine how the four principles of a human-centred governance model might apply to your organisation in practice.** In what ways would it be possible to engage with the four characteristics of human-centred governance proposed in this chapter? If you take a particular service intervention or policy programme, which concrete ways of governing and managing would need to change? You might do this as an exercise where you ask "What if we adopted a relational perspective on this activity? How might we need to change it?"

In the next chapter I explore the wider implications for managing in – and for – a human-centred governance paradigm. How does human-centred governance compare to where we are coming from, and to what extent might it differ from where some organisations are already headed? Are there strengths of our governance legacy that we risk missing by adopting a new approach?

Notes

[1] Darmer subsequently estimated that the annual productivity savings at the ward following the project were in the range of 4 million Danish kroner (Darmer, Boesgaard, Bason et al, 2015).

[2] This may also involve commercial partners and interests. Eggers and Macmillan (2013) have argued that new forms of collaboration between private firms, social innovators, philanthropies and government organisations arise in solution 'ecosystems' to address societal problems.

[3] Electrical patients are patients who have some type of pacemaker.

ELEVEN

Towards human-centred governance

Twenty-first century challenges and the means of addressing them are more numerous and complex than ever before. (Stephen Goldsmith and Bill Eggers, *Governance by Network*, 2004, p 7)

The wider context of applying design approaches in government, can be seen as a shift from a classic 'bureaucratic' paradigm, combined in some degree with 'new public management' components or overlays, towards something else, which has more recently been termed 'networked' or 'collaborative' governance, or 'co-production' (Goldsmith and Eggers, 2004; Hartley, 2005; Alford, 2009; Parsons, 2010; Ansell and Torfing, 2014; Greve, 2015). This emerging paradigm seeks to embrace complexity and emergence.

In this chapter I discuss what the four characteristics I presented in Chapter Ten could mean to the future of governance, given what we already know in terms of emerging 'new' governance models.

I first consider the implications and nature of the emerging governance principles: are they different in nature than the types we already know, and if so, how? Here I especially discuss how human-centred governance can be viewed as an approach to co-production of public services. Second, I discuss how the emerging paradigm seems less specified, and more open, than previous ones – more like a skeleton than a monolith. Third, I consider to what extent the characteristics – *relational*, *networked*, *interactive* and *reflective* – can be seen as incremental additions or 'overlays' to existing ways of governing, and to what extent they might be expressions of more disruptive challenges to, or extensions of, the dominant paradigms. Fourth, I explore how potential new characteristics of a governance paradigm might relate to existing models. I discuss how they would perform in relation to the standards that were originally proposed by Max Weber in terms of government efficiency and performance. Would a different paradigm entail the risk of 'throwing the baby out with the bathwater' and failing to deliver on some of the pillars of what we consider good government? Further, I examine how human-centred governance might compare, or fit, with Benington and Hartley's 2001 ideal-types of governance models.

Fifth, I suggest a holistic model that connects management engagement, design approaches and governance context as a potentially reinforcing cycle, leading to ever-more enabling environments for positive change.

Finally, I conclude with some 'to-dos' for working with and managing by a human-centred governance approach.

Re-humanising public organisations

In some ways the characteristics I described in the previous chapter suggests a form of 're-enchantment' of public governance, as a postmodern reaction to the disenchantment (*Entzauberung* in Max Weber's terms) of the modern organisation. Parsons (2010, p 27) suggests that such a re-enchantment requires that we recognise that the problems we face are of a 'wicked' nature and do not have 'solutions' that can be arrived at 'purely through the exercise of reason and analysis'.

Given the strong emphasis on the subjective experience of human beings – of citizens primarily, but also of workers and managers within public systems – design might contribute to this re-enchantment, or at least to the introduction of a different set of parameters for assessing the success of public management. First and foremost, as this book has illustrated, design approaches tend to place people and their relations with public systems and processes more centrally in public management practice. As Meyer (2011) argues, design's essentially humanistic agenda makes it a powerful tool for enriching organisations. This seems to entail a more subjective, empathic, behavioural, contextual, 'messy' and flexible appreciation of what it means to govern public organisations.

Such somewhat vague concepts do not mean that it should not be possible to suggest some characteristics of an emerging governance model, as I have done above. Its properties may just have to be of a more general, and to some extent fluid, nature than the prescriptive and more fixed principles of classic and 'new' public management. To public managers, especially at first, this might be equally frustrating and liberating.

The core shift that is in play appears to be away from models largely designed around the *delivery of services to people*, and towards a model that is designed to better enable, in various forms and guises, the *co-production of services with people and other actors*. Here we are mainly in the camp of Greve's collaborative governance model, although this risks being reductive (Greve, 2015). Certainly, the model takes into account 'messy' subjective, emotional, relational human dimensions. But is this emergent model at a fundamental level different in character than the governance models most public organisations have inherited? As I mentioned in Chapter Ten, Alford (2009) underlines that a more human-centric, co-productive mode of governance raises questions not only about what clients (users, citizens, people) expect from the public organisation, but also about what the public organisation expects from its clients. Likewise, as Ansell and Torfing (2014) contend, the role of service users is recast from passive consumers of public services to active citizens. This calls into question issues of public value and how it is created (Greve, 2015).

A central point here seems to be that in a human-centred mode of governance *the appropriate modality of governing for public value creation varies*. In other words, the emergent model of governance can probably not be entirely prescribed, or specified, to the same level of detail as its predecessors.

Let me illustrate. In his careful and deep study of three cases of co-production of public services, Alford (2009, p 175) concludes that co-production is 'beneficial' to the organisations studied, but that the kinds of public value generated by governance models of co-production 'reveal no particular pattern of "performance"'.

In other words, the ways in which the new governance paradigm contributes value simply differ across the cases with no discernible pattern. Alford finds that the pattern of value is 'haphazard' (2009, p 175), since the benefits of governance as co-production can accrue both in increased effectiveness (better outcomes) and in reduced costs (higher productivity), or both. Across the cases of postal services, employment programmes and tax administration (of which the latter two policy domains are also addressed in this book), Alford finds that the (co-productive) governance model was valuable to different aspects of the organisations' work, to differing extents and in different ways. As discussed in Chapter Nine, I similarly found a wide spectrum of types of public value resulting from the use of design approaches. This is a profound reflection of the complexity and 'messiness' of the governance model itself, or, as Goldsmith and Eggers have suggested, 'one-size-fits-all solutions have given way to customized approaches as the complicated problems of diverse and mobile populations increasingly defy simplistic solutions' (2004, p 7).

In the following I will consider how we might better understand these properties, first in terms of how specified/ unspecified the model is, and second in terms of how it might differ from existing modes of governance.

On the charm of skeletons

In spite of my attempt to characterise the governance model in the previous chapter, it seems underspecified in the sense that the specific management tools needed to then provide content to its dimensions are tentative, open, even elusive. The cases illustrate that managers come to terms with a certain lack of control, of emergence even, and recognise that the way to creating better outcomes or even higher productivity relies just as much on providing space for users and staff to find their own, meaningful path. The model is more of a framework than a prescription, less of a top-down management strategy and more of a placeholder for bottom-up processes to take place. Of course, part of this could be because the empirical material consists of projects, not of all-encompassing public sector reforms. However, it is at least interesting that there are similar patterns and characteristics across most of the projects that may have implications for the conduct of management and the future potential of the role of design in the public sector.

In their consideration of the implications of complexity for policy making, Colander and Kupers (2014, p 276) suggest that, as a 'far-reaching proposal', governments should create eco-structures that are conducive to more bottom-up policy solutions, providing people with institutional space to self-organise in new ways to solve social problems, and should encourage civil debate inside and outside the policy system. They contend that this implies that policy, and governance, cannot be controlled – but can be influenced. Taking complexity seriously as the ultimate constraint for achieving public outcomes, they argue that policy must be 'designed to play a supporting role in an evolving ecostructure – it is not designed to control the system' (Colander and Kupers 2014, p 10). Similarly, writing a decade earlier, Goldsmith and Eggers (2004) suggested that in a networked mode of governing, the ways in which governments achieve objectives will likely be 'unanticipated'. Flexibility and adaptability, for instance to include new partners and new relationships, become important performance criteria (Goldsmith and Eggers, 2004, pp 183–4).

Karl Weick, building on the arguments discussed in the sections above, contends that good design, understood in the context of managing and governing organisations, is intentionally kept underspecified. He argues that in the search for stable and predictable 'solutions', too often designers don't know when to stop – the result being command-and-control and machine-based management models. However, Weick suggests that there is 'charm' in the notion of underspecification, of keeping design parameters open for interpretation – for managers, for front-line staff and, indeed, for users. Hereby (quoting the innovative founder of VISA, Dee Hock), Weick contends that management becomes much more in tune with what is needed to govern in our contemporary world: understanding and coordinating variability, complexity and effectiveness (Weick, 2004, p 47). Normann and Ramirez similarly argue that as actors carry out their activities in value constellations, 'it is not possible to take given characteristics for granted: co-producers constantly reassess each other' (1994, p 55). The charm of an underspecified, or skeletal, governance model thus implies giving up on clarity. This is perhaps a paradox when we have also seen that a (new) degree of clarity can arise from insights into human behaviour through design approaches. However the lack of clarity I am speaking of now is different: it is not a lack of clarity of insight into what matters; it is lack of clarity in terms of a recipe to 'solve' the problem or capture the opportunity at hand.

Institutional shift: overlay or disruption?

The book has shown that public managers appear to engage with design approaches in ways that catalyse new ideas, concepts, solutions and, in many of the studied cases, implementable organisational change. The kinds of change efforts undertaken tend to embody some or all of the governance principles outlined in the preceding chapter. It is a wider and more open question, however, whether these shifts in understanding and engaging in new relations with citizens are expressions of a paradigmatic, 'radical' or 'disruptive' shift in governance or more of an 'overlay' or 'mix' with existing modes, leading to incremental change at best. To what extent do the types of changes in service provision across the cases really signify breaks away from the current dominating institutional 'template' of classic and new public management, and to what extent are they more like reconfigurations through 'bricolage' (Lawrence and Suddaby, 2006, p 229)?

I will consider these two perspectives of incrementalism and more radical, disruptive change here, and discuss them in the light of the research findings.

As we have seen throughout the book, a wide range of the scholars who have turned their attention to the 'what's next' question of public governance contend that, to the extent that something new may be happening, the new governance instruments – characterised by a balancing of the top–down and bottom–up perspectives, multiplicity of actors, taking complexity seriously and so forth – can be viewed as *additional* elements that are added on top of existing governance mechanisms of bureaucracy and the new public management (NPM) (Bourgon,

2012; Agranoff, 2014; Waldorff et al, 2014). Informed both by executive experience and careful research (Bourgon) and by the long-term view of historical institutionalism (Waldorff et al), the argument here is that change is incremental in nature, and that as new governance instruments arise they do not take something away but, rather, add to the growing complexity or complicatedness of the public service system itself (Christensen, 2012). Waldorff et al (2014) argue in an assessment of multiple public sector innovation cases that bureaucratic and NPM modes of governance tend to cast their 'shadow' over what are at surface more innovative, collaborative or 'new public governance' practices. In line with these findings, institutional theory – arguably a key theoretical school in characterising public organisations – expects that organisations only rarely change, since rationalised institutions create myths of formal structure that in turn shape organisations (Meyer and Rowan, 1977). Over time, organisations become increasingly similar in structure, mainly due to adaptation to a socially constructed environment through three types of pressures: *coercive pressures* that result from politics and power relationships; *mimetic pressures* that arise as organisations, under conditions of uncertainty, take note of successful peers and adopt structures and approaches that are similar; and *normative pressures* that especially characterise highly professionalised organisations that favour practices and structures that are considered morally 'proper' (Boxenbaum and Jonsson, 2008).

A variant of this incremental perspective is Karl Weick's argument, also mentioned in Chapter Three, that any design efforts undertaken by managers are essentially redesigns or reinterpretations because of the 'thrownness' of the situations within which public managers find themselves (Weick, 2004, p 76). Weick asserts that any effort at organisational change must accept the richness and never-ending presence of *context* – empirical organisational, societal, behavioural factors and so forth that imply that the world is 'pre-interpreted' by the actors who occupy it. Weick thus contends that 'thrownness suggests that design is incremental even when it aspires to be much more' (2004, p 77). For designers, this happens because, as they relate to the client's world – briefs, specifications, needs, expectations –

they adjust and tune in and thereby 'typically extend rather than upend' (2004, p 77). Clients (in this book, public managers) also pull design towards incremental, rather than disruptive, change, since they assimilate and 'normalise' design not just to fit with their existing practices, but also 'bending' the solutions their way so that they fit with what is already coming in terms of strategies and plans. This in turn leaves little wiggle room for agency.

Such incremental design need not be negative; rather, for Weick, good design is exactly the kinds of design that take seriously what is already going on in the world and offer useful extensions or amendments to it.

However, it is worth underlining at this point that the cases studied by Waldorff et al, the experience of Bourgon, and for that matter the design perspective taken by Weick, are not based on collaborative design approaches as they have been defined in the present book. Rather, the 'innovation' projects and 'designs' referred to by most other scholars who have examined cases of public sector innovation are very much based on traditional consulting approaches, which as described in Chapter Two distinguish quite sharply between designer, client and end-user. Further, in the 'managing as designing perspective' taken up by Weick, there is no empirical experience of what collaborative design approaches might entail for the managers in terms of access to a different epistemology that can power a different level of reflection, as discussed above.

It is another apparent paradox, then, as documented in the cases in this book, that by taking context and external (user experience) seriously, thrownness is not just embraced; rather, it is in a sense suspended for a while, or put into perspective. Managers seem able, drawing on the design approaches of exploring the problem space, to reflect with more clarity and vision on the fundamental purpose of their organisation. By creating opportunities and affordances that – for a while – suspend thrownness, the purpose can be (re-)examined, reflected upon, and the organisation's engagement with the world can in some cases be reconfigured and reframed.

Madsbjerg and Rasmussen (2014) argue that such 'clarity' is achieved exactly because it allows for new meaning and new interpretations to emerge (here we are again speaking of clarity as insight). Likewise Weick goes so far as to assert that the potential value of design is that it 'stirs up those pre-existing interpretations, throws some of them up for grabs, and encourages people to redecide what matters' (2004, p 77). Here, it sounds somewhat more radical and fundamental to redecide what matters. Perhaps Weick is not so sure about the incremental argument as he contends? The cases discussed above show a range of examples where this does seem to happen: managers reframe, rethink, redecide, reinterpret their relations with users and other stakeholders, and often challenge their fundamental mission. Somehow, the organisation's purpose seems to become more clear, even as the governance approach is loosened up.

In fact, Weick himself contents that 'in a true upending of organizational design, we find ourselves engaged, not in uncertainty absorption, but in uncertainty infusion' (2004, p 48). To the extent that collaborative design approaches 'take in' complexity and uncertainty and help managers to reconcile themselves with it, might they achieve a different kind of stability than the one characterised by (the illusion of) control? In the cases studied, at least, it seems that it is the rule rather than the exception that they do tend to draw on a rich appreciation of the 'pre-interpreted world', as they take qualitative design research as the starting point, drawing in human subjective experience and generating empathy with the perspective of users. The stories shared by many of the managers indicate that the resulting insights were rather profound, in that they gave a reframed perspective of the problem space. The expectations and pre-interpretations embraced by the managers were thrown into question; the stable state was challenged. The new form of stability is, perhaps, instead one of continuous sense making starting with a changed frame.

Perhaps the most significant point here is not a discussion of whether the change towards human-centred governance is 'radical' or 'incremental' but, rather, whether it somehow, to quote Kurt Lewin (1947), 'unfreezes' the existing structures, making them less stable and more open, fluid, amenable to adaptive change. This may not qualify as a 'disruption' or a paradigm shift as Clayton Christensen (1997) or Thomas Kuhn may have argued; it is something different. As collaborative design approaches are brought into public organisations, public managers are empowered to redefine relationships, engage wider networks, make interactions more meaningful and gain new epistemologies. This may not be just temporarily tinkering with change but perhaps permanently managing differently. As such, managers can give new (reframed) direction focusing on citizens and outcomes, while at the same time, perhaps, letting go of some control. Purpose and meaning are shifted to the fore, rather than structure and rationality. As I will discuss later, for managers already engaging in (new) networked forms of governance, this may not feel like a major break from the past. But for organisations anchored more firmly in a traditional bureaucratic paradigm, the change could well be radical.

On the performance of a human-centred paradigm

In the first part of the book I discussed the distinguishing characteristics of Weberian bureaucracy and the outcomes it claimed to deliver. There seems to be no doubt that the triumph of bureaucracy both in public administration and in the business world throughout the 20th century had to do with these outcomes, including efficiency, predictability, objectivity, procedural fairness and democracy. Indeed,

> Because public administration [before the separation of politics from administration] was still infused with pre-bureaucratic forms of patronage and personally motivated favour, scientific management offered the prospect of more rational and systematic procedures and forms of conduct that would help eliminate these features. Its achievements in delivering on this promise should not be underestimated. (du Gay, 2000, p 116)

The question becomes to what degree the positive achievements of traditional public administrations might be sustained, to the extent they are still relevant to a contemporary world, while at the same time coexisting with the principles of human-centred governance? Or are these paradigms or governance models really at either end of a spectrum? Table 11.1 contrasts some of the defining characteristics of the two models.

Table 11.1: Contrasting bureaucratic and human-centred governance

Domain	Bureaucratic governance	Human-centred governance
Citizens	Formal rules Impersonal	Relational
Organisation	Division of responsibility Management hierarchy	Networked
Processes	Transactional	Interactive
Epistemology	Objective	Reflective

As the table illustrates, there are some rather fundamental differences between bureaucratic governance and an emerging human-centred governance. However, the wider question is beyond the descriptive and, rather, the *performative*: how would an emerging human-centred governance paradigm potentially fare against these outcome, or performance criteria, of bureaucratic governance? The answer might be that the principles underlying the two models, at least as ideal-types, are vastly different and that they have different objectives. Table 11.2 illustrates some key issues.

An important – perhaps the most important – point in Table 11.2 is the issue of efficiency. In Weber's traditional bureaucracy there was no mature concept for *outcomes*, understood as the ability to influence a societal challenge or problem and, to quote Herbert Simon, to turn the current situation into a preferred one. So, in Weberian bureaucracy efficiency is in a sense internally defined as productivity, or the ability to churn out a particular output at a particular unit cost. The main concern across the cases studied in this book, and thus a key characteristic of human-centred governance, seems, rather, to be the ability to achieve particular outcomes. This is more a matter of (externally oriented) *effectiveness*.

Table 11.2: Performance factors of bureaucratic governance vs human-centred governance

Performance factor	Bureaucratic governance *achieved through*	Human-centred governance *achieved through*
Efficiency	Scale Standardisation Specialisation Defined as cost per output	Relations Networked Individualisation Prevention Defined *also* as cost of outcomes (*effectiveness*)
Predictability and objectivity	Hierarchical management Recruitment practices Rule-based	Adaptability Empathy Embracing complexity
Procedural fairness	Uniformity of rules, no matter the context Equality in terms of right to certain activities	Differentiation of processes to fit with differing contexts Equality in terms of right to certain outcomes
Democracy	Transparency of *basis* for making decisions	Transparency of *means* to achieve outcomes

We are now ready to take a look at how human-centred governance connects to the different conceptions of the emerging, networked governance that I introduced in Chapter Four and discussed extensively in that chapter. Table 11.3 displays the range of variants I presented and discussed, and adds human-centred governance, essentially as an additional perspective or variation.

I have purposely not included in Table 11.3 the three contextual factors proposed by Benington and Hartley (that the *context* of governance is continuously changing, that the *population* is increasingly diverse and that needs and problems of society are *complex*, volatile and prone to risk). All the governance model variants appear to recognise these conditions as the canvas against which governance is practised. However, it is interesting to contrast the approaches suggested by the four variants across the remaining characteristics: how is strategy shaped? How is governance done? How is public value understood? The table shows some interesting nuances and differences. When it comes to 'human-centred governance', as might be expected, the relations with citizens are at the forefront, the role of networks and interactions are central and continuous reflection on the generation of desired outcomes is an important characteristic.

On balance, it seems that the governance characteristics I have labelled as human-centred governance share many similarities, especially with collaborative governance, but perhaps also partly with public value management. It appears, however, that putting human beings – people and their experiences and behaviour – at the forefront, including potentially reframing the relationship, could be a characteristic that at least in part is particular to human-centred governance, even though co-production is central also to collaborative governance.

Table 11.3: Emerging paradigms: variations over the next governance model

Networked governance overall characteristics	Digital-era governance (Dunleavy)	Public value management	Collaborative governance	Human-centred governance
Strategy Shaped by civil society	Driven by digital and technological opportunities and capabilities	Strategic triangle between legitimising, authorising and organising environment	Primary attention on public-private partnerships, networks, and joined-up services	Shaped by relations, empathy with citizens' experience and design of service journeys
Governance Through networks and partnerships Civic leadership	Priority on centralisation and specialisation to reap benefits of digitisation	Focus on management for results and performance	Emphasises collaborative networks and co-production	Maintained as public managers' domain but organised by citizens' experience and role of other actors (networks and interactions)
Key concept Public value	Focused on radical productivity gains through digitisation	Point of departure for public governance	Prioritises the generation of outcomes	Focuses on continuous reflection, learning on how to create better outcomes

Source: Adapted from Benington and Hartley (2001)

A positive cycle of designing, managing and governing with people

What do the book's insights imply for the future of public governance? This chapter and the previous one have in a sense challenged Abraham Lincoln's classic dictum of 'government of the people, by the people, for the people'. Applying a human-centred governance model means governing *with* the people, in the sense that citizens' experiences and behaviours become an on-going consideration within the organisation, in the minds of managers and staff alike. Human-centred governance certainly represents a break away from traditional public administration, and, arguably, from the new public management. In the context of more networked and collaborative governance models, human-centred governance can be seen as a variation with some particular characteristics that arise from the engagement with design approaches. What is important to understand is that human-centred governance as an operational model is reached, or discovered, through engagement, by public managers, with the design approach.

To put it simply, design powers the journey to human-centred governance.

However, that journey does not have a final destination. Because human-centred governance, among other things, is reflective and interactive by nature, the process of governing becomes an on-going cycle of engaging with design and applying the results back into the governance context. One could say that there is a potentially reinforcing, positive cycle between using design, managing to innovate and changing the governance context. Figure 11.1 illustrates this cycle. It shows how the interaction between the management efforts to drive design projects, the innovation processes themselves and the implications for the governance context can be mutually reinforcing. What I have essentially been exploring across the book is the relationships that unfold between managers' agency as they engage with innovation processes through design approaches, and the impact on, and role of, governance as the context.

Figure 11.1: Cycle of governance (context), management (agency) and innovation (change)

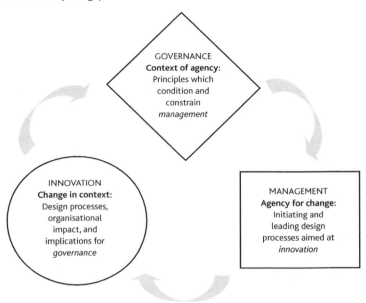

Figure 11.1 illustrates how the governance context sets the stage and defines constraints and opportunities for management's engagement with design processes. In turn, the leveraging of design approaches and the ensuing generation of change may influence the context in which agency is possible.

For managers, this framework offers a holistic view of the role of continuously engaging with design to influence the very governance context, which in turn can allow for more openness to more ambitious use of design. This positive cycle may lead to an ever-increasing ability to achieve desirable outcomes, and to shaping the governance approach and organisational capabilities to that end.

How to do it: governing with people

As this chapter has discussed, human-centred governance entails some interesting implications for public managers, including the following.

- **Be open to type of public value creation.** Managers pursuing human-centred governance should be open to different kinds of value creation. As a form of human-centred governance, co-production calls for a high degree of contextual sensitivity. The approach can lead to a variety of public values, from efficiency gains to better outcomes, or both. Managers must see the discovery of potential for value creation as part of the governing task.
- **Manage underspecification.** If there is one insight that seems clear from what this book has shown about governing in complexity, it is that public organisations must change to become more agile, adaptive and tuned to the types of problems they are facing. Managing with a human-centred governance paradigm requires coming to terms with less tight and specified governance mechanisms, not least in terms of 'unfreezing' and loosening attempts to control behaviour inside and outside the organisation.
- **Brace for disruption.** For managers already working within or towards the 'new' public governance, human-centred governance opens up some new perspectives and practices, but will probably not feel like a major break from the past. Perhaps the biggest change for them will be the strong(er) emphasis on people and on outcomes. However, in organisations that are more deeply anchored in a traditional and bureaucratic governance paradigm, and/or in models heavily dominated by the new public management, human-centred governance will likely be experienced as a disruption. That may be good to keep in mind as you engage with design approaches to leverage the positive cycle of change, especially as it begins to extend across the organisation.

In the next and final chapter I explore the implications of the book's findings for public leadership.

TWELVE

Take the curvy path: leading change by design engagement

> Design is one of the three required competencies
> for being an effective manager. (Richard Boland and
> Fred Collopy, *Managing as Designing*, 2004, p 265)

Close to my home, north of Copenhagen, an old mill stream cuts through a wooded area.[1] Runners or ramblers can choose between two different paths, not far apart but offering markedly different experiences. One path cuts a straight line through the area, and from start to finish, the algae-green waters of the mill stream are visible at the end of it. The other path, by contrast, twists and turns, and all one sees is birch trees and the dense undergrowth until one is just a few metres from the bank of the stream. And what is the difference? The straight path feels much, much faster than the curvy path. Maybe even twice as fast, although in fact they are almost exactly the same length.

The markedly different experience of running on the two paths is reminiscent of the difference between a traditional development process and a design process – the kind of process that this book has explored. A traditional development process typically has a clearly defined goal. When the project team set out, they have a pretty good idea of what a successful outcome should look like. They also usually have a fairly clear understanding (often passed down from top management) of the problem at hand. They have a well-defined brief that suggests a particular type of solution. The manager to whom the project team refer to can therefore rest assured that the team will be able to deliver. This type of process is linear in nature – like my local nature path

– and even if it may not be without challenges and difficulties, it is fairly predictable. As a consequence, the management task is standard: initiating the process, prioritising resources, establishing deadlines and milestones and eventually deciding whether the resulting proposed solution should be implemented. There is a clear and definite path that will take them out of the woods. But the process is not exactly exciting – nor innovative.

As we have seen throughout this book, design processes are markedly different from the scenario described above. Typically, one of the first things designers do when they are handed an assignment is to question it: challenging the underlying premises and assumptions behind the brief, or going into the world to observe whether clients or users actually behave as described in the brief. Or it may involve coming up with preliminary solutions, prototypes, to be used as development tools. Deliberately influencing the practices of users, stakeholders and suppliers gives the designers access to early feedback, which helps them to determine whether a prospective solution should be rejected or developed further.

Designers thrive when they challenge the problem space. They also thrive when they create new, visionary possibilities by insisting on giving shape to future solutions. They thrive in situations characterised by ambiguity, uncertainty and disruption. The best designers are able to keep an open mind while working on a practical solution. The catch is that this approach is extremely challenging for many managers. Thus, managers who wish to reap the full benefit from working with designers need to engage with them in ways that facilitate a fruitful design and change process.

This book has shown the dynamic interplay between collaborative design approaches to public sector innovation and the problem-solving, opportunity-finding reflections and activities of public managers. A key theme has been *design engagement* as a way to understand the management processes that may catalyse shifts from current modes of governance. I have proposed that these shifts seem to lean toward a more relational, networked, interactive and reflective mode of governance. In the previous chapter I suggested that this set of emerging characteristics might, as a whole, be termed *human-centred governance*.

However, what have we learned more specifically about the *leadership* role of public managers as they engage with design processes, and possibly about their role as 'designers'? What model, or models, of management engagement with design emerge? How do public managers learn and gain confidence and skill in collaborating with designers, and how does this influence their view of their own agency and opportunities?

This chapter is structured in three sections, each of which provides a different perspective on the relationship between public managers and design.

First, I summarise the book's key points on leadership through *design engagement*. Second, I examine how managers in the book's cases have built confidence in using design approaches as part of their leadership practice, and have taken on a new vocabulary as a result.

Third, I reflect on design as *decision making* versus *future making*. How can managers relate to the options presented to them for making decisions as prompts that may lead to the pursuit of alternative futures?

These perspectives constitute the book's conclusion on the emergence of a potentially different approach to leading change in government, which unfolds in the space between managers and designers.

Design as engagement

I have found six types of engagements with design, which can be understood as the patterns of management attitudes and behaviours that unfolded as design methods were carried out in the organisations I studied. The engagements are expressions, in essence, of *what happens between managers and design processes*. The six engagements were the following.

- *Questioning assumptions*, including an a priori tendency to seek ways of questioning one's own assumptions as a manager, as well as the role of design approaches in enabling the manager to ask new questions as to 'what is going on' as the organisation interacts with its users

- *Leveraging empathy*, which is the propensity for managers to take and actively utilise the 'empathic data' generated by ethnographically inspired design research in order to initiate processes of change in their organisation
- *Stewarding divergence*, which means the ability to open, and keep open, space and time in the organisation for a diversity of possible ideas to flourish, and linger, while maintaining for the staff an overall sense of direction and purpose.
- *Navigating the unknown*, which is in many ways the ability of managers to handle their own insecurity and worries about where the design process may take them, their staff and the organisation.
- *Making the future concrete*, which was tightly connected to the design practice of prototyping and testing possible solutions together with end-users, staff and other stakeholders. Making the future concrete is a management engagement, in the sense that many of the managers insist that solutions must become concrete and tangible. Additionally, some are even themselves inclined to build concrete expressions of what a new future could look like.
- *Insisting on public value*, which reflects an engagement with outcomes of the organisation's mission and a dedication to producing multiple kinds of value. Productivity gains are certainly often an important dimension, but most often it is the generation of more and different kinds of value for citizens or businesses that managers, at the end of the day, choose to engage with.

As the managers I have studied engage with design across the dimensions mentioned here, it seems right to say, with Herbert Simon, that they seek to change the situations in which they find themselves into preferred ones. However, does this make them 'designers'?

As I have discussed extensively as I uncovered these six engagements in the book, there are variations in the degree to which the managers a priori, or intrinsically, display certain attitudes or behaviours, and the extent to which management action is prompted, or triggered, by what one might call extrinsic influences by the design work. The interplay here is complex.

For instance, I show how 'questioning assumptions' is both an intrinsically driven propensity as well as influenced extrinsically by the 'empathic data' generated by design research. Likewise, as design methods challenge the manager to allow for a wider and richer divergence of possible solutions, the question becomes why this happens: is it because the manager is (intrinsically) inclined to allow for extended periods of uncertainty and is ready to steward this divergence; or is it because the methodology of design-led ideation and concept development more or less forces the manager to take a certain stance? Could it be that because the manager has invested his or her personal prestige in working with designers that they are more likely to allow the designers to have some leeway as the process moves forward and becomes, in terms of content, unpredictable? Or is it that because the design process itself is often quite well-described (even as problems and outcomes are left open), managers can still feel somewhat 'safe'?

As I have hinted on multiple occasions throughout the book, it does at least seem that part of the answer is that there is *something* about these managers' way of thinking that enables rather powerful uses of design work to initiate or drive change in the organisations studied. Are they simply thinking differently, in general? If one were to ask Roger Martin (2007; 2009), long-time proponent of design thinking as a management approach to innovation, he might answer that these managers were in various ways displaying design thinking. At the very least, they find themselves involved with methods, tools, activities and ways of thinking that are broadly associated with the design profession. One could say that they are growing their design confidence.

Building design confidence

As I showed in Chapter Nine, there are changes flowing from the design engagements: tangible design outputs as well as less tangible, and in some cases certainly discernible changes to the organisation and the ways in which it relates to and interacts with its surrounding environment. I showed that a range of the cases I have studied demonstrated signs of the creation of public value, including productivity gains, democratic value, stronger service experience and tentative signs of better outcomes.

One would think that if these kinds of value were actually partly or wholly generated, managers would be inclined to continue to collaborate with designers and to leverage design approaches. Or at the least, it should make them inclined to adopt some of the practices that inspired them, and bring them more permanently into their own organisation.

However, does the experience of engaging with design also influence how these managers undertake work on organisational change *the next time they have the opportunity to do so*? Or, put in a different way: once they have collaborated with designers, has this changed the managers' perspective and confidence in how they can lead change in their organisations? Do they, for instance, embrace more of a design attitude?

Through the book I have been occupied with the question of the relationship between the use of designers and managers' engagement with the acts and processes of designing. However, this relationship is not static. As managers gain experience and confidence in the use of design approaches, their appetite for and ability to engage with design changes. Part of this is because their wider organisation, collectively, has also gained experience and confidence. Part of it is because they themselves are changed by the experience.

As the Norwegian scholar of organisations Tor Hernes (2008, p 145) says, in organisations, actors change during processes. 'They act in a fluid world, which changes them in turn.' Part of the change that seems to have happened with managers throughout the processes I have studied is their ability to reflect. Such reflections seem to be enabling them to be more confident in taking particular forms of action. Hernes (2008, p 145) notes, 'Unconsciously, decision makers know that the world is far more complex and fluid because they live in that world every day.' Through the design work, and the collective experience if it, dealing with that complexity has somehow become more natural, both for the manager and for the staff who were involved. This was demonstrated in a variety of ways across the book, as I also discussed in the previous chapter's consideration of designing in 'thrownness' (Weick, 2004). From the experience of dealing constructively with that thrownness comes confidence. For instance, Mette Rosendal Darmer at Rigshospitalet says:

"there is so much uncertainty in terms of which way we can go. But no doubt these methods provide a level of maturity in the organisation."

Darmer feels more confident that positive change can take place. And she feels confident that she knows which tools to use: "My leadership role is that I have become even more aware of the role of facilitation." The notion of organisational maturity and reflection is also experienced by Jesper Wiese, the manager of the institution for the disabled at Skansebakken. Here he shares his thoughts about the next innovation project on which his organisation is going to venture out:

> "We are now running the next innovation project and it is a completely different organisation and with completely different people. And the really interesting thing is that we are running it with the same designers again. And [the designers] they say, 'Oh my God, these are not at all the same people as two years ago.' Now the employees know what it's about, now it makes sense to say, 'We need to innovate here, we need to make a service design. You know what it is, so come and join us ...' Now they know. They still don't know, none of us knows where we'll end up, but now they know the process. They can rely on the process."

The interesting point here is how the managers Darmer and Wiese draw on a different vocabulary, at least in part as a consequence of the design work. Boland and Collopy argue that the awareness of language as well as work practice is key for managers as they seek to engage with design as a way of problem solving:

> An awareness of one's own vocabulary is the first step to questioning it with a design attitude and exploring how different vocabularies yield more creative problem representations and enable the development of better designs. (Boland and Collopy, 2004, p 15)

What Boland and Collopy indicate is that this ability to be aware of, but also to adapt, one's vocabulary as a manager is an expression of design attitude. The question is whether the engagement with design not only builds a form of higher *competence* to undertake the next engagement. Does the engagement with design also stimulate and develop a *confidence* of being future oriented? As discussed earlier, some managers were a priori prone to question their own assumptions, just as some managers seemed inclined to put citizens and public value before anything else. In that sense, as illustrated in the previous section, they were already displaying attitudes related to 'embracing complexity and ambiguity' and 'deep empathy'. But does the managers' exposure to design approaches then amplify or catalyse latent inclinations towards more 'mature' design engagement? Or would they have thought and acted the same in the absence of their concrete experience with design work?

There seem to be signs that the design work inspires some degree of behaviour change, and perhaps confidence, in the managers, in terms of embracing a different way of working. The managers have discarded their 'stable state' (Churchman, 1971) and taken on more designerly roles, so to speak. For instance, Elspeth Gibson, in Suffolk, is inspired by the designers and then independently chooses to make her team to go and do field-work. Sune Knudsen, working on the Branchekode project, seems to know better what to ask for (and what to expect) in the current project due to his past experience with designers. Mette Rosendal Darmer at Rigshospitalet takes the lead to engage her team in developing prototypes. One gets the sense that perhaps the design work stimulates their thinking and perhaps teases out a more designerly way of addressing current and maybe also future problems. Is design in this sense a catalyst of design attitude?

Flipped management: the public manager as future maker

In educational circles a novel paradigm is gaining ground. Instead of asking students to prepare for class by first doing their homework and then listening to a lecture, the new paradigm flips this around: the students watch the lecture, usually as a video online, *before* they enter the classroom, freeing up time for an informed and critical dialogue with the teacher. The model is called *flipped classroom*.

The notion of managing as *future making*, discussed earlier in this book, represents a similar shift. In flipped classroom, the model is a shift from a teacher-centric to a learner-centric model. To view management as a design activity challenges the current paradigm of public management from a decision-centric model to a future-centric one by suggesting a different orientation in management practice.

For the manager as a *decision maker*, the assumption is that the alternative courses of action to be decided upon already exist. Public managers are presented with options by their staff, or options to be decided upon are presented top-down through the hierarchy. Solutions are, to put it a bit crudely, assumed to exist 'out there' already. 'Should I choose A or B or C?' becomes the question. Sometimes the alternatives are weighed in terms of costs and benefits. Decision making becomes a data-driven, analytical exercise.

For the manager as a *future maker*, the approach is different. As we have seen throughout the book, the manager (working with designers) seeks to inquire into the nature of the problem and is at the same time curious about what might be a better future situation. This is also what Boland and Collopy (2004) and Michlewski (2008; 2015) call design attitude. Here, the exploration of the problem and the articulation of possible futures go hand in hand. Future making does not assume that solutions pre-exist. Rather than focusing immediately, or at least in the short term, on reaching a decision, the question becomes 'What new solutions can we create, or design?' This is really akin to a 180-degree shift in the orientation that public managers bring to development work, anchoring it in future visions and potential new practices rather than in past analysis. It is to take the curvy path rather than the straight one.

Table 12.1 summarises the difference between a decision-making and a future-making approach to management.

Table 12.1: From decision making to future making

Decision making	Future making
What is the decision space? What is the current or past situation? Which decision should I make?	What is the problem- or opportunity space? What could be a better future situation? How might we expand our range of options to decide about?
The decision is there to be found	*The decision is there to be created.*

Of course, real-world management situations are not quite as simple. Every day, managers must make decisions on the fly, in the face of limited or almost no information about what would be the better course of action. Often, there simply is not time to engage in future-making or design activities.

The premise of this book is not that somehow, by magic, enough space, time and opportunity materialise to entirely shift management activity towards future making. My hope is, rather, to raise the awareness of more public managers that under some conditions, and given the many and increasingly complex problems they are dealing with, it can make sense to insist on engaging with design to create better futures.

Leading from the future: managing for human-centred governance

As public managers engage with design, are they also empowered to 'flip' the public management model on its head? And to the extent that they do, as they reframe the very model of management, are they also challenging the governance model? One might say that the appreciation of human action, and thus of outcomes, that is characteristic of management engagement with design is also characteristic of the emerging governance model I discussed in the previous chapter. Consider this scenario: as managers transform, or 'flip' the way in which they work to create better future outcomes, the public governance model is also transformed to be more human- and outcome-centric. Leaders used to manage inputs and principles as the foundation of governance. As they engage with design, they manage for outcomes *back to* activities, inputs and, ultimately, to (re)assess their core mission. One could say that they lead from the future.

Leading from the future implies managing on the basis of intuition, of creativity and of vision. It implies, to some extent, to manage with only the imagination as one's guide. What then of evidence, what of basing decisions on best practice and on 'what works'? To some extent, these questions become less relevant, because managers find themselves in a space where there is not yet any sound evidence on which to base their decision. In fact, the process of designing is to create new solutions which in turn might then be assessed and evaluated as evidence.

This is perhaps also a key to why the emerging governance model must necessarily be more of a scaffolding, more loosely coupled, than before. Because leading from the future, whether it is near or far, can never be done with the same certainty, stability or control as leading from the past. Rather than extrapolate *to* possible consequences of their past or current actions, managers must engage in 'leaps of faith' that what they decide will actually bring about the future they hope for.

How to do it: leading by future making

This chapter has summarised the six management engagements with design that are proposed in this book, but has also moved beyond them to discuss how to build design confidence and how to view managing as a design activity of future making rather than decision making.

As a manager, consider how you might embrace a designerly approach to management as a radical new orientation.

- **Across the six engagements with design, where do you as a manager need to develop your own attitude and stance?** As you reflect on the types of design processes and engagements, where are you challenged the most? Where is your own development need the greatest? What could you do to get started on the curvy path?
- **What is the next challenge or opportunity where you could take a future-making approach?** Often, as we have seen, this can be triggered by particular events or by data showing something problematic. Or it can be triggered by a vision or opportunity that you (or your political leadership)

wish to pursue. How would you carve out the time and space you need? How would you access design skills and processes? Who would you want to lead the work, and what kind of team should it be?

- **What would be your ultimate motivation for engaging with design?** What do you hope to achieve for society? For your organisation? For your end-users? For your staff? For yourself?

Note

[1] This section is based on Bason (2016).

Glossary

Bureaucracy: A system of organisation distinguished by characteristics such as rigid division of labour; clear (managerial) hierarchy of authority; formal selection based on merit; career-oriented and impartial employees; written, formal and inflexible rules, regulations and procedures; impersonal relationships.

Business case: A business case seeks to capture the business justification for initiating a task or a project or implementing a solution. The business case can be presented as a comparison between expected costs or investments and expected benefits or value creation.

Co-design: Collective creativity as it is applied across the whole span of a design process. In *co-design*, diverse experts come together, such as researchers, designers or developers, and (potential) customers and users – who are also experts, that is, 'experts of their experiences'.

Complexity: Complex characteristics refer to systems with large numbers of interacting elements; where interactions are non-linear so that minor changes can have disproportionately large consequences; that are dynamic and emergent; and where hindsight cannot lead to foresight because external conditions constantly change.

Concept development: Concept development is the process of selecting, prioritising, synthesising and creating a single whole out of ideas that have been developed by combining key elements from different ideas into a complete proposal for a solution. Concepts can in turn be made into testable prototypes.

Co-production: Co-production refers to an arrangement where citizens are viewed and treated not as passive recipients of a service, but are engaged in a reciprocal relationship as co-producers of the service.

Design approaches: Systematic, creative processes that engage people in exploring problems and opportunities, developing ideas and visualising, testing and creating new solutions. In the public sector, the use of such methods is often framed in the context of new forms of citizen involvement and collaborative innovation.

Design attitude: Design attitude is an expression of the professional culture of designers, and can be seen as the expectations and orientations one brings to a design project. This entails viewing new projects as opportunities for invention, including questioning basic assumptions, and a resolve to leave the world a better place than one found it. *Design attitude* can be framed in opposition to a *decision attitude*, which portrays the manager as facing a fixed set of alternative courses of action from which a choice must be made.

Design thinking: Design thinking can be viewed as 'design for managers', as it proposes an iterative method for resolution of problems or realising opportunities that draws on design methods. In some versions it incorporates two different cognitive styles: an analytical-logical mind-set and an interpretative, intuitive mindset.

Field research: Any activity aimed at collecting primary (original or otherwise unavailable) data, using methods such as face-to-face interviewing and a variety of observation methods.

Governance: Governance is derived from the ancient Greek word *kubernáo*, which is also the origin of the word government, and which means the steering of a ship or cart (Wikipedia, 2016). Hufty (2011) has suggested that governance is the processes of interaction and decision making among the actors involved in a collective problem that lead to the creation, reinforcement or reproduction of social norms and institutions.

Ideation: Ideation can be seen as the explicit process of generating, developing and communicating ideas, where 'idea' is understood as a basic element of thought that can be visual, concrete or abstract. A variety of creativity and brainstorming techniques are often used to drive the ideation process.

New public management: New public management is a public management reform ideology and governance model that builds on two key ideas: first, that it is possible to insert competition and market-like mechanisms, such as user choice and contracting out, into the public sector to make it more innovative and efficient; and second, that it is possible to render the public sector more effective by introducing management measures and tools, such as performance metrics and targets, that seem to work in the private sector.

Persona: A persona is a representation of a user, typically based on user research (quantitative and qualitative) and incorporating factors such as statistically validated characteristics, user properties, goals, challenges, needs and interests.

Prototyping: A prototype is a tentative, draft version of a product, service or system that allows the design team to explore ideas and show the intention behind a feature or an overall concept to users before investing additional time and money in further development. A prototype can be anything from paper drawings (low-fidelity) to something that allows digital click-through of a few pieces of content to a fully functioning solution (high-fidelity).

Public administration: Public administration comes from the term *ministrare*, meaning 'to serve, and hence later, to govern'. It can be viewed as an activity serving the public, where public servants carry out policies that are set by others. Public administration is concerned with procedures for translating policies into practice and with on-going management tasks.

Public management: The term management is derived from the term *manus*, meaning 'to control by hand'. Public management, in addition to the activities listed above as public administration, thus places more emphasis on the role of managers and their organising and controlling activities of achieving objectives with optimal efficiency.

Public value: Public value emphasises the difference between managing a public and private realm, and emphasises that policy and management strategies must be substantively valuable to the citizens, politically legitimate, feasible and sustainable, operationally possible and practical. Public value can take the form of (positive changes in) productivity, service experience, outcomes, and democratic transparency and participation.

Service design: Service design covers the design of systems, processes and intangible services that aim at delivering a service to a user. Service design is a composite of well-known design disciplines such as communication design, interaction design and digital design and ethnographic methods, which is fundamentally about the involvement of user needs and behaviour.

User journey: A user journey is a series of steps and events, often presented visually, that represent a scenario in which a user interacts with the product, service or system. The user journey can be a mapping of existing processes and user experiences, or it can be a blueprint for a future process and desired experiences.

Visualisation: Visualisation is the representation of business or scientific data, often quantitative – but it can also be qualitative – as graphics or images that can aid in understanding the meaning of the data.

Wicked problems: Wicked problems are characterised by the following: (1) causal relationships are unclear and dynamic, (2) the problem does not fit into a known category, (3) attempts at problem-solving change the problem, (4) not having a stopping rule, that is, solutions cannot be judged as true or false, but merely as 'better or worse'.

References

Ackoff, R.L., J. Magidson and H.J. Addisson (2006) *Idealized design: Creating an organization's future*, Upper Saddle River: Wharton School Publishing

Agranoff, R. (2014) 'Reconstructing bureaucracy for service: innovation in the governance era', in Ansell, C. and J. Torfing (eds) *Public innovation through collaboration and design*, Abingdon: Routledge

Alford, J. (2009) *Engaging public sector clients: From service-delivery to co-production*, Hampshire: Macmillan

Ansell, C. and J. Torfing (eds) (2014) *Public innovation through collaboration and design*, Abingdon: Routledge

Ariely, D. (2009) *Predictably irrational: The hidden forces that shape our decisions*, New York, NY: HarperCollins

Arnstein, S.R. 'A ladder of citizen participation', *JAIP*, vol. 35, no. 4, July 1969, pp 216–224

Attwood, M. (2003) *Leading change: A guide to whole systems working*, Bristol: Policy Press

Australian Government (2011) *Australian Public Service Innovation Action Plan*, http://www.industry.gov.au/innovation/publicsectorinnovation/Pages/Library%20Card/APS_Innovation_Action_Plan.aspx

Banerjee, B. (2014) 'Innovating large-scale transformations', in Bason, C. (ed) (2014) *Design for policy*, Farnham: Gower Ashgate

Bason, C. (2007) *Velfærdsinnovation: Ledelse af innovation i den offentlige sektor [Innovating welfare: Leading innovation in the public sector]*, Copenhagen: Børsens Forlag

Bason, C., S. Knudsen and S. Toft (2009) *Sæt borgeren i spil: Sådan involverer du borgere og virksomheder i offentlig innovation [Put the citizen into play: How to involve citizens and businesses in public sector innovation]*, Copenhagen: Gyldendal Public

Bason, C. (2010) *Leading public sector innovation: Co-creating for a better society*, Bristol: Policy Press

Bason, C. (2012) 'Public managers as designers: Can design-led approaches lead to new models for public service provision?' *Danish Journal of Management & Business*, vol 77, no 4

Bason, C. (2013) 'Design-led innovation in government', in *Stanford Social Innovation Review*, 10th Anniversary Issue, Spring 2013

Bason, C. (2014a) 'Design as an innovation catalyst', in C. Ansell and J. Torfing (eds) (2014) *Public innovation through collaboration and design Collaborative innovation and design in the public sector*, Abingdon: Routledge

Bason, C. (2014b) 'Introduction', in *Design for policy*, Farnham: Gower Ashgate

Bason, C. (2014c) 'The design/policy nexus', in *Design for policy*, London: Gower Ashgate

Bason, C. (2016) *Design leadership: Take the curvy path*, http://ddc.dk/en/2015/11/design-leadership-take-the-curvy-path/

Bate, P. and G. Robert (2007) *Bringing User experience to healthcare improvement: the concepts, methods and practices of experience-based design*, Abingdon: Radcliffe Publishing

Benington, J. and J. Hartley (2001) 'Pilots, paradigms and paradoxes: Changes in public sector governance and management in the UK', for International Research Symposium on Public Sector Management (Barcelona)

Benington, J. and M. Moore (2011) *Public value: Theory and practice*, London: Palgrave Macmillan

Body, J. and Terrey, N. (2014) 'Tools for intent: strategic direction by design', in Bason, C. (ed) (2014) *Design for policy*, Farnham: Gower Ashgate

Boland, R.J. and F. Collopy (2004) *Managing as designing*, Stanford, CA: Stanford University Press

Borins, S. (2000) 'Loose cannons and rule breakers, or enterprising leaders?', *Public Administration Review*, November/December 2000, vol 60, no 6.

Bourgon, J. (2008) 'The future of public service: A search for a new balance', Keynote Address to the 2008 IPAA National Conference, Sydney, NSW, June 2008

References

Bourgon, J. (2012) *A new synthesis of public administration: Serving in the 21st century*, Canada: McGill-Queen's University Press

Boxenbaum, E. and S. Jonsson (2008) 'Isomorphism, Diffusion and Decoupling', in R. Greenwood et al (eds) *The Sage handbook of organizational institutionalism*, Sage Publications

Boyer, B., J.W. Cook and M. Steinberg (2011) *In studio: Recipes for systemic change*, Helsinki: Sitra

Boyle, D. and M. Harris (2009) *The challenge of co-production: How equal partnerships between professionals and the public are crucial to improving public services*, London: NESTA

Bridges, W. (1980) *Transitions: Strategies for coping with the difficult, painful, and confusing times in your life*, Cambridge: Perseus

Brown, T. (2009) *Change by design: How design thinking transforms organizations and inspires innovation*, New York: HarperCollins.

Buchanan, R. (1990) 'Wicked problems in design thinking', essay based on paper presented at Colloque Recherches sur le Design: Incitations, implications, interactions, at l'Université de Technologie de Compiègne, Compiègne, France

Cahn, E. (2004) *No more throwaway people* (2nd edn), Washington, DC: Essential Books

Carlsson, B. (2004) 'Public policy as a form of design', in R. Boland and F. Collopy (eds) *Managing as designing*, Stanford Business Books

Christensen, C. (1997) *The innovator's dilemma: When new technology cause great companies to fail*, Boston: Harvard Business School Press

Christensen, T. (2012) 'Post-NPM and changing public governance', in *Meiji Journal of Political Science and Economics*, vol 1. Available at: http://mjpse.meiji.jp/articles/files/01-01/01-01.pdf

Christiansen, J. (2014) *The irrealities of public innovation*, doctoral thesis (submitted), Aarhus University

Churchman, C.W. (1967) 'Wicked problems', *Management Science*, vol 4, no 14, December

Churchman, C.W. (1971) *The design of inquiring systems: Basic concepts of systems and organization*, London: Basic Books

Cliffe, S. (2011) 'When your business model is in trouble: an interview with Rita Gunther McGrath', *Harvard Business Review*, January

Colander, D. and R. Kupers (2014) *Complexity and the art of public policy: Solving society's problems from the bottom up.* Princeton University Press Crafting Stories for Better Design, New York, NY: Rosenfeld Media

Cole, M. and G. Parston (2006) *Unlocking public value: A new model for achieving high performance in public service organizations*, Wiley Community Matters (2012) *Family by Family evaluation report 2011–12*. Available at http://www.tacsi.org.au/wp-content/uploads/2014/08/TACSI-FbyF-Evaluation-Report-2012.pdf

Cooper, R. and S. Junginger (2011) 'General introduction: Design management – A reflection,' in Cooper, R., S. Junginger and T. Lockwood (eds) *The handbook of design management,* Oxford: Berg Publishers

Cooper, R., S. Junginger and T. Lockwood (2011) *The handbook of design management*, Oxford: Berg Publishers

Corbin, J. and A. Strauss (2008) *Basics of qualitative research* (3rd edn), London: Sage

Cottam, H. (2012) 'Relational welfare', *Soundings*, https://relationalwelfare.files.wordpress.com/2012/11/soundings48_cottam1.pdf

Danish Commerce and Companies Agency et al (2012) *Clear, user-friendly, simple: New visions for digital government*, http://mind-lab.dk/wp-content/uploads/2014/07/Tv_rg_ende_opsamling_UK.pdf

Darmer, M.R., S. Boesgaard, P. Preisler, L.V. Høyer, M. Kynemund and C. Bason (2015) 'Co-creating new meaning: towards the patient-centric hospital?', *Danish Journal of Management and Business*, vol 3, pp 23–41

Design Council (2014) *Case study: Lewisham Council: Service design delivers £368,000 efficiency savings*, http://www.designcouncil.org.uk/resources/case-study/lewisham-council

Dewey, J. (1938) *Logic: The theory of inquiry.* Henry Holt & Company

Donahue, J.D. and R.J. Zeckhauser (2011) *Collaborative governance: Private roles for public goals in turbulent times*, Princeton, NJ: Princeton University Press

Dorst, K. (2015) *Frame innovation: Create new thinking by design*, Cambridge, MA: The MIT Press

Doz, Y. and Koskonen, M. (2014) *Governments for the future: Building the strategic and agile state*, Helsinki: Sitra

Dragoman, L. and K. Kühl (2014) *Evaluating new housing services*, New York, NY: Public and Collaborative

du Gay, P. (2000) *In praise of bureaucracy: Weber, organization, ethics*, London: Sage Publications

Dunleavy, P., H. Margetts, S. Bastow and J. Tinkler (2006) *Digital era governance: IT corporations, the state, and e-government*, Oxford: Oxford University Press

Edmondson, A. and S.E. McManus (2007) 'Methodological fit in management', *Academy of Management Review* 32(4), 1155–1179.

Eggers, W. and P. Macmillan (2013) *The solution revolution*, Boston: Harvard Business Review Press

Eggers, W. and J. O'Leary (2009) *If we can put a man on the moon … getting big things done in government*, Boston, MA: Harvard Business Press

Eggers, W.D. and S. Singh (2009) *The public innovators playbook*, Harvard Ash Center for Democratic Governance and Innovation

Ellis, T. (2010) *The new pioneers: Sustainable business success through social innovation and social entrepreneurship*, Chichester: Wiley

European Commission (2012) *Design for growth and prosperity: Report and recommendations of the European Design Leadership Board*, http://europeandesigninnovation.eu/wp-content/uploads/2012/09/Design_for_Growth_and_Prosperity_.pdf

European Commission (2013a) *A vision for public services* (version 13/06/2013), https://ec.europa.eu/digital-single-market/en/news/vision-public-services

European Commission (2013b) *Powering European public sector innovation: Towards a new architecture*, Brussels: The European Commission

Friedman, K. and E. Stolterman (2014) 'Series foreword', in *Situated design methods*, Cambridge, MA: MIT Press

Gadsdon, P. (2012) 'Putting partnership into practice'. Presentation, 19 March

Gillinson, S., M. Horne, and P. Baeck (2010) *Radical efficiency*, NESTA

Giudice, M. and C. Ireland (2014) *Rise of the DEO: Leadership by design*, New Riders

Goldsmith, S. and W.D. Eggers (2004) *Governing by network: The new shape of the public sector*, Washington DC: Brookings Press

Greve, C. (2015) 'Ideas in public management reform for the 2010s: Digitalization, value creation and involvement', in *Public Organization Review*, vol 15, no 1, pp 49–65

Halse, J. (2014) 'Tools for ideation: Evocative visualization and playful modelling as drivers of the policy process', in C. Bason (ed) *Design for policy*, Abingdon: Routledge

Halse, J., E. Brandt, B. Clark and T. Binder (2010) *Rehearsing the future*, Copenhagen: Danish Design School Press

Hartley, J. (2005) 'Innovation in governance and public services: Past and present,' *Public Money and Management*, 25, 1: 27–34.

Hassan, Z. (2014) *The social labs revolution: A new approach to solving our most complex challenges*, San Francisco, CA: Berrett-Koehler Publishers

Hasse, C. (2003) 'Mødet: den antropologiske læreproces' ['The meeting: The anthropological learning process'] in Hastrup, K. (ed) *Ind i verden: En grundbog i antropologis kmetode* [*Into the world: An introduction to anthropological methods*], Copenhagen, Hans Reitzel

Hernes, T. (2008) *Understanding organization as process: Theory for a tangled world*, Abingdon: Routledge

Heskett, J. (2002) *Toothpicks and logos: Design in everyday life*, New York/Oxford: Oxford University Press

Hood, C. (1991) 'A public management for all seasons?', in Lodge, M., Page, E.C. and Balla, S.J. (eds) *The Oxford handbook of classics in public policy and administration*, Oxford: Oxford University Press

Hood, C. and R. Dixon (2015) *Government that worked better and cost less? Evaluating three decades of reform and change in UK central government*, Oxford: Oxford University Press

Hufty, M. (2011) 'Governance: Exploring four approaches and their relevance to research' in Wiesmann, U. and H. Hurni (eds) *Research for sustainable development: foundations, experiences, and perspectives*, Bern: NCCR North-South/Geographica Bernensia

Jakobsen, M. and L. Truelsen (2013) 'How to design social relationships with disabled citizens', in *Touchpoint Magazine*, http://www.service-design-network.org/products-page/article/tp6–3p30/

Jenkins, J. (2008) 'Creating the right environment for design', *Design Management Review*, Summer 2008

Junginger, S. (2014) 'Towards policymaking as designing: policymaking beyond problem-solving and decision-making', in Bason, C. (ed) *Design for policy*, Farnham: Gower Ashgate

Kahneman, D. (2011) *Thinking, fast and slow*, New York, NY: Farrar, Straus and Giroux

Kelley, T. (2005) *The ten faces of innovation*, New York, NY: Doubleday

Kimbell, L. (2014) *The service innovation handbook*, London: BIS Publishers

Klijn, E.-H. and Skelcher, C. (2008) 'Democracy and governance networks: compatible or not?', *Public Administration*, vol 85, no 3, pp 587–608

Latour, B. (2007) 'How to think like a state', Lecture on 22 November at the WRR Anniversary

Lawrence, T.B. and R. Suddaby (2006) 'Institutions and institutional work', in Stewart, R., Clegg, C.H., Thomas B.L. and Walter R.N. (eds) *Sage handbook of organization studies*, 2nd edn, London: Sage, 215-254

Leonard, D. and J.F. Rayport (1997) 'Spark innovation through empathic design', *Harvard Business Review*, November-December, pp 102–13

Lewin, K. (1947) 'Frontiers in group dynamics: concept, method and reality in social science; social equilibria and social change', *Human Relations*, vol 1, no 1, pp 5–41

Liedtka, J., A. King and K. Bennett (2013) *Solving problems with design thinking: 10 stories of what works*, New York: Columbia Business School Publishing

Lippmann, W. (1925) *The phantom public*, New Brunswick: Transaction Publishers

Madsbjerg, C. and Rasmussen, M.B. (2014) *The moment of clarity: Using the human sciences to solve your toughest business problems,* Boston, MA: Harvard Business Review Press

Manzini, E. (2011) 'Introduction', in Meroni, A. and D. Sangiorgi (eds) *Design for services*, Farnham: Gower Publishing

Manzini, E. (2015) *Design: When everybody designs: An introduction to design for social innovation*, Cambridge, MA: The MIT Press

Manzini, E. and E. Staszowski (eds) (2013) *Public and collaborative: Exploring the intersection of design, social innovation and public policy.* DESIS Network

Martin, R. (2007) *The opposable mind,* Cambridge, MA: Harvard Business Press

Martin, R. (2009) *The design of business: Why design thinking is the next competitive advantage,* Cambridge: Harvard Business Press

Mattelmäki, T. (2008) 'Probing for co-exploring', *Co-design,* vol 3, no 1, pp 65–78

Mazzucato, M. (2014) *The entrepreneurial state: Debunking public vs. private sector myths,* London: Anthem

Meroni, A. and D. Sangiorgi (2011) *Design for services,* Farnham: Gower

Meyer, A. (2011) 'Embedding design practice within organisations,' in Cooper, R., S. Junginger and T. Lockwood (eds) *The handbook of design management,* Oxford: Berg Publishers

Meyer, A. (2014) 'Embedding design practice within organisations', in Cooper, R., S. Junginger and T. Lockwood (eds) *The handbook of design management,* Oxford: Berg Publishers

Meyer, J. W. and B. Rowan (1977) 'Institutionalized organizations: Formal structure as myth and ceremony', in *American Journal of Sociology,* vol 83, no 2, 1977, pp 340–363

Michlewski, K. (2008) 'Uncovering design attitude: Inside the culture of designers', *Organization Studies* 29, 2: 229–248

Michlewski, K. (2015) *Design attitude,* Farnham: Gower

MindLab (2012) 'New industry code website reaps rewards for companies and for business', http://www.mind-lab.dk/en/cases/nyt-branchekodesite-hoester-gevinster-baade-hos-myndigheder-og-virksomheder

Mintzberg, H. (2009) *Managing,* Harlow: Pearson Education

Moggridge, W. (2007) *Designing interactions,* Cambridge, MA: MIT Press

Moore, M. (1995) *Creating public value: Strategic management in government,* Cambridge, MA: Harvard University Press

Mulgan, G. (2009) *The art of public strategy,* Oxford: Oxford University Press

Mulgan, G. (2014) *Design in public and social innovation: What works and what could work better?,* London: Nesta

Mulgan, G. and D. Albury (2003) *Innovation in the public sector*, London: Strategy Unit. Available at: http://www.michaellittle. org/documents/Mulgan%20on%20Innovation.pdf

Mulgan, G. and N. Wilkie, S. Tucker, R. Ali, F. Davis and T. Liptror (2006) *Social Silicon Valleys*, London: Young Foundation

Murray, R., J. Caulier-Rice and G. Mulgan (2009) *Social venturing*, London: Nesta. Available at: http://www.nesta.org. uk/publications/reports/assets/features/social_venturing

National Audit Office (NAO) (2006) *Achieving innovation in central government organisations*

Nesta (2014) *i-Teams: The teams and funds making innovation happen in governments around the world*, London: Nesta with Bloomberg Philanthropies

Newman, J. and J. Clarke (2009) *Publics, politics and power: Remaking the public in public services*, London: Sage

Norman, D. (1988) *The design of everyday things*, New York, NY: Basic Books

Norman, D. (2007) *The design of future things*, Philadelphia, PA: Basic Books

Normann, R. and R. Ramirez (1994) *Designing interactive strategy: From value chain to value constellation*, Chichester: John Wiley & Sons

Nussbaum, B. (2011) 'Design thinking is a failed experiment so what's next', in *FastCoDesign*, accessed 11 March 2014 at: http://www.fastcodesign.com/1663558/design-thinking-is-a-failed-experiment-so-whats-next

O'Leary, R. and Bingham, L.B. (2009) *The collaborative public manager: New ideas for the twenty-first century*, Washington, DC: Georgetown University Press

Osborne, S.P. (2006) 'The new public governance?', *Public Management Review*, vol 8, no 3, pp 377–387

Osborne, D. and T. Gaebler (1992) *Reinventing government: How the entrepreneurial spirit is transforming the public sector*, Reading: Addison Wesley

Osborne, S.P. and K. Brown (2005) *Managing change and innovation in public service organisations*, New York: Routledge.

Paquet, G. (2009) *Scheming virtuously: The road to collaborative governance*, Ottawa: Invenire

Parker, S. and J. Heapy (2006) *The journey to the interface: How public service design can connect users to reform*, London: Demos

Parsons, W. (2010) 'Modernism redux: po-mo problems and hi-mo public policy', in Fenwick, J. and J. McMillan, *Public management in the postmodern era: Challenges and prospects*, Cheltenham: Edward Elgar

Pascal, R., J. Sternin and M. Sternin (2010) *The power of positive deviance: How unlikely innovators solve the world's toughest problems*, Cambridge, MA: Harvard Business Press

Pestoff, V. (2012) 'Innovations in public services: co-production and new public governance in Europe', in Botero, A., A.G. Paterson and J. Saad-Sulonen *Towards peer production in public services: Cases from Finland*, Helsinki: Aalto University publication series Crossover 15/2012

Peters, G.B. (2010) 'Still the century of bureaucracy? The roles of public servants', in Fenwick, J. and J. McMillan (eds) *Public management in the postmodern era: Challenges and prospects*, Northampton: Edward Elgar

Peters, T. (1997) *The circle of innovation*, London: Hodder & Stoughton

Peters, B.G. and Pierre, J. (2003) *Handbook of public administration*, London: Sage

Piore, M.J. and R.K. Lester (2006) *Innovation: The missing dimension*, Cambridge, MA: Harvard University Press

Polaine, A., L. Lövlie and B. Reason (2013) *Service design: From insight to implementation*, New York, NY: Rosenfeld Media

Pollitt, C. (2003) *The essential public manager*, Maidenhead: Open University Press

Potter, N. (2002) *What is a designer: things. places. messages*, London: Hyphen Press

Pruitt, J. and A. Tamara (2006) *The persona lifecycle: Keeping people in mind throughout product design*, San Francisco, CA: Morgan Kaufmann

Quesenbery W. and K. Brooks (2010) *Storytelling for user experience*, New York, NY: Rosenfeld Media

Raffnsøe, S. (2013) *The human turn: The makings of a contemporary relational topography*, Copenhagen: Copenhagen Business School

Reagan, R. (1981) Inaugural address, accessed 03.12.2015 at http://www.reagan.utexas.edu/archives/speeches/1981/12081a.htm

Rist, R.C. and J. Zall Kusek (2004) *Ten steps to a results-based monitoring and evaluation system*, Washington, DC: World Bank

Ritchey, T. (2011) *Wicked problems – social messes: Decision support modeling with morphological analysis*, Berlin: Springer

Rittel, H. and Webber, M. (1973) 'Dilemmas in a general theory of planning', *Policy Sciences*, vol 4, Amsterdam: Elsevier Scientific Publishing

Rowe, P.G. (1987) *Design thinking*, Cambridge, MA: MIT Press.

Sanders, E. (2014) 'Co-designing can seed the landscape for radical innovation and sustainable change', in Christensen, P. R. and S. Junginger (eds) *The highways and byways to radical innovation: Design perspectives*, Design School Kolding and University of Southern Denmark

Sanders, E. and P.J. Stappers (2008) 'Co-creation and the new landscapes of design,' *CoDesign: International Journal of CoCreation in Design and the Arts*, 1745–3755, 4, 1: 5–18

Sangill, P. (2013) *Det gode køkken* [*The good kitchen*], presentation to 2013 Design Days conference

Schön, D. (1971) *Beyond the stable state*, Toronto: The Norton Library

Schön, D. (1983) *The reflective practitioner*, Aldershot: Ashgate

Seddon, J. (2008) *Systems thinking in the public sector: The failure of the reform regime and a manifesto for a better way*, Devon: Triarchy Press

Shove, L., Watson, M., Hand, M. and Ingram, J. (2007) *The design of everyday life*, Oxford: Berg Publishers

Simon, H.A. (1996) *The sciences of the artificial*, Cambridge, MA: MIT Press

Simon, H.A. (1997) *Administrative behaviour*, New York, NY: The Free Press

Simonsen, J., Svabo, C., Strandvad, S.M., Samson, K., Hertzum, M. and Hansen, O.E. (2014) *Situated design methods*, Cambridge, MA: MIT Press

Siodmok, A. (2014) 'Tools for insight: design research for policymaking', in Bason, C. (ed) (2014) *Design for policy*, Farnham: Gower Ashgate

Snowden, D. and Boone, M. (2007) 'Leader's framework for decision-making', *Harvard Business Review*, November

Sparke, P. (2004) *An introduction to design and culture: 1900 to present*, Abingdon: Routledge

Steinberg, M. (2014) 'Strategic design and the art of public sector innovation', in Bason, C. (ed) *Design for policy*, Farnham: Gower Ashgate

Suddaby, R. (2006) 'From the editors: What grounded theory is not', *Academy of Management Journal*, vol 49, no 4: 633–42

Sunstein, C. (2013) *Simpler: The future of government*, New York, NY: Simon & Schuster

Surowiecki, J. (2004) *The wisdom of crowds: Why the many are smarter than the few and how collective wisdom shapes business, economies, societies and nations*, London: Little, Brown

Tapscott, D. and A.D. Williams (2006) *Wikinomics: How mass collaboration changes everything*, New York, NY: Penguin

Terwiesch, C. and K.T. Ulrich (2009) *Innovation tournaments: Creating and selecting exceptional opportunities*, Cambridge, MA: Harvard Business Press

Thaler, R. and C. Sunstein (2008) *Nudge: Improving decisions about health, wealth and happiness*, New Haven, CT: Yale University Press

The Economist (2011) 'Welcome to the Anthropocene' [Front cover], 26 May

The Economist (2014) 'Test-tube government', 6 December

The Guardian (2010) 'Social innovation is my motivation', http://www.theguardian.com/service-design/social-innovation, 12 March

Tsoukas, H. (1989) 'The validity of idiographic research explanations', *Academy of Management Review*, 14: 551–61

Tufte, E. (1983) *The visual display of information*, Cheshire: Graphics Press

Van de Ven, A. (2007) *Engaged scholarship*, Oxford/New York: Oxford University Press

van Wart, M. (2008) *Leadership in public organizations*. Armonk: M.E. Sharpe

Vejle Municipality and Social Service Agency (2014) *Evaluering af Design af Relationer* [*Evaluation of design of relations*], http://socialstyrelsen.dk/filer/handicap/udviklingshaemning/evalueringsrapport-design-af-relationer-3.pdf

Verganti, R. (2009) *Design-driven innovation: Changing the rules of competition by radically innovating what things mean*, Boston: Harvard Business Press

Von Hippel, E. (2005) *Democratizing innovation*, Cambridge: MIT Press

Waldorff, S.B., Kristensen, L.S. and Ebbesen, B.V. (2014) 'The complexity of governance: challenges for public sector innovation', in Ansell, C. and J. Torfing (eds) *Public innovation through collaboration and design*, Abingdon: Routledge

Weber, M. (1964) *The theory of social and economic organization*, New York: The Free Press

Weick, K. (2004) 'Rethinking organizational design', in Boland, R.J. and F. Collopy (eds) *Managing as designing*, Stanford, CA: Stanford University Press

Wetter-Edman, K. (2014) *Design for service: A framework for exploring designers' contribution as interpreter of users' experience*, PhD dissertation. University of Gothenburg

Wildevuur, S. (2013) *Connect: Design for an empathic society*, Amsterdam: Waag Society and BIS Publishers

Wilson, J.Q. (1989) *Bureaucracy: What governments do and why they do it*, New York: Basic Books

Winhall, J. and Maschi, S. (2014) 'Tools for implementation', in Bason, C. (ed) *Design for policy*, Farnham: Gower Ashgate

Wren, D.A. and Bedeian, A.G. (2009) *The evolution of management thought*, John Wiley & Sons, Inc

Index

Printed and bound by CPI Group (UK) Ltd, Croydon, CR0 4YY

09/06/2025

14685899-0001